PARALLEL COMPUTING
USING THE PREFIX PROBLEM

PARALLEL COMPUTING USING THE PREFIX PROBLEM

S. Lakshmivarahan
Sudarshan K. Dhall

School of Computer Science
University of Oklahoma
Norman, Oklahoma

New York   Oxford
OXFORD UNIVERSITY PRESS
1994

Oxford University Press

Oxford   New York   Toronto
Delhi   Bombay   Calcutta   Madras   Karachi
Kuala Lumpur   Singapore   Hong Kong   Tokyo
Nairobi   Dar es Salaam   Cape Town
Melbourne   Auckland   Madrid

and associated companies in
Berlin   Ibadan

Library of Congress Cataloging-in-Publication Data
Lakshmivarahan, S.
Parallel computing using the prefix problem /
S. Lakshmivarahan, Sudarshan K. Dhall.
p.   cm.   Includes bibliographical references and index.
ISBN 0-19-508849-2
1. Parallel programming (Computer science)
2. Computer algorithms.
I. Dhall, Sudarshan Kumar, 1937-
II. Title.
QA76.642.L353   1994   005.2—dc20   94-3070

9 8 7 6 5 4 3 2 1

Printed in the United States of America
on acid-free paper

Dedication

To my brothers

Sankaran, Narayanan, and Krishnamurthy

S. Lakshmivarahan

To

Pushpa, Alka, Vandana, and Komal

Sudarshan K. Dhall

Preface

In the parlance of serial computation outside of the realm of Automata Theory and Formal Languages, there is hardly any reference to the notion of prefix. As a part of the construction for a fast binary adder, Ofman, a Russian Mathematician, in 1963 introduced the notion of prefix circuits. Simultaneously, in 1962, Kenneth Iverson introduced the concept of a vector operation called **compress** as a part of the library of vector operations in the programming language, APL. This **compress** operation may be considered as the precursor to the present day notion of prefix computations. Since then, with the emergence of parallel computing, the notion of *prefix* computation has gained considerable importance in the literature. It is now recognized as one of the fundamental building blocks in the development of parallel algorithms. Consequently, a variety of parallel algorithms for computing prefixes have been developed by various authors. These algorithms may be broadly classified into two groups — (a) algorithms for *shared memory* models, and (b) those for *circuit* models. In general, while it is true that an algorithm on either class of models can be easily implemented on the other, these algorithms have certain nuances that are characteristic of the models in question. Further, this problem has been well understood and many *efficient* algorithms are known. Accordingly, a comprehensive account of the development of various algorithms for this *ubiquitous* problem is in order. In fact, most of the contents of Chapters 3 through 8 appear for the first time in book form.

There is a second and perhaps more compelling reason for our interest in this project. Thanks to the support from the National Science

Foundation to initiate undergraduate students into research in parallel processing, we faced the challenge of introducing the basic principles and tools for the design and analysis of parallel algorithms to a heterogeneous mix of very bright juniors and seniors drawn from several institutions with varying backgrounds and training. We had two choices. First, and most tempting, was to follow the beaten track by choosing one of the many excellent text books, in which event, it would have been just another course. Instead, we decided to pick a problem simple enough to understand, and using it as a focus, introduce various aspects of parallel algorithms. The basic principles and tools introduced in this exposition include the following: parallel models — PRAM models and circuit models, relations between these models, the notion of parallel complexity, divide and conquer, recursive doubling, symmetry breaking, pointer jumping, lower bounds, optimality, size *vs.* depth trade-off analysis, principles of randomized *vs.* deterministic algorithms, mapping algorithms onto parallel architectures, impact of unbounded *vs.* bounded fan-out, unbounded *vs.* bounded fan-in, and above all, several applications of the prefix problem. This book is eminently suitable for a one semester introductory course on parallel algorithms for Computer Science / Computer Engineering / Mathematics students at the senior/honors/first-year graduate level.

This book is divided into four parts and three Appendices, with each part, divided into two Chapters. The exercises constitute an integral part of the development of the material, and the section on Notes and References provides comments, historical perspectives, and citations to the literature. Several research projects worthy of attention are mentioned throughout the book.

The first part, entitled Getting Started, consists of Chapters 1 and 2. In Chapter 1, following the definition of the problem, we present examples of the application of the prefix problem — ranking, packing, radix sort, addition of two integers, computing the output of a finite state transducer, linear recurrences, polynomial interpolation, several problems from graph theory, and pattern matching. To render the presentation self-contained, Chapter 2 contains a brief description of parallel computers, parallel models — the shared memory and circuit models — their relations, performance measures (parallel time, optimal speed up, efficiency, depth and size, fan-in and fan-out), and a discussion of the parallel complexity class, namely the *NC*. Chapter 2 concludes with a discussion of Brent's inequalities and a derivation of a simple lower bound used in proving optimality of algorithms of interest in this book.

Chapters 3 and 4, which constitute Part Two, deal with *parallel algorithms for prefix computation on the shared memory models.* Chapter 3 describes parallel prefix algorithms when the input is in the form of an array, and Chapter 4 deals with the analogous algorithms for the input in the form of linked lists. This part contains deterministic and randomized algorithms and introduces the reader to several basic principles including recursive doubling, pointer-jumping, symmetry breaking *via* coloring, methods for finding a k-ruling set *via* deterministic coin tossing schemes and randomized symmetry breaking.

Part Three, consisting of Chapters 5 and 6, introduces the reader to the elegance of *parallel algorithm* design using the *circuit model.* Chapter 5 provides an introduction to the design of parallel prefix circuits. This chapter develops the notion of the depth-optimal circuits and exhibits the presence of depth *vs.* size trade-off in parallel prefix circuits. In turn, Chapter 6 derives a lower bound on the (size + depth) for a class of circuits with unbounded fan-out. Based on this lower bound, a number of optimal (with respect to this lower bound) designs are presented in this chapter.

Part Four, the conclusion, examines the effect of bounded *vs.* unbounded fan-in and fan-out. Chapter 7 describes algorithms for bounding fan-out and derives expressions for the increase in size and depth resulting from bounding fan-out. Little is known about the structure of optimal circuits (in the sense of depth, or (size + depth), etc.) with bounded fan-out. Chapter 8 contains an elaborate analysis of the design of unbounded fan-in circuits for computing prefixes. It is shown that unbounded fan-in circuits of linear size and depth, proportional to the inverse of Ackermann's function, exist for computing prefixes, the sum of two integers, and any associative function. These results depend critically on a number of factors — the underlying semigroup being group-free, the non-existence of constant depth and polynomial size circuits for computing parity, and the strong relation between group-free semigroups, star-free regular expressions and a class of finite automata known as **RS** machines.

To render our exposition self-contained, Appendix A summarizes the properties of semigroups and monoids. A succinct summary of the relation between group-free semigroups, star-free regular expressions and **RS** machines is contained in Appendix B. An analysis of the complexity of computing parity is given in Appendix C.

A note on notations. Chapters are divided into sections which in turn are divided into subsection. Thus, section (a.b.c) refers to the cth subsection of the bth section in Chapter a. The equations within each subsection are numbered independently in increasing order. Within the same subsection, the equations are referred to by their number as in " From equation (5) ....", and elsewhere as " ... from equation (k) in Section (a.b.c) ... ". References are listed in alphabetical order and citations are referred to by the last names of the authors followed by the year of publication in brackets, as in Ladner and Fischer [1980].

Acknowledgments

We have received considerable help in the form of comments and criticism from several of our friends and colleagues. Narsingh Deo (University of Central Florida) and Sajal Das (North Texas State University) have spend considerable time reviewing earlier drafts of this book. Çetin Kaya Koç (Oregon State University), E. Gallopoulos (University of Illinois), and Ömer Eğecioğlu (University of California, Los Angeles), in addition to providing us with copies of their latest papers, have also reviewed different parts of the book. Richard Cole (Columbia University) and Uzi Vishkin (University of Maryland) have been generous in answering our questions related to the algorithms in Section 4.4. Jung-Sing Jwo (Providence University, Taiwan) taught a course on *Parallel Computation* based on an earlier version of our manuscript. His insightful suggestions on the entire manuscript were very useful. Justin Smith (Drexel University) and Tanasis Tsantilas (Columbia University), as reviewers for the Oxford University Press, provided many valuable comments. Sridhar Radhakrishnan (University of Oklahoma) has been a source of constant encouragement and support. We are grateful to all these individuals for their contributions.

The final organization of the book was, in large part, a result of continued interaction with several of our students. We are grateful to Chi-Ming Yang for his collaborative efforts in the development of LYD circuits, described in Chapter 6, as a part of his Master's thesis. By way of introducing the basic principles of parallelism to a group of students who participated in the NSF program on Research Experience for Undergraduates, we have used several chapters for a seminar course on *Introduction to Parallelism*. Our thanks are due to Kerry Bourque, Jimmy Kerl, Aimee Oleniczak, Landon Henderson, Michael Eddy, and Barry Jacobson, for their participation in these seminars, and their comments on the contents and organization of the book.

We wish to record our thanks to Donald Jackson of the Oxford University Press for his interest and constant encouragement. It has been a great pleasure to work with him on this project. Our thanks are also due to Bill Zobrist for introducing us to Don Jackson in the first place.

Finally, we thank the members of our family for their enthusiasm and support, without which we could not have taken up this project.

CONTENTS

Part One

Getting Started

Chapter 1

The Prefix Problem
And Its Applications

With the emergence of parallel computing, the notion of prefix computation has gained considerable attention in the literature and it plays a central role in parallel algorithm design. This introductory chapter begins with the definition of the prefix problem. The ubiquitous nature of this problem is then illustrated using a host of examples drawn from a variety of application areas. Readers unfamiliar with a particular application area may choose to consult the appropriate references given in Section 1.4, Notes and References. After gaining sufficient familiarity with the remainder of this book, the reader will profit by revisiting Chapter 1 to apply the parallel prefix algorithms to several of the problems introduced here. In fact, many interesting class projects can be developed by cleverly mixing the problems and the algorithms.

1.1 The Prefix Problem

Let A be a set and o be a binary operation defined over the elements of A. It is assumed that

C1. *A* is *closed* under the binary operation o, that is, if a and b are in A, then so is a o b, and

C2. the operation o is *associative,* that is, if a, b, and c are in A, then

$$(a \text{ o } b) \text{ o } c = a \text{ o } (b \text{ o } c) = a \text{ o } b \text{ o } c.$$

The system (A, o) satisfying conditions **C1** and **C2** is called a *semi-group* (Birkhoff and Bartee [1970]). Examples include, (a) A is the set of integers (or real or complex numbers) and o denotes either the *addition* or the *multiplication* operation, and (b) A is a set of finite alphabet and o denotes the *concatenation.* To render our exposition self-contained, in Appendix A we discuss various properties of semigroups of interest to us in this book.

Let $d = (d_1, d_2, \cdots, d_N)'$, where $d_i \in A$, for $1 \le i \le N$. Consider the problem of computing

$$x_i = x_{i-1} \text{ o } d_i$$

for $2 \le i \le N$, given that $x_1 = d_1$. Since

$$x_i = d_1 \text{ o } d_2 \text{ o } \cdots \text{ o } d_i,$$

this problem of computing x_i's from d_i's is called the *prefix* problem (Ladner and Fischer [1980]). It is also useful to look at this prefix problem as a *vector operation.* Let $\mathbf{x} = (x_1, x_2, \cdots, x_n)'$. Then,

$$\mathbf{x} = prefix(\mathbf{d})$$

denotes the operation of computing $x_i = d_1 \text{ o } d_2 \text{ o } \cdots \text{ o } d_i$, for $1 \le i \le n$, where $\mathbf{d}$ is the input vector and $\mathbf{x}$ is the output vector. Likewise, if $\mathbf{y} = (y_1, y_2, \cdots, y_N)'$, then

$$\mathbf{y} = suffix(\mathbf{d}),$$

where

$$y_i = d_i \text{ o } d_{i+1} \text{ o } \cdots \text{ o } d_N,$$

for $1 \le i \le n$, is the *suffix* operation of computing suffixes of $\mathbf{d}$.

When the binary operation is the usual addition operation, then the prefix problem is also known as *all partial sums* problem (Schwrartz [1980]) or as the *cascade sum* problem (Hockney and Jesshope [1981]). Blelloch [1989] calls the prefix operation the **scan** operation. In particular, it is called **+scan**, **max-scan**, **min-scan** when the binary operation is addition, maximum, or the minimum operation, respectively.

The serial computation of all the prefixes takes $N - 1$ binary operations.

1.2 Why Prefix Problem

The importance of the prefix problem stems from the fact that it arises naturally in a number of application areas.

1.2.1 Ranking, Packing, and Radix Sort

Given an array of N elements, let r of these elements be *marked* and the remainder of the $(N - r)$ elements be *unmarked*. The *packing* problem consists of creating another array where all the marked elements are moved to the lower (or left) part of the array and the unmarked ones to the upper (or right) part of the array without changing their relative order. One method for packing consists of assigning a value 1 to each of the marked elements and a value 0 to each of the unmarked elements. Clearly, the problem of computing the *ranks* of the marked elements reduces to the problem of prefix computation on the 0-1 array obtained above. Likewise, one can compute the ranks of the unmarked elements by interchanging 0's and 1's. Knowing the ranks, the elements can be *packed* into their final positions.

We now illustrate the packing operation using an example. Referring to Figure 1, the problem is to pack the even elements to the left and the odd elements to the right. The first row contains the input, and the second, a vector of flags, where T denotes an odd, and F denotes an even integer. (Recall that an integer is odd or even, if the least significant bit in its binary representation is one or zero, respectively.) Considering T as integer 0 and F as integer 1, perform *prefix* (*FLAG*), as given in the third row, and *suffix* ($\neg FLAG$), as given in the fourth row. Then, compute the fifth row as $N + 1 - suffix$ ($\neg FLAG$). The key to packing is to obtain the row of Index I, where

$$I(i) = \begin{cases} i^{th} \text{ element of } 3^{rd} \text{ row} & \text{if } FLAG(i) = F \\ i^{th} \text{ element of } 5^{th} \text{ row} & \text{if } FLAG(i) = T. \end{cases}$$

The packed array is obtained by permuting the input array A using the index array I. Here, the operation *permute* (A, I) denotes the assignment

$$A(I(i)) = A(i), \quad \text{for} \quad 1 \leq i \leq N.$$

We can readily use the packing operation to perform *radix sort* [Aho, Hopcroft and Ullman [1974]]. Radix sort consists in repeatedly sorting elements based on the values of the bits starting from the least significant to the most significant. Figure 1 shows the packing operation based on the least significant bits. Figures 2 and 3 demonstrate the sorting based on the second least significant and third most significant bits of the input. Since the input integers range from 1 through 7, radix sort using packing is accomplished in three steps.

Array Index	1	2	3	4	5	6	7	8
Input A	5	7	3	1	4	2	7	2
FLAG	T	T	T	T	F	F	T	F
prefix (FLAG)	0	0	0	0	1	2	2	3
suffix ($\neg$ FLAG)	5	4	3	2	1	1	1	0
$N + 1 -$ suffix ($\neg$ FLAG)	4	5	6	7	8	8	8	9
Index, I	4	5	6	7	1	2	8	3
Permute (A, I), $A\,(I\,(i)) = A\,(i)$	4	2	2	5	7	3	1	7

Figure 1. An illustration of packing on an array of size 8.

In the programming language APL (Iverson [1962], Hellerman and Smith [1976]), the packing operation is performed using the array operator called *COMPRESS,* which is considered as the precursor to the present day notion of prefix computation (Blelloch [1989]).

Array Index	1	2	3	4	5	6	7	8
Input A	4	2	2	5	7	3	1	7
FLAG	F	T	T	F	T	T	F	T
prefix (FLAG)	1	1	1	2	2	2	3	3
suffix ($\neg$ FLAG)	5	5	4	3	3	2	1	1
$N + 1 -$ suffix ($\neg$ FLAG)	4	4	5	6	6	7	8	8
Index, I	1	4	5	2	6	7	3	8
Permute (A, I), $A\,(I\,(i) = A\,(i)$	4	5	1	2	2	7	3	7

Figure 2. Packing based on the second significant bit.

Array Index^{1}	1	2	3	4	5	6	7	8
Input A	4	5	1	2	2	7	3	7
FLAG	T	T	F	F	F	T	F	T
prefix (FLAG)	0	0	1	2	3	3	4	4
suffix ($\neg$ FLAG)	4	3	2	2	2	2	1	1
$N + 1 -$ suffix ($\neg$ FLAG)	5	6	7	7	7	7	8	8
Index, I	5	6	1	2	3	7	4	8
Permute (A, I), $A\,(I\,(i) = A\,(i)$	1	2	2	3	4	5	7	7

Figure 3. Packing based on the third significant bit.

1.2.2. Carry-Look-Ahead Addition

Let

$$a = a_N\, a_{N-1}\ \cdots\ a_2\, a_1$$

and

$$b = b_N\, b_{N-1}\ \cdots\ b_2\, b_1$$

be two N-bit binary numbers, and let

$$s = a + b = s_{N+1}\, s_N\ \cdots\ s_2\, s_1$$

be their sum in binary. The conventional algorithm for addition computes $s_i's$ as follows:

$$s_i = a_i\ \oplus\ b_i\ \oplus\ c_{i-1}, \qquad i = 1\ \cdots\ N \tag{1}$$

$$s_{N+1} = c_N$$

where

$$c_0 = 0$$

$$c_i = (a_i \wedge b_i) \vee (a_i \wedge c_{i-1}) \vee (b_i \wedge c_{i-1}), \qquad i = 1\ \cdots\ N.$$

The symbol $\oplus$ refers to the exclusive-or (or the modulo-2 addition), $\wedge$ is the Boolean AND, $\vee$ is the Boolean OR, and c_i is the carry from the ith bit position. By simplifying the right-hand-side of the equation defining c_i, it can be shown that (Brent and Kung [1982]),

$$c_0 = 0$$
$$c_i = g_i \vee (p_i \wedge c_{i-1}) \qquad\qquad (2)$$

where

$$g_i = a_i \wedge b_i, \quad \text{for } i = 1 \cdots N,$$

and

$$p_i = a_i \oplus b_i, \quad \text{for } i = 1 \cdots N.$$

It is customary to call the g_i the *carry generate bit* and p_i the *carry propagate bit* at position i. Thus, c_i is either generated by a_i and b_i, or propagated from the previous carry c_{i-1}. 'It readily follows that s_i in (1) can be computed in parallel, provided all the c_i's are available. In other words, a great portion of the time required to add two N-bit binary integers is primarily spent computing the carry-bits.

In the following, we present a parallel method for computing the carry-bits and show that it reduces to computing prefixes in parallel. To this end, rewrite the first-order linear recurrence (2), defining c_i in a functional form as follows:

$$c_0 = 0$$

$$c_i = f_i(c_{i-1}) = g_i \vee (p_i \wedge c_{i-1}),$$

where g_i and p_i depend only on the input and can be computed in parallel. Clearly,

$$c_{k+1} = f_{k+1}(c_k) = f_{k+1}(f_k(c_{k-1})).$$

Now, defining the composition of functions as

$$f_k \circ f_{k+1}(c_{k-1}) = f_{k+1}(f_k(c_{k-1})),$$

it is readily seen that computation of all the c_i's in parallel is equivalent to computing

$$f_1 \circ f_2 \circ \cdots \circ f_i(c_0),$$

for all $i = 1$ to N, in parallel.

Recall that f_i is uniquely determined by the pair $[g_i, p_i]$. Thus, we denote f_i as

$$f_i(x) = [g_i, p_i](x).$$

Since

$$f_i \circ f_j(x) = f_j(f_i(x)) = (g_j \vee (p_j \wedge (g_i \vee (p_i \wedge x))))$$

$$= [g_j \vee (p_j \wedge g_i)] \vee [(p_j \wedge p_i) \wedge x],$$

we can essentially denote

$$f_i \circ f_j = [g_i, p_i] \circ [g_j, p_j] = [g_j \vee (p_j \wedge g_i), p_j \wedge p_i].$$

Since the operation $\circ$ is associative (Exercise 1.1), it readily follows that

$$f_1 \circ f_2 \circ \quad \cdots \quad \circ f_i$$

can be computed in any order. (Also, refer to Brent [1970], Han, Carlson, and Levitan [1987], Krapchenko [1970], and Ofman [1963].)

Computation of the carry bit can also be reformulated as a semigroup product as follows. For each i, define

$$x_i = \begin{cases} s & \text{if } a_i = b_i = 1 & (g_i = 1 \text{ and } p_i = 0) \\ p & \text{if } a_i \neq b_i & (g_i = 0 \text{ and } p_i = 1) \\ r & \text{if } a_i = b_i = 0 & (g_i = 0 \text{ and } p_i = 0) \end{cases}$$

that is, s may be thought of as *set carry*, p as *propagate carry*, if it exists, and r is the *reset carry*. Let $S = \{s, p, r\}$ and define an associative binary operation

$$\alpha : S \times S \to S,$$

where $\alpha(y, z) = yz$ is given by

$$ys = s \qquad yr = r \qquad \text{and} \qquad yp = y.$$

This operation α may be represented in a tabular form as follows:

y	z		
	s	r	p
s	s	r	s
r	s	r	r
p	s	r	p

It can be verified that the set S with the binary operation defined above constitutes a semigroup (refer to Appendix A, particularly Example 7).

It can also be verified that there is a carry bit into the $(i + 1)^{th}$ bit exactly when the semigroup product is

$$x_1\, x_2\, \cdots\, x_i = s.$$

As an example, let

$$a = a_5\, a_4\, a_3\, a_2\, a_1 = 1\,0\,1\,1\,1$$

and

$$b = b_5\, b_4\, b_3\, b_2\, b_1 = 1\,0\,1\,1\,0.$$

Then,

$$x_1 = p, \qquad x_2 = s, \qquad x_3 = s, \qquad x_4 = r, \qquad x_5 = s.$$

Clearly, $c_0 = 0$, and

$$\left. \begin{aligned} c_1 &= 0 \\ c_2 &= 1 \\ c_3 &= 1 \\ c_4 &= 0 \\ c_5 &= 1 \end{aligned} \right\} \quad since \quad \left\{ \begin{aligned} x_1 &= p \\ x_1 x_2 &= s \\ x_1 x_2 x_3 &= s \\ x_1 x_2 x_3 x_4 &= r \\ x_1 x_2 x_3 x_4 x_5 &= s. \end{aligned} \right.$$

1.2.3. Finite State Transducers

The above example can be readily generalized to the design of combinational or Boolean circuits for simulating a sequential processor defined by finite-state transducers. Consider the general Mealy model (Hopcroft and Ullman [1979]) of a deterministic finite-state transducer M, defined by the six-tuple

$$M = (\, K,\, \Sigma,\, \Delta,\, \delta,\, \lambda,\, p_0),$$

where

> K $-$ is the finite set of states
> Σ $-$ is the finite set of the input alphabet
> Δ $-$ is the finite set of the output alphabet
> δ : $K \times \Sigma \rightarrow K$ is the state transition function
> λ : $K \times \Sigma \rightarrow \Delta$ is the output function
> $p_0 \in K$ is the initial state of a Mealy finite-state transducer.

Corresponding to each input symbol a, there is a function

$$M_a : K \rightarrow K,$$

where

$$M_a(p) = \delta(p, a).$$

If $x = a_1 a_2 \cdots a_N$ is an input string, then define M_x as

$$M_x(p_0) = M_{a_1 a_2 \cdots a_N}(p_0) = M_{a_1} \circ M_{a_2} \circ \cdots M_{a_N}(p_0)$$

$$= M_{a_N}(M_{a_{N-1}}(\cdots (M_{a_2}(M_{a_1}(p_0)) \cdots).$$

Thus given the initial state p_0 and the input $x = a_1 a_2 \cdots a_N$, we can readily compute the output string in parallel as follows:

Step 1: Compute the functions M_{a_i}, for $1 \leq i \leq N$ in parallel.

Step 2: Compute $M_i = M_{a_1} \circ M_{a_2} \circ \cdots \circ M_{a_i}$, for $i = 1$ to N.

Step 3: Compute $p_i = M_i(p_0)$ in parallel.

Step 4: Compute $b_i = \lambda(p_{i-1}, a_i)$, for $1 \leq i \leq N$.

Note that step 2 corresponds to the prefix problem, and $b = b_1 b_2 \cdots b_N$ is the output string. A practical method for computing M_x is pursued in Exercise 1.3.

1.2.4. Solution of Linear Recurrences

Consider an mth order linear recurrence defined by

$$x_i = a_{i1} x_{i-1} + a_{i2} x_{i-2} + \cdots a_{im} x_{i-m} + b_i,$$

for $i > m$, where $a_{i1}, a_{i2}, \cdots a_{im}$, and b_i, for all $i > m$, and $x_1, x_2, \cdots, x_m$ are known. The above relation may be rewritten as (Fich [1983])

$$\bar{x}_i = \bar{x}_{i-1} A_i,$$

where

$$\bar{x}_i = (x_i, x_{i-1}, \cdots, x_{i-m+1}, 1)$$

$$\bar{x}_{i-1} = (x_{i-1}, x_{i-2}, \cdots, x_{i-m}, 1),$$

and

$$\mathbf{A}_i = \begin{bmatrix} a_{i,1} & 1 & 0 & \cdots & & 0 & 0 \\ a_{i,2} & 0 & 1 & \cdots & & 0 & 0 \\ \cdot & \cdot & \cdot & \cdots & & \cdot & \cdot \\ \cdot & \cdot & \cdot & \cdots & & \cdot & \cdot \\ \cdot & \cdot & \cdot & \cdots & & \cdot & \cdot \\ a_{i,m-1} & 0 & 0 & \cdots & & 1 & 0 \\ a_{i,m} & 0 & 0 & \cdots & & 0 & 0 \\ b_i & 0 & 0 & \cdots & & 0 & 1 \end{bmatrix}.$$

Define, for $i \geq 2$,

$$\mathbf{B}_i = \mathbf{A}_{(i-1)m+1} * \mathbf{A}_{(i-1)m+2} * \cdots * \mathbf{A}_{im},$$

where $*$ is the matrix multiplication operation. Likewise, define

$$\mathbf{y}_i = \left[\mathbf{x}_{im}, \mathbf{x}_{im-1}, \cdots, \mathbf{x}_{(i-1)m+1}, 1 \right].$$

Then, clearly

$$\mathbf{y}_i = \mathbf{y}_1 \, \mathbf{B}_2 * \mathbf{B}_3 * \cdots * \mathbf{B}_i,$$

where

$$\mathbf{y}_1 = (x_m, x_{m-1}, \cdots, x_1, 1)$$

is given.

As an example, let $m = 2$. Then, for $i \geq 3$, let

$$x_i = a_{i1} x_{i-1} + a_{i2} x_{i-2} + b_i \tag{1}$$

where the initial conditions x_1 and x_2 are assumed to be known. Clearly,

$$\overline{\mathbf{x}}_i = (x_i, x_{i-1}, 1),$$

and

$$\mathbf{A}_i = \begin{bmatrix} a_{i1} & 1 & 0 \\ a_{i2} & 0 & 0 \\ b_i & 0 & 1 \end{bmatrix}.$$

The recurrence (1) may be rewritten as

$$(x_i, x_{i-1}, 1) = (x_{i-1}, x_{i-2}, 1) \begin{bmatrix} a_{i1} & 1 & 0 \\ a_{i2} & 0 & 0 \\ b_i & 0 & 1 \end{bmatrix}.$$

Consider the computation of x_i, for $3 \le i \le 8$. Then,

$$
\left.
\begin{aligned}
\overline{\mathbf{x}}_8 &= \overline{\mathbf{x}}_7 \, \mathbf{A}_8 = \overline{\mathbf{x}}_6 \, (\mathbf{A}_7 * \mathbf{A}_8) \\
\overline{\mathbf{x}}_6 &= \overline{\mathbf{x}}_4 \, (\mathbf{A}_5 * \mathbf{A}_6) \\
\overline{\mathbf{x}}_4 &= \overline{\mathbf{x}}_2 \, (\mathbf{A}_3 * \mathbf{A}_4)
\end{aligned}
\right\} .
\tag{2}
$$

and

Define,

$$
\mathbf{y}_1 = \overline{\mathbf{x}}_2 = (x_2, x_1, 1), \qquad \mathbf{B}_2 = \mathbf{A}_3 * \mathbf{A}_4
$$

$$
\mathbf{y}_2 = \overline{\mathbf{x}}_4 = (x_4, x_3, 1), \qquad \mathbf{B}_3 = \mathbf{A}_5 * \mathbf{A}_6
$$

$$
\mathbf{y}_3 = \overline{\mathbf{x}}_6 = (x_6, x_5, 1), \qquad \mathbf{B}_4 = \mathbf{A}_7 * \mathbf{A}_8
$$

$$
\mathbf{y}_4 = \overline{\mathbf{x}}_8 = (x_8, x_7, 1).
$$

The computations in (2) can now be expressed as follows:

$$
\begin{aligned}
\mathbf{y}_1 \ & \textit{is given.} \\
\mathbf{y}_2 &= \mathbf{y}_1 \, \mathbf{B}_2 \\
\mathbf{y}_3 &= \mathbf{y}_1 \, (\mathbf{B}_2 * \mathbf{B}_3) \\
\mathbf{y}_4 &= \mathbf{y}_1 \, (\mathbf{B}_2 * \mathbf{B}_3 * \mathbf{B}_4).
\end{aligned}
$$

It is readily seen that the vectors $\mathbf{y}_2, \ \cdots \ \mathbf{y}_N$ can be computed in parallel as follows.

Step 1: Compute $\mathbf{B}_i$, $i = 2$ to N in parallel.

Step 2: Compute $\overline{\mathbf{B}}_i = \mathbf{B}_2 * \mathbf{B}_3 * \cdots * \mathbf{B}_i$, for all $i = 2$ to N in parallel.

Step 3: Compute $\mathbf{y}_i = \mathbf{y}_1 \overline{\mathbf{B}}_i$ in parallel.

Note that step 2 corresponds to the prefix computation.

1.2.5. Polynomial Evaluation and Interpolation

The relation between the problem of evaluating a polynomial at a consecutive set of lattice points and the prefix computation is explored in Exercise 1.4. In the following, we consider the polynomial interpolation problem. Polynomial interpolation schemes constitute the basis for computer graphics and geometric modeling using computers (Bartels, Beatty, and Barsky [1987]).

A. Newton's Interpolation

Let $f(x)$ be a function defined for $x \in [a, b]$, where $a < b$. Let $a \le x_0 < x_1 < x_2 < \cdots < x_n \le b$ be a set of $N + 1$ *distinct* points, and let $f_i = f(x_i)$. Given the collection of $N + 1$ pairs (x_i, f_i), the problem of constructing a polynomial $p_N(x)$ of degree N, such that $p_N(x_i) = f_i$, for $i = 0, 1, 2, \cdots, N$, is known as the *polynomial interpolation problem*. A classic approach due to Newton is to express $p_N(x)$ in the following form (Hildebrand [1974]):

$$p_N(x) = f_0 + f_{01}(x - x_0) + f_{012}(x - x_0)(x - x_1) + f_{0123}(x - x_0)(x - x_1)(x - x_2)$$

$$+ \cdots + f_{012 \cdots N}(x - x_0)(x - x_1) \cdots (x - x_{N-1}), \qquad (1)$$

where $f_{012 \cdots t}$, for $t = 0, 1, \cdots, N$ are called the *divided differences* of f which are computed recursively as follows:

$$f_{i,i+1, \cdots, i+t} = \frac{(f_{i,i+1, \cdots, i+t-1} - f_{i+1,i+2, \cdots, i+t})}{(x_i - x_{i+t})}. \qquad (2)$$

Thus,

$$f_{i,i+1} = \frac{f_i - f_{i+1}}{(x_i - x_{i+1})} \qquad (3)$$

$$f_{i,i+1,i+2} = \frac{f_{i,i+1} - f_{i+1,i+2}}{(x_i - x_{i+2})}, \qquad (4)$$

and so on (Exercise 1.5). These computations can be arranged in the form of a table as follows:

x_0	f_0					
x_1	f_1	f_{01}				
x_2	f_2	f_{12}	f_{012}			
x_3	f_3	f_{23}	f_{123}	f_{0123}		
x_4	f_4	f_{34}	f_{234}	f_{1234}	f_{01234}	
x_5	f_5	f_{45}	f_{345}	f_{2345}	f_{12345}	f_{012345}

Note that the diagonal entries are the required coefficients in (1).

In recasting Newton's interpolation scheme described above as a prefix problem, substitute (3) in (4) to obtain

$$f_{i,i+1,i+2} = \frac{f_i}{(x_i - x_{i+1})(x_i - x_{i+2})} + \frac{f_{i+1}}{(x_{i+1} - x_i)(x_{i+1} - x_{i+2})}$$

$$+ \frac{f_{i+2}}{(x_{i+2} - x_i)(x_{i+2} - x_{i+1})}, \tag{5}$$

that is, $f_{i,i+1,i+2}$ can be expressed as a linear combination of f_i, f_{i+1}, and f_{i+2}. Generalizing this trend, let $d_{ij} = (x_i - x_j)^{-1}$, for $i \neq j$. It can be verified that

$$f_{012\cdots t} = (d_{01}\, d_{02}\, \cdots\, d_{0t})f_0 + (d_{10}\, d_{12}\, \cdots\, d_{1t})f_1 + \cdots$$

$$+ (d_{t0}\, d_{t1}\, \cdots\, d_{t,t-1})f_t. \tag{6}$$

Since the coefficients of f_0 in $f_{012\cdots t}$, for $t = 1, 2, \cdots, N$, are d_{01}, $d_{01}\, d_{02}$, $d_{01}\, d_{02}\, d_{03}$, $\cdots$, $d_{01}\, d_{02}\, \cdots\, d_{0N}$, respectively, these coefficient terms can be obtained through the prefix computation on $(y_1, y_2, \cdots, y_N)$, where $y_i = d_{0i} = (x_0 - x_i)^{-1}$, for $i = 1, 2, \cdots, N$, with o as the usual multiplication operation (Eğecioğlu, Gallopoulos and Koç [1989, a, b], [1990]).

The computation of the coefficients of f_i, for $1 \leq i \leq t$, in $f_{012\cdots t}$, for $t = 1, 2, \cdots, N$, can likewise be recast as a prefix problem. Thus, Newton's interpolation over $N + 1$ points gives rise to a total of $N + 1$ distinct prefix problems.

B. Hermite Interpolation

We now consider another type of interpolation scheme called the *Hermite* interpolation, wherein the aim is to construct an Nth degree polynomial $p(x)$ that interpolates $f(x)$ from the given values of

$$f(x_i), f^{(1)}(x_i), f^{(2)}(x_i), \cdots, f^{(n_i - 1)}(x_i),$$

for $i = 0, 1, 2, \cdots, N$, where $f^{(j)}(x_i)$ denotes the jth derivative of $f(x)$ at $x = x_i$. For simplicity in notation, let

and
$$\left.\begin{array}{c} f_i = f(x_i) \\[2em] f_{ik} = \dfrac{f^{(k-1)}(x_i)}{(k-1)!}. \end{array}\right\} \tag{7}$$

Express $p(x)$ as

$$p(x) = f_0 + f_{0^2}(x - x_0) + f_{0^3}(x - x_0)^2 + \cdots + f_{0^n}(x - x_0)^{n_0 - 1}$$

$$+ f_{0^n 1}(x - x_0)^{n_0} + f_{0^n 1^2}(x - x_0)^{n_0}(x - x_1)$$

$$+ f_{0^n 1^n}(x - x_0)^{n_0}(x - x_1)^{n_1 - 1} + f_{0^n 1^n 2}(x - x_0)^{n_0}(x - x_1)^{n_1}$$

$$+ \cdots + f_{0^n 1^n 2^n}(x - x_0)^{n_0}(x - x_1)^{n_1}(x - x_2)^{n_2 - 1}$$

$$+ \cdots +$$

$$+ f_{0^n 1^n 2^n \ldots N^{n_N}}(x - x_0)^{n_0}(x - x_1)^{n_1} \cdots (x - x_N)^{n_N}, \tag{8}$$

where the coefficients for $i < j$

$$f_i{}^{a_i} \ldots {}_j{}^{a_j} = d_{ij}[f_i{}^{a_i} \ldots {}_j{}^{a_j - 1} - f_i{}^{a_i - 1} \ldots {}_j{}^{a_j}] \tag{9}$$

are called the *generalized divided differences (GDD)* of f and $d_{ij} = (x_i - x_j)^{-1}$. Let us first illustrate the recursive computation of the *GDD* using an example. Consider $f_{0^2 1^3}$. Applying (9) repeatedly, we obtain

$$f_{0^2 1^3} = d_{01}[f_{0^2 1^2} - f_{0 1^3}]$$

$$f_{0^2 1^2} = d_{01}[f_{0^2 1} - f_{0 1^2}]$$

$$f_{0^2 1} = d_{01}[f_{0^2} - f_{0 1}]$$

$$f_{0 1} = d_{01}[f_0 - f_1]$$

$$f_{0 1^3} = d_{01}[f_{0 1^2} - f_{1^3}]$$

$$f_{0 1^2} = d_{01}[f_{0 1} - f_{1^2}].$$

Combining these, it can be verified that

$$f_{0^2 1^3} = -3\, d_{01}^4\, f_0 + 3\, d_{01}^4\, f_1 + d_{01}^3\, f_{0^2} + 2\, d_{01}^3\, f_{1^2} + d_{01}^2\, f_{1^3}, \tag{10}$$

that is, $f_{0^2 1^3}$ is a linear combination of the input data. These computations can be arranged in the form of a binary tree given in Figure 1, where the node label $0^r 1^s$ corresponds to $f_{0^r 1^s}$. The root of this tree is at level 1. Each leaf is assigned a *signed weight* equal to the product of the weights of the edges along the path from the root to that leaf. It can be verified that the length of the string that constitutes the label of a node at level i is $(L - i + 1)$, where $L = r + s$, and the magnitude of the weight of the leaf at level i is d_{01}^{i-1}. For example, the weight of the left-most leaf node with label 0^2, is d_{01}^3, and that of the left-most leaf with label 0, is $-d_{01}^4$.

Let $0^r 1^s |_0$ denote the coefficient of f_0 in the expansion of $f_{0^r 1^s}$ obtained above. It can be shown (Exercise 1.6) that the sign of this coefficient is $(-1)^{r-1}$. If m_0 is the number of nodes with label 0, then

$$0^r 1^s \,|_0 = (-1)^{r-1} \, m_0 \, d_{01}^{r+s-1} \tag{11}$$

(recall that all the leaves with label 0 are at the same level), where (Exercise 1.7),

$$m_0 = \binom{r+s-2}{s-1}. \tag{12}$$

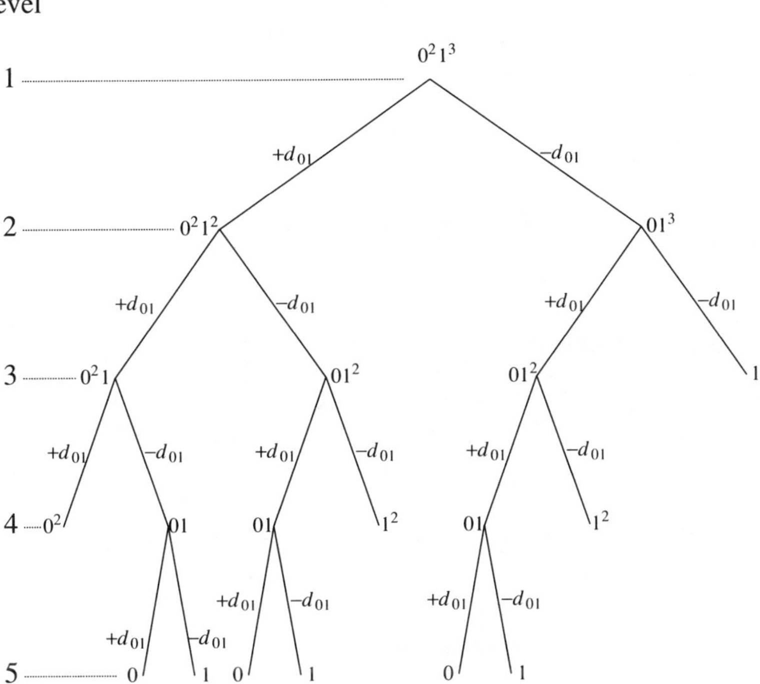

Figure 1. A method for computing the GDD, $f_{0^2 1^3}$.

By suitably modifying the above argument, explicit expressions for

$$0^{a_0} 1^{a_1} \mid_{0^i}, \qquad 0^{a_0} 1^{a_1} \mid_{1^i}, \qquad 0^{a_0} 1^{a_1} 2^{a_2} \cdots N^{a_N} \mid_0,$$

and

$$0^{a_0} 1^{a_1} 2^{a_2} \cdots N^{a_N} \mid_{j^k}$$

can be obtained (see Exercises 1.8 and 1.9).

We now illustrate the above method using a practical case when $n_i = 2$, for all $i = 0$ to N, that is,

$$f_i = f(x_i) \qquad \text{and} \qquad f_{i^2} = f^{(1)}(x_i)$$

are given, for $i = 0$ to N. In this case

$$p(x) = f_0 + f_{0^2}(x - x_0) + f_{0^2 1}(x - x_0)^2 + f_{0^2 1^2}(x - x_0)^2(x - x_1)$$

$$+ f_{0^2 1^2 2}(x - x_0)^2(x - x_1)^2 + f_{0^2 1^2 2^2}(x - x_0)^2(x - x_1)^2(x - x_2)$$

$$+ \cdots + f_{0^2 1^2 \ldots N^2}(x - x_0)^2(x - x_1)^2(x - x_2)^2 \cdots (x - x_N)^2.$$

It can be verified by either direct calculation (refer to Figure 2) or by specializing the formulae in Exercise 1.9 that

$$0^2 1 \mid_{0^2} = d_{01}$$

$$0^2 1^2 \mid_{0^2} = d_{01}^2$$

$$0^2 1^2 2 \mid_{0^2} = d_{01}^2 \, d_{02}$$

$$0^2 1^2 2^2 \mid_{0^2} = d_{01}^2 \, d_{02}^2.$$

Generalizing this, we obtain, for $1 \leq k \leq N$,

$$\left. \begin{aligned} 0^2 1^2 2^2 \cdots (k-1)^2 \, k \mid_{0^2} &= d_{01}^2 \, d_{02}^2 \cdots d_{0(k-1)}^2 \, d_{0k} \\[2em] 0^2 1^2 2^2 \cdots k^2 \mid_{0^2} &= d_{01}^2 \, d_{02}^2 \cdots d_{0k}^2 \end{aligned} \right\} . \tag{13}$$

Clearly, these coefficients can be computed as the prefixes of

$$(d_{01}, d_{01}, d_{02}, d_{02}, \cdots, d_{0N}, d_{0N}).$$

Similarly, it can be verified that

$$0^2 1 \mid_0 = -d_{01} \, [d_{01}]$$

$$0^2 1^2 \mid_0 = -d_{01}^2 \, [2 d_{01}]$$

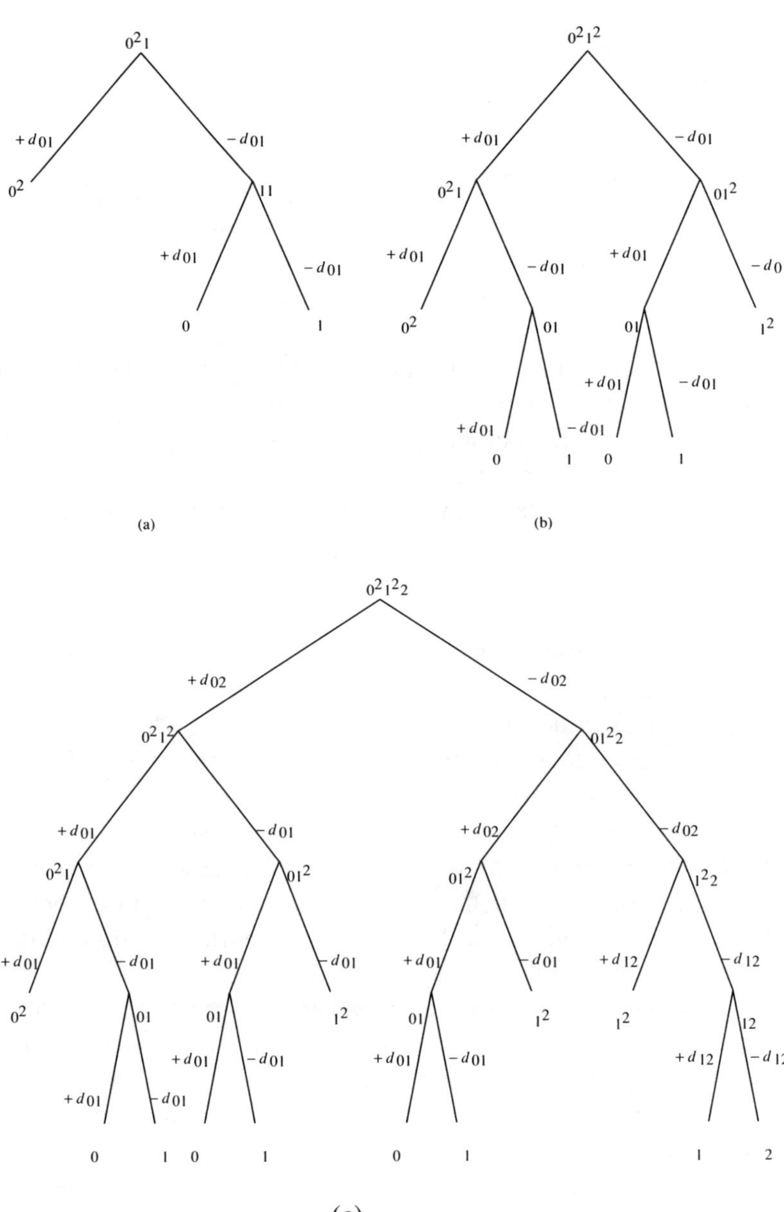

Figure 2. Examples of computation of *GDD*'s.

$$0^2 1^2 2 \mid_0 = -d_{01}^2 \, d_{02} \, [2d_{01} + d_{02}]$$

$$0^2 1^2 2^2 \mid_0 = -d_{01}^2 \, d_{02}^2 \, [2d_{01} + 2d_{02}].$$

Generalizing this trend, we obtain

$$\left.\begin{array}{l} 0^2 1^2 2^2 \cdots (k-1)^2 k \mid_0 = -d_{01}^2 \, d_{02}^2 \, \cdots \, d_{0k} \, [2d_{01} + 2d_{02} + \cdots + d_{0k}] \\[2ex] 0^2 1^2 2^2 \cdots k^2 \mid_{0^2} = -d_{01}^2 \, d_{02}^2 \, \cdots \, d_{0k}^2 \, [2d_{01} + 2d_{02} + \cdots + 2d_{0k}] \end{array}\right\} . \qquad (14)$$

Half of the terms inside the brackets in equation (14) can be obtained as the prefixes of

$$(2d_{01}, 2d_{02}, 2d_{03}, \cdots, 2d_{0N})$$

and the other half can be obtained by adding d_{0i} to the ith prefix sum. The terms outside the brackets are given in equation (13). By repeating the above method, coefficients of other terms in $p(x)$ can be obtained using the prefix computation.

Another important practical case of Hermite interpolation, when $f(x_i)$, $f^{(1)}(x_i)$, and $f^{(2)}(x_i)$ are given, for $i = 0$ to N, is pursued in Exercise 1.11.

1.2.6 Tree Computations Based on Euler Tour Technique

In this Section, we describe many of the graph problems that are commonly solved by invoking the prefix computation. We begin by reviewing several related notions from graph theory. Let $G = (V, E)$ be an *undirected* graph. G is said to be *connected* if there is a path connecting every pair of vertices in G. A *directed* graph $G = (V, E)$ is said to be *connected* if the underlying, undirected graph (obtained by ignoring the orientation of the edges) is connected. In the following, by a graph, we mean an undirected graph.

Let G be a graph. An *Euler tour* in G is a cycle that contains every edge in G exactly once. It is well known that an undirected graph has an Euler tour if, and only if, it has zero or two vertices of odd degree.

Let G be a connected, directed graph. A *directed Euler tour* in G is a directed cycle that contains each edge exactly once. It is well known that a directed graph contains an Euler tour if, and only if, the *in-degree* of each vertex is equal to its *out-degree*. Graphs containing Euler tours are called Eulerian graphs. If we remove an edge from an Euler tour, it becomes an Euler path. A little reflection reveals that an *Euler path* corresponds to a traversal of a graph.

A graph G containing no cycles is called *acyclic*. A *connected acyclic* graph is called a *tree*. Let $G = (V, E)$ be a tree with $|V| = N$ vertices. Then, $|E| = N - 1$. Let $G' = (V, E')$ be a *directed* graph obtained by replacing each edge by two directed edges in opposite directions in a tree $G = (V, E)$. Since the in-degree equals the out-degree for each node in G', clearly, G' has a directed Eulerian tour. Refer to Figure 1 for an example. There are efficient serial algorithms for finding Euler tours for general graphs. Refer to Exercise 1.15. In the following, it is assumed that the reader is familiar with the algorithm for generating the Euler tour in trees. Refer to Figure 1 for an example.

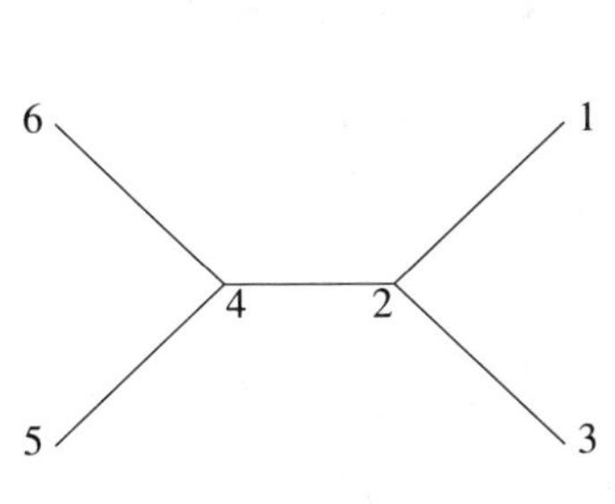

Nodes	Adjacency List
1	2
2	4, 1, 3
3	2
4	2, 6, 5
5	4
6	4

(a) The given tree.

(2, 4), (4, 6), (6, 4), (4, 5), (5, 4), (4, 2), (2, 1), (1, 2), (2, 3), (3, 2)

(b) An Euler tour for the tree in (a).

2, 4, 6, 4, 5, 4, 2, 1, 2, 3, 2

(c) A node traversal corresponding to the Euler tour in (b).

Figure 1. A 6-node tree along with an Euler tour for it.

A. Rooting a Given Tree

Let $G = (V, E)$ be a tree. Let $r \in V$ be a distinguished node in G, called the *root*. The problem is to find the parent of each node $x \neq r$, when G is rooted at r. This problem is called the *rooting of a tree*.

An algorithm for rooting a tree, given below, assumes that the tree $G = (V, E)$, the required root node $r \in V$, and a directed Eulerian path in G are given.

Step 1: First, open up the Euler tour starting and ending at the root node (see Figure 1 for an illustration), and assign a weight of unity to each edge in the resulting Euler path. This induces an ordering of the edges in the tree.

Step 2: Compute the prefix sum of the weights on the edges with respect to this ordering.

Step 3: The node a is the parent of node b, if the prefix sum of the edge (a, b) is less than that of the edge (b, a).

Refer to Table 1 for an illustration. Figure 2 gives the tree rooted at node 2, corresponding to the tree in Figure 1.

Table 1. An illustration of the rooting algorithm.

Edge	Initial Weights	Prefixes
(2, 4)	1	1
(4, 6)	1	2
(6, 4)	1	3
(4, 5)	1	4
(5, 4)	1	5
(4, 2)	1	6
(2, 1)	1	7
(1, 2)	1	8
(2, 3)	1	9
(3, 2)	1	10

Given a rooted tree, several interesting questions relating to the structure of the tree often arise in practice. These relate to computing, (a) the level of a given vertex, (b) the number of descendants of a given vertex, and (c) the order in which the nodes in the tree are visited, for example, in the pre-order traversal, etc. These questions can be readily answered by a clever combination of Euler tours in a rooted tree and prefix computation.

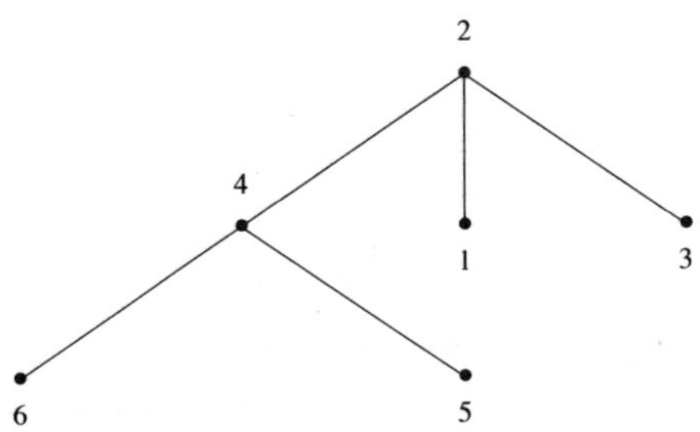

Figure 2. A rooted tree.

B. Computing the Level of a Node

Let $G = (V, E)$ be a rooted tree with $r \in V$ as the root. For any $x \in V$, *level*(a) is the length of the path from r to a. First, construct an Euler path starting at r for any node $x \in V$, let $p(x)$ denote the parent of x. The edges $(p(x), x)$ and $(x, p(x))$ will be denoted as the *forward edge* and the *backward edge,* respectively.

Step 1: Assign a weight of $+1$ to the forward edge and -1 to the backward edge.

Step 2: Perform the prefix computation on the ordered list of directed edges corresponding to an Euler path starting at r.

Step 3: The *level*(x) is the prefix sum associated with the forward edge $(p(x), x)$.

Table 2 contains the results of the level calculations for the tree in Figure 2. For example, the level of node 5 is 2, which is the prefix sum of the edge $(4, 5)$.

Table 2. An example of level calculation.

Edge	Weights	Prefix Sum
(2, 4)	1	1
(4, 6)	1	2
(6, 4)	− 1	1
(4, 5)	1	2
(5, 4)	− 1	1
(4, 2)	− 1	0
(2, 1)	1	1
(1, 2)	− 1	0
(2, 3)	1	1
(3, 2)	− 1	0

C. Computing the Number of Descendants of a Node

Let $G = (V, E)$ be a rooted tree with $r \in V$ as the root. For any $x \in V$, and $x \neq r$, consider the sub-tree G_x rooted at x. The set of all elements of this tree G_x is called the *descendant* of x. Let $des(x)$ denote the number of descendants of x, and let $p(x)$ be the parent of x. The following algorithm computes $des(x)$ for each x in G.

Step 1:   Assign a weight of zero to the edge $(p(x), x)$, and a weight of unity to the edge $(x, p(x))$.

Step 2:   Compute the prefix sum of the edges along the Euler path starting at the root r.

Step 3:   Along the Euler path, the sequence of edges embedded between $(x, p(x))$ and $(p(x), x)$ constitutes the Euler tour for the subtree rooted at x. Clearly, $des(x)$ is given by the difference of the prefix sum of $(x, p(x))$ and $(p(x), x)$.

Table 3 illustrates this algorithm. The difference of the prefix sums between (4, 2) and (2, 4) is 3, which is the number of nodes in the subtree rooted at 3.

Table 3. An example for descendant computation.

Edge	Weight	Prefix Sum
(2, 4)	0	0
(4, 6)	0	0
(6, 4)	1	1
(4, 5)	0	1
(5, 4)	1	2
(4, 2)	1	3
(2, 1)	0	3
(1, 2)	1	4
(2, 3)	0	4
(3, 2)	1	5

Algorithms for finding the order in which the nodes of a tree are visited in a given traversal, for example, preorder or postorder, are pursued in Exercise 1.16.

D. Tree Contraction

Let $G = (V, E)$ be a *rooted* tree with r as its root and size, $| V | = N$. Given $1 < M \leq N$, the problem is to derive a new tree $G' = (V', E')$ from G of size $| V | = O(N/M)$. The process of obtaining G' from G is called *tree contraction*. The interest in tree contraction stems from the fact that it arises naturally in the parallel evaluation of arithmetic expressions. While there are several approaches to tree contraction, in the light of our interest, in the following, we describe the one due to Gazit, Miller and Teng [1987], that is based on prefix computation.

The first step in the tree contraction is to *split* the given tree into a certain number of subtrees, called *bridges*. To this end, let $S \subseteq V$. Two edges, say, e_1 and e_2 in G are said to be *S-equivalent* if a path exists (which is a sequence of edges) connecting e_1 and e_2 that does *not pass through the nodes in S. The subtrees formed by the* equivalence classes of *S*-equivalent edges are called the *bridges*. A bridge consisting of only one edge is called a *trivial* bridge. If B is a bridge, then the nodes of B in S are called *attachments*.

As an example, refer to the tree of size $N = 19$ given in Figure 3. Let $S = \{b, e, g\}$. Clearly, S partitions the given tree into seven bridges B_i, $1 \le i \le 7$, shown in Figure 4. Clearly, B_1 is a trivial bridge. The node g is an attachment to the bridge B_2. Also, the nodes b and e are the attachments to the bridge B_4.

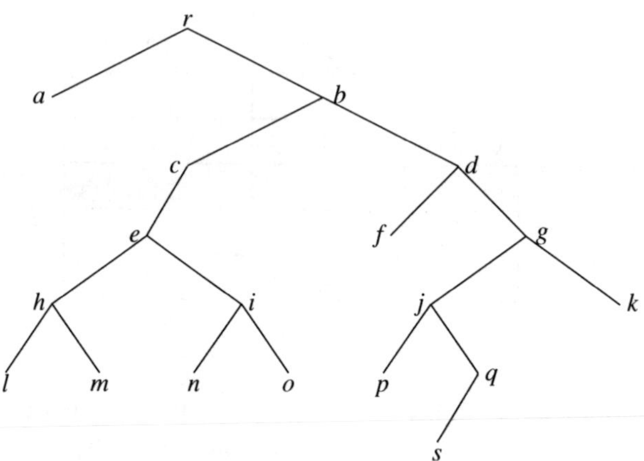

Figure 3. The given tree with root r.

We now describe the process of picking the subset S used in defining the bridges. Define the weight $w(x)$ of a node x in G as the number of nodes in the subtree rooted at x. Clearly, $w(x) = des(x)$ can be readily computed using the algorithm given in subsection 1.2.6C. Figure 5 indicates the weights of the tree in Figure 3. Then,

$$S_M = \{ x \in V \mid \left\lceil \frac{w(x)}{M} \right\rceil \ne \left\lceil \frac{w(y)}{M} \right\rceil \text{ for all descendents } y \text{ of } x \}.$$

Referring to Figures 3 and 5, with $M = 5$, it can be verified that the vertex $g \in S_M$, since $\left\lceil \dfrac{w(g)}{M} \right\rceil = 2$, and $\left\lceil \dfrac{w(y)}{M} \right\rceil = 1$, for all the descendents y of g.

Also, $d \notin S_M$ since $\left\lceil \dfrac{w(d)}{M} \right\rceil = \left\lceil \dfrac{w(g)}{M} \right\rceil$, where g is a descendent of d.

Following this argument, it can be verified that $S_M = \{ b, e, g \}$. Any node in S_M is called *M-critical* node. The bridges in G corresponding to the equivalence partition induced by S_M are called *M-bridges*. Referring to Figure 4, bridges B_1 through B_7 are the seven 5-bridges induced by the set S_M of 5-critical nodes.

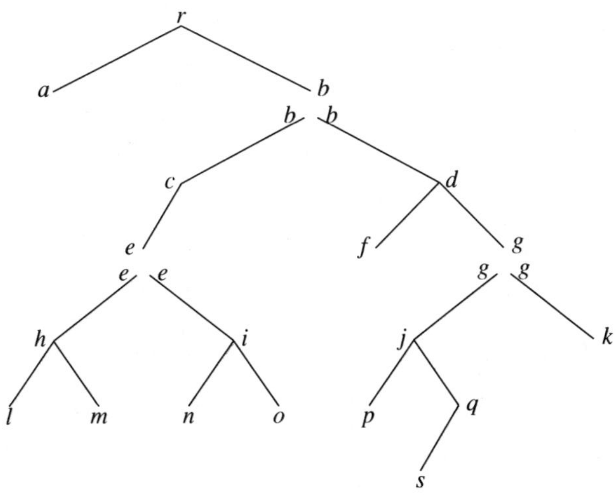

$$B_1 = \{\, g, k \,\} \qquad B_2 = \{\, g, j, p, q, s \,\} \qquad B_3 = \{\, b, d, g, f \,\}$$
$$B_4 = \{\, b, c, e \,\} \qquad B_5 = \{\, e, h, l, m \,\} \qquad B_6 = \{\, e, i, n, o \,\}$$
$$B_7 = \{\, a, r, b \,\}$$

Figure 4. The S-equivalent partitions of the tree
in Figure 3 with $S = \{\, b, e, g \,\}$.

We now state, without proof, several properties of M-bridges. For details of proof, refer to Gazit, Miller and Teng [1987], (Exercise 1.19).

Property 1. Let B be an M-bridge in G. Then, B has at most one attachment which is a leaf of B (recall leaf is a node of degree unity).

Since $M \leq N$, there will be no attachment only when $M = N$. Referring to Figure 4, all the attachment nodes b, e and g are leaves in the respective bridges.

Property 2. The number of nodes in any M-bridge B in G is bounded by $M + 1$.

The largest size of the 5-bridges in Figure 4 is five, which is bridge B_2.

Property 3. The number of M-critical nodes in a tree of size N is, at most, $\dfrac{2N}{M} - 1$. That is, $\mid S_M \mid \leq \dfrac{2N}{M} - 1$.

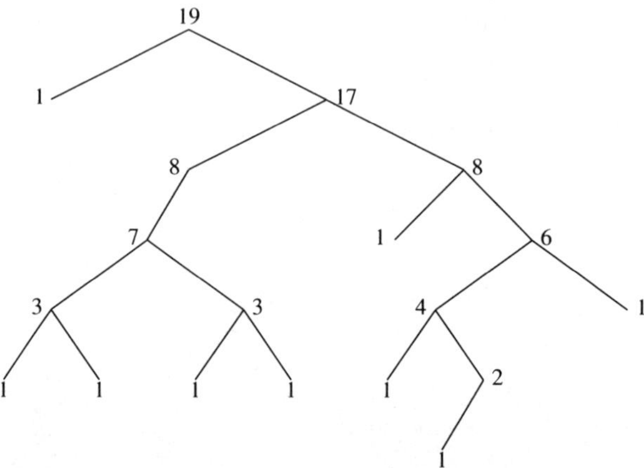

Figure 5. The tree with the weights of the corresponding vertices.

There are clearly three, 5-critical nodes in the tree of size 19 given in Figure 3. (See Exercise 1.20).

The M-contraction of a tree $G = (V, E)$ with root r is a tree $G_M = (V_M, E_M)$, such that $V_M = S_M \cup \{ r \}$, and

$$E_M = \{ (x, y) \mid x, y \in V_M \text{ and } x \text{ and } y \text{ belong to the same bridge } M \},$$

that is, two nodes in V_M are connected exactly when they both are in the same bridge. Combining this with Property 3, we have $|V_M| \leq \dfrac{2N}{M}$ (Exercise 1.21). The 5-contraction of the tree in Figure 4 is given in Figure 6.

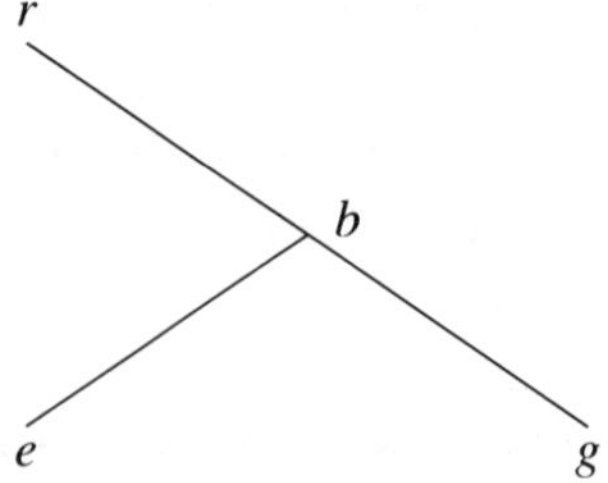

Figure 6. The M-contraction of the tree in Figure 3 for $M = 5$.

It is clear from the above developments that the key to M-contraction of a tree is to identify the M-critical nodes in it. We conclude this discussion with an algorithm for picking the *M*-critical nodes. It is useful to distinguish two cases — the degree *d* of the tree (which is the maximum of the degrees of the nodes in the tree) is *bounded,* that is, *d* is fixed and is independent of the size *N* of the tree and the degree *d* is *unbounded,* that is, *d* varies as a function of *N*. For simplicity, in the following, we consider the case of bounded degree. The algorithm for the unbounded case is quite similar but more involved and the reader is referred to Gazit, Miller and Teng [1987] for details.

Step 1:   Given the tree $G = (V, E)$, first compute the Euler tour and the weights of each node using the prefix computation of the Euler tour as explained in Section 1.2.6C.

Step 2:   Using the weight computed in step 1, compute the maximum of the weights of the children of each node. This maximum can be found using the **max-scan** or **max-prefix** operation (refer to Section 1.1).

Step 3:   By dividing the weight of each node and the maximum weight found in step 2 by *M* we can determine the *M*-critical set.

Note that the prefix computation is used in both steps 1 and 2.

It is assumed that the tree is given by the set of pointers from each child to its parent and that the children of a vertex are ordered from left to right. It is assumed that each node has an associated array with the label of that node followed by that of its children in the left to right order. It is into this array, the weight of a node and its children are stored when they are computed in step 1. Refer to Figure 7 for an illustration. These arrays containing the node and their children play a crucial role in determining the *M*-critical sets in step 2.

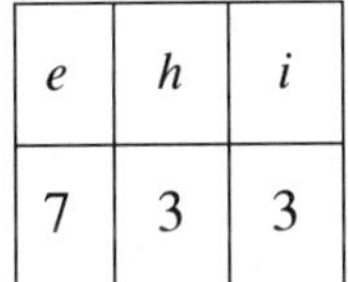

e	h	i
7	3	3

d	f	g
8	1	6

i	n	o
3	1	1

Figure 7. An illustration of the array associated with each node. This array is used in the computation of *M*-critical set.

E. Breadth-First Tree-Traversal

Efficient sequential algorithms for traversing a tree in the breadth-first order require $O(n)$ time for an n-node tree (Aho, Hopcroft and Ullman [1983]). Recently, Chen and Das [1990], [1992], presented a parallel algorithm for breadth-first tree-traversal which takes $O(\frac{n}{p} + \log n)$ time for an n-node tree using p processors. The major steps in the algorithm make use of the parenthesis matching, list ranking, and prefix-sum. Parallel algorithms for list ranking are given in Chapter 4.

The first step for the tree-traversal is the construction of an Euler tour of the given tree, starting at the root. In Table 4, the first row gives the sequence of directed edges traversed in the Euler tour of the tree given in Figure 8.

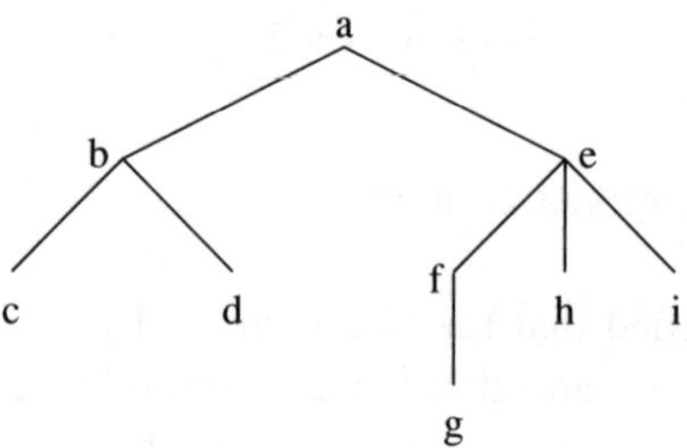

Figure 8: A given tree.

Let the *level of a directed edge* be defined as the level of the child node with which it is incident. The level of the directed edges can be obtained as in Section 1.2.6B. Refer to lines 2, 3, and 4 of Table 4 for the given example.

With each backward (forward) edge, except the rightmost (leftmost) edge at each level, assign a left (right) parenthesis. This sequence of parentheses is referred to as the *Euler sequence*. To identify the leftmost edge at each level, proceed as follows. Let $(e_1, e_2, \cdots, e_k)$ be the edge-sequence according to the Euler tour. First, note that e_1 is a leftmost edge at level 1. Let level (e_i) denote the level of edge e_i. Define

$$L(e_i) = \max\{\, level(e_j) \mid 1 \le j \le i \,\}, \quad 1 \le i \le k.$$

Then, e_i, $2 \le i \le t$, is a leftmost edge, if $|\, L(e_i) - L(e_{i-1})\, | > 0$. Similarly, to identify the rightmost edge at any level, repeat this procedure on the reversed edge-sequence of the Euler tour. Refer to lines 5-8 in Table 4 for identification of leftmost and rightmost edges at each level.

Table 4. Computations leading to the *successor* function.

Euler tour edge-sequence	ab	bc	cb	bd	db	ba	ae	ef	fg	gf	fe	eh	he	ei	ie	ea
Weights	+1	+1	-1	+1	-1	-1	+1	+1	+1	-1	-1	+1	-1	+1	-1	-1
Prefix sum of weights	1	2	1	2	1	0	1	2	3	2	1	2	1	2	1	0
Level of edges	1	2	2	2	2	1	1	2	3	3	2	2	2	2	2	1
$L(e_i)$	1	2	2	2	2	2	2	2	3	3	3	3	3	3	3	3
Leftmost edges	×	×							×							
$L(e_i)$ reversed order	3	3	3	3	3	3	3	3	3	3	2	2	2	2	2	1
Rightmost edges										×					×	×
Euler sequence			(	)	(	(	)	)			(	)	(	)		

Assume the edges at each level are numbered from left to right, starting with 1. At any level, the *successor* of an edge numbered k is the edge numbered $k+1$ at the same level, if there is any, or the edge numbered 1 at the next level, if any. The definition implies that the rightmost edge at the highest level has no successor. It is desired to find the successor of all backward edges. Since the leftmost and rightmost edges have already been identified, the successor of the rightmost backward edge at each level can be easily determined from this information. To identify the successor of the remaining backward edges, solve the parenthesis matching problem (Exercise 1.22) corresponding to the Euler sequence. The successor of a backward edge is the edge which corresponds to the right parenthesis which matches the left parenthesis corresponding to the backward edge.

To order the nodes in the breadth-first order, define the function *next* as follows. Let edge ij be the successor of the backward edge lm. Then,

$next\,[l] = j$. If lm is the first edge in the Euler tour, let $next\,[l] = m$. Refer to Table 5 for computation of the *next* function for the given example.

Table 5. Computation of the *next* function.

Arc pair (backward, successor)	*next* function
$(cb,\ bd)$	$next\,(c) = d$
$(db,\ ef)$	$next\,(d) = f$
$(ba,\ ae)$	$next\,(b) = e$
$(fe,\ eh)$	$next\,(f) = h$
$(he,\ ei)$	$next\,(h) = i$
$(ie,\ fg)$	$next\,(i) = g$
$(ea,\ bc)$	$next\,(e) = c$
first edge ab	$next\,(a) = b$

Finally, by applying a linked-list ranking algorithm to the *next* function, we obtain the breadth-first traversal of the tree. Refer to Table 6 for an example. The complete algorithm for breadth-first traversal is given in Figure 9.

Table 6. Rank of nodes in breadth-first order.

Node	Next	Rank
a	b	1
b	e	2
c	d	4
d	f	5
e	c	3
f	h	6
g	$\times$	9
h	i	7
i	$g^{\star}$	8

Step 1: Compute the Euler tour of the given tree.

Step 2: Assign levels to edges in the Euler tour.

Step 3: Identify and delete the leftmost and rightmost edges at each level of the tree from the Euler tour. Call the remaining edges the Euler sequence.

Step 4: Assign a left parenthesis to each backward edge and a right parenthesis to each forward edge in the Euler sequence.

Step 5: Solve the parentheses matching problem corresponding to the Euler sequence. (Exercise 1.22.) This will define the *successor* for each backward edge except the rightmost edge at each level. The *successor* of the rightmost edge at each level is the leftmost edge at the next level, if any.

Step 6: Order the nodes by assigning the *next* function as follows. Let ij be a backward edge and let lm be its successor. Then, $next[i] = m$. If ij is the first edge in the Euler tour, then, $next[i] = j$.

Step 7: Obtain the breadth-first order by using the list ranking algorithm on the *next* function.

Figure 9. Algorithm for breadth-first traversal of a tree.

1.2.7 Pattern Matching

Let $X = x_1 x_2 x_3 \cdots x_N$ be an N-bit binary string denoting the text, and let $Y = y_1 y_2 \cdots y_m$ be the m-bit binary string denoting the pattern, where $m \leq N$. The problem is to find all the occurrences of the pattern Y in the text X. For $i \leq j$, let $X[i:j] = x_i x_{i+1} \cdots x_j$ denote the segment of X of length $j - i + 1$ starting at position i. Let $I = \{i \mid 1 \leq i \leq N - m + 1\}$. The pattern matching problem reduces to one of finding the subset $M \subseteq I$, such that

$$X[i : i + m - 1] = Y \quad \text{for all} \ \ i \in M.$$

Let $\{0, 1\}^m$ denote the set of all m-bit binary strings. Let D be an appropriately chosen domain. Let

$$f : \{0, 1\}^m \rightarrow D$$

be a function called the *fingerprint* function.

As an example, let D denote the set of all 2×2 non-singular matrices (Exercise 1.17). Let

$$f(0) = \begin{bmatrix} 1 & 0 \\ 1 & 1 \end{bmatrix} \quad \text{and} \quad f(1) = \begin{bmatrix} 1 & 1 \\ 0 & 1 \end{bmatrix}.$$

In extending f from symbols to strings, let

$$f(ab) = f(a) f(b)$$

and

$$f(\lambda) = \begin{bmatrix} 1 & 0 \\ 0 & 1 \end{bmatrix},$$

where λ is the null string, ab denotes the concatenation of strings a and b, and $f(a) f(b)$ denotes the usual matrix product. Thus,

$$f(01) = \begin{bmatrix} 1 & 0 \\ 1 & 1 \end{bmatrix} \begin{bmatrix} 1 & 0 \\ 0 & 1 \end{bmatrix} = \begin{bmatrix} 1 & 1 \\ 1 & 2 \end{bmatrix}$$

It can be verified that f so defined is a one-to-one function, that is, $f(a) = f(b)$ implies $a = b$. Clearly,

$$f^{-1}(0) = \begin{bmatrix} 1 & 0 \\ -1 & 1 \end{bmatrix} \quad \text{and} \quad f^{-1}(1) = \begin{bmatrix} 1 & -1 \\ 0 & 1 \end{bmatrix}$$

Let, for $1 \le k \le N - m + 1$,

$$A_k = f(x_1) f(x2) \cdots f(x_k)$$

and

$$B_k = f^{-1}(x_k) f^{-1}(x_{k-1}) \cdots f^{-1}(x_2) f^{-1}(x_1).$$

Clearly,

$$f(x[i : i + m - 1]) = B_{i-1} \cdot A_{i+m-1}.$$

The pattern matching algorithm may be stated as follows.

Step 1:   For $1 \le k \le N$, compute the set of all A_k's.

Step 2:   For $1 \le k \le N + m - 1$, compute the set of all B_k's.

Step 3:   For $1 \le i \le N - m+1$, if $B_{i-1} \cdot A_{i+m-1} = f(Y)$, then $i \in M$.

Note that steps 1 and 2 involve prefix computation involving 2×2 matrices.

A number of observations are in order. If $a \in \{0, 1\}^k$, then the elements of $f(a)$ can be exponentially large. Indeed, it can be verified (Exercise 1.18) that each element of $f(a)$ is less than or equal to $F(k + 1)$, the $(k + 1)^{th}$ Fibonacci integer, where $F(k + 1) \approx \phi^k$ and $\phi = 1.618$. Thus, for large n and m, the above fingerprint function presents the challenge of performing arithmetic with exponentially large numbers. To circumvent this difficulty, the fingerprint function is modified as follows. Let

$$P = \{ p \mid p \text{ is a prime and } p \leq L \text{ for some integer } L \}.$$

Define, for $a \in \{0, 1\}^k$,

$$f_p(a) = f(a)(mod\ p).$$

that is, $f_p(a)$ is a 2×2 matrix of non-negative integers, where each element of $f_p(a)$ is the residue mod p of the corresponding elements of $f(a)$. It can be verified that

$$f_p^{-1}(0) = \begin{bmatrix} 1 & 0 \\ p-1 & 1 \end{bmatrix} \quad \text{and} \quad f_p^{-1}(1) = \begin{bmatrix} 1 & p-1 \\ 0 & 1 \end{bmatrix}$$

and a new pattern matching algorithm is obtained by replacing f by f_p. In other words, we can control the growth of the elements of $f(a)$ by the *folding* operation resulting from the residue computation. An unpleasant side effect of this folding is that f_p is no longer a one-to-one function. That is, $f_p(a)$ may be equal to $f_p(b)$ even when $a \neq b$ leading to a false match. Thus, the pattern matching algorithm based on the fingerprint function f_p may lead to false matches and hence, is called a *randomized pattern matching* algorithm.

For a given N (the size of the text X) and m (the size of the pattern Y), choose $L = Nm^2$. Now, by picking a prime p randomly in the range $[1, Nm^2]$, we can compute the probability of false match *a priori*. Such computations are beyond the scope of this book and the reader is referred to Karp and Rabin [1987] for details.

1.3 Exercises

1.1   Show that the binary operation o defined by

$$[g_i, p_i] \circ [g_j, p_j] = [g_j \vee (p_j \wedge g_i), p_j \wedge p_i]$$

is associative.

1.2   (Brent and Kung [1982]) Define

$$[G_i, P_i] = \begin{cases} [g_1, p_1] & \text{for } i = 1 \\ [g_i, p_i] \circ [G_{i-1}, P_{i-1}] & \text{for } i = 2 \ to \ N \end{cases}$$

where o is as defined in problem 1 above. Show by induction that

$$G_i = c_i, \text{ the } i^{th} \text{ carry bit}, \ 1 \le i \le N.$$

(G_i may be denoted as the *block carry generate* and P_i as *block carry propagate* condition quite similar to g_i and p_i, respectively.)

1.3   Given a finite-state transducer $M = (K, \Sigma, \Delta, \delta, \lambda, p_0)$, the computation of the output string corresponding to an input string can be expressed in terms of certain matrix-vector operations as follows. Let $K = \{ p_1, p_2, \cdots, p_k \}$. If $p_0 = p_i$ for some $1 \le i \le k$, then the initial state p_0, may be denoted by a k-vector $\bar{p}_0$ whose i^{th} component is unity and all the other components are zero, that is $\bar{p}_0$ is a row vector,

$$\bar{p}_0 = (0, 0, \cdots, 1, 0, \cdots, 0)$$

Likewise, the function M_a may be denoted by a $k \times k$ Boolean matrix $\overline{M}_a$, where

$$\overline{M}_a(i, j) = 1 \text{ if and } only \text{ if } \delta(p_i, a) = p_j$$

$$= 0 \ otherwise.$$

(a) Show that if $M_a(p) = q$, then

$$\bar{q} = \bar{p} \, \overline{M}_a.$$

(b) Show that if $x = a_1 a_2 \cdots a_N$, then M_x corresponds to the matrix $\overline{M}_x$, where

$$\overline{M}_x = \overline{M}_{a_1} * \overline{M}_{a_2} * \cdots * \overline{M}_{a_{N-1}} * \overline{M}_{a_N},$$

where $*$ denotes the matrix multiplication.

(c) Using this matrix notation, recast the parallel computation of the output string of a finite-state transducer.

1.4　　(Fich [1983]) Let L and U be two integers, with $L < U$. Let $p(x)$ be a polynomial of degree N. It is required to evaluate $p(.)$ at consecutive lattice points $k\delta$ where k is an integer in the range $L \leq k \leq U$. This exercise suggests a parallel algorithm based on parallel prefix computation for this problem. Define a sequence of difference polynomials as follows. Let

$$p^{(0)}(x) = p(x).$$

For $1 \leq i \leq N$, define

$$p^{(i)}(x) = p^{(i-1)}(x) - p^{(i-1)}(x - \delta).$$

Clearly, $p^{(i)}(x)$ is a polynomial of degree $N - i$. Since $p^{(N)}(x)$ is a zero-degree polynomial, it follows, that

$$p^{(N)}(k\delta) = p^{(N)}(L\delta) \text{ for } all \ L \leq k \leq U.$$

Observe that

$$p^{(j)}(k\delta) = p^{(j)}((k-1)\delta) + [p^{(j)}(k\delta) - p^{(j)}((k-1)\delta)]$$

$$= p^{(j)}((k-1)\delta) + p^{(j+1)}(k\delta).$$

Likewise,

$$p^{(j)}((k-1)\delta) = p^{(j)}((k-2)\delta) + p^{(j+1)}((k-1)\delta).$$

Substituting back into the previous equation, the latter becomes

$$p^{(j)}(k\delta) = p^{(j)}((k-2)\delta) + p^{(j+1)}((k-1)\delta) + p^{(j+1)}(k\delta).$$

Continuing in this fashion, we readily obtain that

$$p^{(j)}(k\delta) = p^{(j)}(L\delta) + p^{(j+1)}((L+1)\delta) + \cdots$$
$$+ p^{(j+1)}((k-1)\delta) + p^{(j+1)}(k\delta).$$

This relation immediately suggests that the problem of computing $p^{(j)}(k\delta)$, for $L \leq k \leq U$ is, in fact, a *prefix* problem. Thus, to compute $p(k\delta)$, for all $L \leq k \leq U$, first compute $p^{(N)}(k\delta)$ which is constant, for all $L \leq k \leq U$. Then, compute $p^{(j)}(k\delta)$, for all $L \leq k \leq U$, for $j = N - 1, N - 2, ..., 1, 0$. Clearly, $p^{(0)}(k\delta)$ is the solution. In other words, by repeatedly applying the parallel prefix algorithm, $p(x)$ is calculated at all the required points.

(a) Compute the computational complexity of this approach.

(b) Compare this with the method of repeatedly applying the best known serial method, namely, the Horner's method.

1.5   Verify the correctness of the formula in equation (2) of Section 1.2.5 for computing the divided differences.

1.6   (Eğecioğlu, Gallopoulos and Koç [1989]) Show that the sign of the leaf node with label 0 in the binary tree expansion, for $f_{0^r 1^s}$ is $(-1)^{r-1}$, and that all the leaf nodes with label 0 are at level $r + s - 1$.

1.7   (Eğecioğlu, Gallopoulos and Koç [1989]) Consider the string $0^r 1^s$. Starting with $0^{r-1} 0 1 1^{s-1}$, consider the number of ways of parenthesizing the string $0^r 1^s$ such that each new pair of parentheses contains one more symbol than the previous pair. For example, $((((0(01))1)1)$, $((0((01)1))1)$, and $(0(((01)1)1))$ correspond to the three leaf nodes with label 0 from left to right, respectively, in Figure 1 of Section 1.2.5.

Let $a_{r,s}$ denote the number of ways of parenthesizing the string $0^r 1^s$. From the recursive structure of the binary tree, it follows that

$$a_{r,s} = a_{r-1,s} + a_{r,s-1},$$

where $a_{r,1} = 1 = a_{1,s}$. Show that

$$a_{r,s} = \binom{r+s-2}{s-1},$$

where $\binom{n}{r}$ denotes the number of *combinations* of r things taken

out of n things.
Hint: Use induction.

1.8   (Eğecioğlu, Gallopoulos and Koç [1989]) By considering 11 as a single symbol, it can be seen that there are two ways of parenthesizing $0^2 1^3$ as $((0(011))1)$ and $(0((011)1))$. Again, considering 00 as a single symbol, it can be verified that there is only one way of parenthesizing $0^2 1^3$ as $(((001)1)1)$. First, verify these claims by comparing with the binary tree in Figure 1 of Section 1.2.5. By following the computing procedure in Exercise 1.7, show that

(i) $0^r 1^s \mid {}_{0^2} = (-1)^{r-2} \begin{bmatrix} r+s-3 \\ s-1 \end{bmatrix} d_{01}^{r+s-2}.$

(ii) $0^r 1^s \mid {}_{0^i} = (-1)^{r-i} \begin{bmatrix} r+s-i-1 \\ s-1 \end{bmatrix} d_{01}^{r+s-i}, \quad i \le r.$

(iii)   Derive similar expressions for $0^r 1^s \mid {}_{1^2}$, and $0^r 1^s \mid {}_{1^i}$, for $i \le s$.

1.9   (Eğecioğlu, Gallopoulos and Koç [1989]) (a) Show that, for $i \ge 1$,

$$
0^{a_0} 1^{a_1} \cdots N^{a_N} \mid {}_{0^i} = (-1)^{a_0 - i} \sum_P \begin{bmatrix} \lambda_1 - 1 \\ \lambda_1 \end{bmatrix} \begin{bmatrix} \lambda_2 - 1 \\ \lambda_2 \end{bmatrix}
$$

$$
\cdots \begin{bmatrix} \lambda_N - 1 \\ \lambda_N \end{bmatrix} d_{01}^{\lambda_1} d_{02}^{\lambda_2} \cdots d_{0N}^{\lambda_N},
$$

where $\lambda_j = \lambda_j + a_j$ and P is the set of all ordered N-tuples that constitute all the partitions of $a_0 - i$, that is,

$$
P = \{ (\lambda_1, \lambda_2, \cdots, \lambda_N) \mid \sum_{j=1}^{N} \lambda_j = a_0 - i, \ \lambda_j \ge 0 \}.
$$

Remark: When $a_j = 1$ for $j = 0 \cdots N$ and $i = 1$, we obtain

$$
012 \cdots N \mid {}_0 = d_{01} d_{02} \cdots d_{0N},
$$

which is the formula obtained for Newton's interpolation scheme.

(b) Show that, for $i \geq 1$ and $1 \leq k \leq N$,

$$0^{a_0} 1^{a_1} \cdots N^{a_N} \,|_{k^i} = (-1)^{a_k - i} \sum_P \begin{bmatrix} \lambda_0 - 1 \\ \lambda_0 \end{bmatrix} \cdots \begin{bmatrix} \lambda_{k-1} - 1 \\ \lambda_{k-1} \end{bmatrix} \begin{bmatrix} \lambda_{k+1} - 1 \\ \lambda_{k+1} \end{bmatrix}$$

$$\cdots \begin{bmatrix} \lambda_N - 1 \\ \lambda_N \end{bmatrix} d_{k0}^{\lambda_0} \, d_{k1}^{\lambda_1} \cdots d_{k,k-1}^{\lambda_{k-1}} \, d_{k,k+1}^{\lambda_{k+1}} \cdots d_{kN}^{\lambda_N},$$

where $\lambda_j = \lambda_j + a_j$ and P is such that

$$P = \{(\lambda_0, \lambda_1, \cdots, \lambda_{k-1}, \lambda_{k+1}, \cdots, \lambda_N) \mid \sum_{j=1}^{N} \lambda_j = a_k - i, \ \lambda_j \geq 0\}.$$

1.10   Verify the expression in (13) of Section 1.2.5.

1.11   (Eğecioğlu, Gallopoulos and Koç [1989]) In many practical applications of the Hermite interpolation scheme, usually $f(x_i)$, $f^{(1)}(x_i)$ and $f^{(2)}(x_i)$ are given, for $i = 0 \cdots N$. Combining the definitions in (8) and (9) of Section 1.2.5, show that

(a) $0^3 1^3 2^3 \cdots k \,|\, 0^3 = d_{01}^3 \, d_{02}^3 \cdots d_{0(k-1)}^3 \, d_{0k}$

        $0^3 1^3 2^3 \cdots k^2 \,|\, 0^3 = d_{01}^3 \, d_{02}^3 \cdots d_{0(k-1)}^3 \, d_{0k}^2$

        $0^3 1^3 2^3 \cdots k^3 \,|\, 0^3 = d_{01}^3 \, d_{02}^3 \cdots d_{0(k-1)}^3 \, d_{0k}^3$

(b) $0^3 1^3 2^3 \cdots k \,|\, 0^2 = -d_{01}^3 \, d_{02}^3 \cdots d_{0(k-1)}^3 \, d_{0k}$

                    $(3d_{01} + 3d_{02} + \cdots + d_{0k})$

        $0^3 1^3 2^3 \cdots k^2 \,|\, 0^2 = -d_{01}^3 \, d_{02}^3 \cdots d_{0(k-1)}^3 \, d_{0k}^2$

                    $(3d_{01} + 3d_{02} + \cdots + 2d_{0k})$

        $0^3 1^3 2^3 \cdots k^3 \,|\, 0^2 = -d_{01}^3 \, d_{02}^3 \cdots d_{0(k-1)}^3 \, d_{0k}^3$

                    $(3d_{01} + 3d_{02} + \cdots + 3d_{0k})$

(c) $\quad 0^3 1^3 2^3 \cdots k \,|\, 0 = \frac{1}{2}\, d_{01}^3 \; d_{02}^3 \; \cdots \; d_{0(k-1)}^3 \; d_{0k}$

$$[3d_{01}^2 + 3d_{02}^2 + \cdots + 3_{0(k-1)}^2 + d_{0k}^2$$

$$+ (3d_{01} + 3d_{02} + \cdots + d_{0k})^2]$$

$\qquad 0^3 1^3 2^3 \cdots k^2 \,|\, 0 = \frac{1}{2}\, d_{01}^3 \; d_{02}^3 \; \cdots \; d_{0(k-1)}^3 \; d_{0k}^2$

$$[3d_{01}^2 + 3d_{02}^2 + \cdots + 3_{0(k-1)}^2 + 2d_{0k}^2$$

$$+ (3d_{01} + 3d_{02} + \cdots + 2d_{0k})^2]$$

$\qquad 0^3 1^3 2^3 \cdots k^3 \,|\, 0 = \frac{1}{2}\, d_{01}^3 \; d_{02}^3 \; \cdots \; d_{0(k-1)}^3 \; d_{0k}^3$

$$[3d_{01}^2 + 3d_{02}^2 + \cdots + 3_{0(k-1)}^2 + 3d_{0k}^2$$

$$+ (3d_{01} + 3d_{02} + \cdots + 3d_{0k})]$$

1.12 Consider a collection of $I_t = [l_t, r_t]$, $t = 1, 2, \cdots, N$ of intervals on a real line. Consider an interval $I_j = [l_j, r_j]$. The left-end point l_j is said to be *covered* by an interval I_k if $l_j \in I_k$. The problem is to find the number of intervals covering l_t for $t = 1, 2, \cdots, N$. This problem can be solved using the following idea which essentially involves prefix computation.

Step 1: Sort the $2N$ end points $\{l_t, r_t | t = 1 \cdots N\}$ to obtain a list $c_1 \le c_2 \le \cdots \le c_{2N}$.

Step 2: Define

$$f(c_i) = \begin{cases} +1 & \text{if } c_i = l_j \text{ for some } j \\ -1 & \text{if } c_i = r_j \text{ for some } j. \end{cases}$$

Compute $\;L_j = \sum_{i=1}^{j-1} f(c_i)$, $1 \le j \le N$, using the prefix algorithm.

Prove that L_j denotes the number of intervals covering l_j.

Note: These types of calculations arise in the analysis of algorithms for Interval graphs (Liang, Dhall and Lakshmivarahan [1990]).

1.13 (Knuth [1969]) If the prefix circuit inputs $x_i = 1$, $1 \le i \le N$, then the circuit is said to *construct* all the integers 1 through N. There is a natural connection between the prefix circuits for constructing integers and the well known problem of *addition chain,* which may be stated as follows. Given an integer N, the *addition chain* for N is an integer sequence

$$1 = b_0, \ b_1, \ b_2, \ \cdots \ , \ b_m = N$$

where

$$b_i = b_j + b_k, \qquad k \leq j < i,$$

that is, the ith member of the sequence is obtained as the sum of two (not necessarily distinct) previous elements of the sequence. The index m is called the length of the addition chain. For example, $b_0 = 1$, $b_1 = 2$, $b_3 \in \{2, 3, 4\}$, $b_4 \in \{2, 3, 4, 5, 6, 7, 8\}$, etc. Without loss of generality, we can require that the addition chain be *ascending,* that is,

$$1 = b_0 < b_1 < b_2 < \cdots < b_m = N.$$

Let $a(N)$ denote the minimum length of the (ascending) addition chain for N. It can be verified that $a(7) = 4$ and $a(8) = 3$.

(a) Show that the minimum number of multiplications required in computing x^N is $a(N)$.

Hint: Multiplication of powers of x reduces to the addition problem for indices.

(b) Compute $a(N)$ for $2 \leq N \leq 100$.

(c) For $1 \leq k \leq N$, compare the value of $a(k)$ with the number of operations performed in constructing the integer k using N input, (i) d-optimal circuit, (ii) (s, d)-optimal circuit.

1.14   (Bilardi and Preparata [1986]) Consider the expression

$$x_t = F^t x_0 + \sum_{k=0}^{t-1} F^k y_{t-k-1}, \qquad 0 \leq t \leq n,$$

where x_t, y_t, and F are matrices of suitable dimensions. Thus,

$$x_1 = F x_0 + y_0$$

$$x_2 = F^2 x_0 + y_1 + F y_0$$

$$x_3 = F^3 x_0 + y_2 + F y_1 + F^2 y_0$$

$$x_4 = F^4 x_0 + y_3 + F y_2 + F^2 y_1 + F^3 y_0.$$

Given x_0, y_0, y_1, y_2, and y_3, x_i's, for $1 \le i \le 4$ can be computed using the following algorithm.

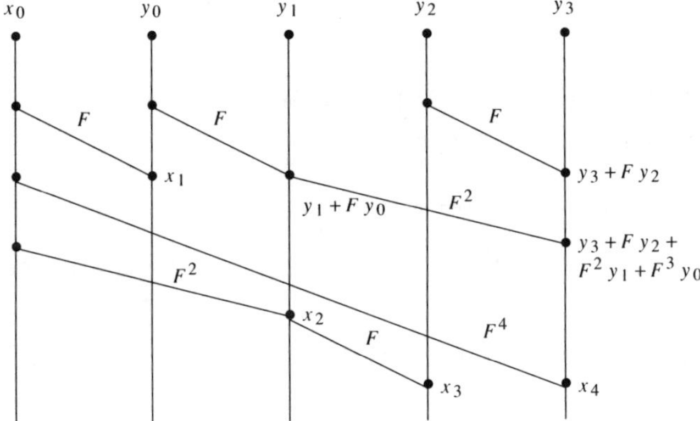

From this example, the similarity of this problem to parallel prefix computation is obvious. Generalize this algorithm for any $n = 2^m$.

Remark: This type of computation naturally arises in the VLSI realization of digital filters. See Bilardi and Preparata [1986] for more details.

1.15   In this exercise, we describe an algorithm for finding an Euler tour in a tree $G = (V, E)$. Let $a \in V$ and $\{ b_0, b_1, \cdots, b_{d-1} \}$ be the ordered set of neighbors of a. Let $G' = (V, E')$ be the corresponding directed graph obtained by replacing each edge in G by two edges directed in *opposite* directions. Let $s{:}E' \to E'$, such that $s((b_i, a)) = (a, b_{i+1})$, where $i + 1$ is computed modulo d. s is called the *successor* function on the edges of G'. As an example consider

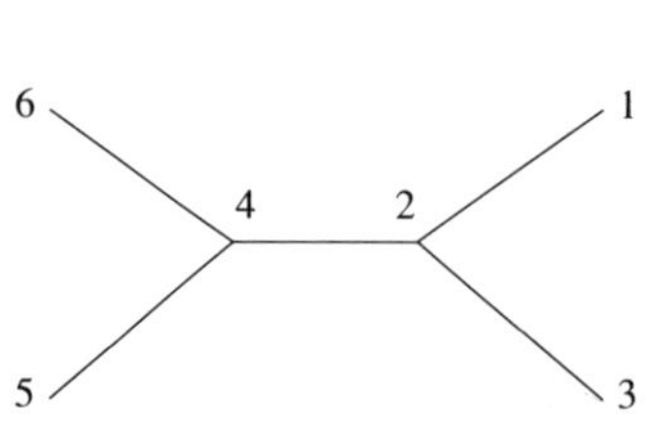

Nodes	Adjacency List
1	2
2	4, 1, 3
3	2
4	2, 6, 5
5	4
6	4

It is clear that $s((2, 4)) = (4, 6)$, $s((6, 4)) = (4, 5)$, etc., and we obtain the following table.

e	(1, 2)	(2, 1)	(2, 3)	(3, 2)	(2, 4)	(4, 2)	(4, 6)	(6, 4)	(4, 5)	(5, 4)
$s(e)$	(2, 3)	(1, 2)	(3, 2)	(2, 4)	(4, 6)	(2, 1)	(6, 4)	(4, 5)	(5, 4)	(4, 2)

The Euler tour can be readily identified using this table.

(a) Derive a constant time parallel algorithm for tracing an Euler tour in an N-node tree using N processors.

(b) Verify that the traversal induced by the Euler tour of $G' = (V, E')$ gives rise to *depth-first search* of the graph $G' = (V, E')$.

1.16   Let $G = (V, E)$ be a tree with $r \in V$ as its root. Let $post(x)$ be the order in which the node x is visited in the post-order traversal of G. An algorithm for finding the post-order number is given below.

Step 1: Assign a weight of 1 for each edge $(x, p(x))$, and zero to the edge $(p(x), x)$.

Step 2: Compute the prefixes along the Euler path starting at root r.

Step 3: For each $x \neq r$, $post(x)$ is equal to the prefix sum of $(x, p(x))$. For $x = r$, clearly, $post(r) = N$, the number of nodes in V.

(a) Verify the correctness of this algorithm.

(b) Modify this algorithm to find the *pre-order number*.

Note: Pre-order numbering has been successfully used in identifying biconnected components in a graph, JáJá [1992].

1.17   For any $a \in \{0, 1\}^n$, compute the determinant of $f(a)$.

1.18   Let $f(0) = \begin{bmatrix} 1 & 0 \\ 1 & 1 \end{bmatrix}$ and $f(1) = \begin{bmatrix} 1 & 1 \\ 0 & 1 \end{bmatrix}$. If $a \in \{0, 1\}^k$, then show that each element of the matrix $f(a)$ is less than or equal to $F(k+1)$, the $(k+1)^{th}$ Fibonacci integer defined by $F(k) = F(k-1) + F(k-2)$, where $F(0) = 0$ and $F(1) = 1$. In particular, verify that $F(k+1) \approx \phi^k$, where $\phi = 1.618$, called the *golden ratio*.

1.19   Prove the properties 1 through 3 in Section 1.2.6D.

1.20   Find an N-node tree with $\dfrac{2N}{M} - 1$ M-critical nodes in it.

1.21   Construct an N-node tree such that the root r is an M-critical node.

1.22   (Prasad, Das, and Chen [1992]) This exercise develops a parallel algorithm for parentheses matching used in Section 1.2.6E. Consider a string α of parentheses of length N. For any substring β of α, let $U(\beta)$ denote the string of parenthesis that is obtained from β by deleting the matched pairs of parentheses. Obviously, the string $U(\beta)$ has the form $\cdots)) \cdots)((\cdots (.$ The string $U(\beta)$ can be written in a shorthand form as $d)_i (_j e$, where d is the consecutive number of right parentheses ending at the parenthesis at position i, and e is the number of consecutive left parentheses starting with the left parenthesis at position j. The right parenthesis at position i is called the *right representative* of the sequence of right parentheses ending at position i. Similarly, the left parenthesis at position j is called the *left representative* of the sequence of left parentheses starting at position j.

Let β and γ be two consecutive substrings of a string of parentheses. Let $U(\beta) = d)_i \;(_j e$, and $U(\gamma) = f)_k \;(_l g$. Then, for the string $\alpha\beta$ obtained by concatenating the strings α and β,

$$U(\beta\gamma) = \begin{cases} d)_i \;(_j e - f \;(_l g & \text{if } e \geq f \\ d)_i \; f - e)_k \;(_l g & \text{if } f \geq e \end{cases}$$

where $0)_i$ and $(_i 0$ represent null strings. Thus, for any string α obtained by concatenation of substrings, $U(\alpha)$ may be written as

$$U(\alpha) = d_1)_{i_1}^{u_1} \; d_2)_{i_2}^{u_2} \; \cdots \; d_k)_{i_k}^{u_k} \; (_{j_r}^{v_r} e_r \; \cdots \; (_{j_2}^{v_2} e_2 \; (_{j_1}^{v_1} e_1,$$

where

$$u_t = d_1 + d_2 + \cdots + d_t, \text{ for } 1 \leq t \leq k,$$

and

$$v_t = e_1 + e_2 + \cdots + e_t, \text{ for } 1 \leq t \leq r.$$

We now define a *tree of unmates* for a string α of parentheses as follows. For the sake of simplicity, let p be a power of 2. Let $\alpha = \alpha_1 \alpha_2 \cdots \alpha_p$. The leaves of the tree are $U(\alpha_1)$, $U(\alpha_2)$, $\cdots$, $U(\alpha_p)$. Let the level of leaves be 0. Then, the nodes at level 1 are $U(\alpha_1 \alpha_2)$, $U(\alpha_3 \alpha_4)$, $\cdots$. The nodes at level 2 are $U(\alpha_1 \alpha_2 \alpha_3 \alpha_4)$, $\cdots$, and so on, with $U(\alpha = \alpha_1 \cdots \alpha_p)$ at the root. The *matching tree* is the tree of unmates with the unmate strings at each node represented in the coded form defined above. We may label the nodes of this tree as follows. The root node is labeled 1. For any node labeled j, its left child is labeled $2j$, and its right child is labeled $2j + 1$.

For any node j, with children $2j$ and $2j + 1$, the *span of a node j* is the pair (r_j, l_j), where r_j and l_j are the number of right and left unmates, respectively, in the string obtained by concatenating the strings at the leaves rooted at node j. Obviously,

$$(r_j, l_j) = (r_{2j}, l_{2j}) + (r_{2j+1}, l_{2j+1}) - (m_j, m_j),$$

where $m_j = \min\{\, l_{2j}, r_{2j+1} \,\}$ is the number of pairs of parentheses matched at node j.

In the following, we describe an algorithm for parentheses matching from Prasad, Das and Chen [1992], for the EREW model using p processors. For the given string α of parentheses of length N, the algorithm provides the matching information in array *MATCH*, where the parenthesis at position *MATCH*[i] matches with the parenthesis at position i. Each processor maintains some local data giving the values of *current_node*, *right_rep*, *left_rep*, *r_value*, *l_value*. In addition, other data structure used for book keeping purposes includes two arrays, each of size $\frac{N}{2}$, called *LMATCH* and *RMATCH*, which maintains the mates of left and right parentheses, respectively, as the algorithm progresses, an array m of size $p - 1$ and an array *pm* also of size $p - 1$, which keeps the prefix sum values of array m, and an array *LIST* of size $p \log p$.

The algorithm proceeds as follows. Assume the number of processors p is a power of 2.

Step 1: Divide the given string of length N into p equal substrings of length $\frac{N}{p}$. Process P_i, $1 \le i \le p$ scans the ith substring to find the matched pairs. The relevant information is saved in the output array *MATCH*, and remaining parentheses are packed together. As mentioned above the unmatched substrings are coded, and for each substring its (r, l) values, and the corresponding left and right representatives are saved. A left representative has the form $({}^{u}_{l_i}, l'_i\ d$, where l_i is the original position of the left parenthesis, and l'_i is the position in the packed array. Similarly, for the right representative. This takes $(\frac{N}{p})$ time.

Step 2: For $1 \le j \le p - 1$, compute m_j. Also compute $pm[j] = m_1 + m_2 + \cdots + m_j$, for $1 \le j \le p - 1$. For $1 \le j \le p - 1$, processor P_i at the child node of j, computes a copy of $pm[i]$ and stores it in *LIST*[$hp + i$], where h is the level of the child node. This step takes $O(\frac{N}{p} + \log p)$ time.

Step 3: The match-finding proceeds as follows. For a node j of the matching tree, consider the action of the left child at node $2j$. Processor P_i checks its variable *current_node*. If it is an even number, it immediately knows that it is working on a left child. First, it computes m_j. Assume, the variable *left_rep* contains $({}^{u}_{l_i}, l'_i\ d$ in its local memory. Three cases arise.

(a) $m_j \geq u$. In this case, all d left unmates have a match. Therefore, copy the *left_rep* into $LMATCH[pm[j] - (m_j - u)]$. This will leave a gap of $d - 1$ cells in $LMATCH$ which can be filled later.

(b) $u > m_j > u - d$. In this case $u - m_j$ parentheses do not match. Let $(_{l_i, h}$, where h is the level of the child node $2j$, be the leftmost matched parenthesis of the d-block under consideration. Since $(_{l_i, l'_i}$ is stored in position l_i, $(_{l_i, h}$ is stored in position $l'_i + u - m_j$, and, therefore, can be retrieved in constant time. Thus, copy $(_{l_i, h}^{m_j} m_j - (u - d)$ in $LMATCH[pm[j]]$. The variable *left_rep* is updated to $(_{l_i, l'_i}^{u - m_j + l_{2j+1}} u - m_j$.

(c) $u - d \geq m_j$. In this case, there is no match. The variable left_rep is updated to $(_{l_i, l'_i}^{u - m_j + l_{2j+1}} d$.

Analogously similar action is taken at node $2j + 1$. This step requires $O(\log p)$ time.

Step 4: This step fills the gaps in the arrays $LMATCH$ and $RMATCH$ from the information produced in step 3. Processor P_i scans arrays $LMATCH$ and $RMATCH$ starting from positions $i \dfrac{N}{2p}$ moving downwards. As each processor scans the allotted portion of the arrays, it fills in the gaps in the arrays by computing appropriate values in unfilled positions subject to the following rules. Each processor marks the first non-empty position. A processor will stop when it comes across a marked position, or has scanned the first element of the array, or has visited its allotted positions. This step takes $O(\dfrac{N}{p})$ time.

Step 5: The output array $MATCH$ is updated from the information stored in arrays $LMATCH$ and $RMATCH$. Note that the left parenthesis in $LMATCH[i]$ matches with the right parenthesis in $RMATCH[i]$. This step can also be completed in time $O(\dfrac{N}{p})$.

The reader is invited to check the correctness of the algorithm and to verify the claim on the time complexities of various steps.

1.4 Notes And References

Section 1.1: To our knowledge there are at least two early and yet independent references to the use of prefix computation. In the context of the design of fast parallel circuits for the addition of two integers in binary, Y. Ofman, in the early 60's introduced the first parallel algorithm for computing prefixes (Ofman [1963]). (Refer to Section 1.2.2.) Simultaneously, K.E. Iverson [1962], introduced the notion of a selection operator called *COMPRESS* as a member of a wide class of special array operators in the programming language APL. If A is an array containing, for example, 3, 5, 7, 1, 8, 9, and U is a Boolean array, for example, 1, 0, 1, 0, 1, 0, then, U/A denotes the *COMPRESS* operation which leads to an output vector containing only those elements of A that correspond to the elements 1 in the array U. Thus, in the above example U/A is 3, 7, 8. This operation is the same as the packing operation discussed in Section 1.2.1.

Recognizing the importance of the prefix operation in diverse applications, Blelloch [1989] has argued that the operation of computing the prefixes may be considered as a *primitive* operation much like addition, multiplication, memory access, etc. Blelloch refers to the problem of computing prefixes as **scan** operation. In fact, the **scan** primitive has been implemented in microcode on the Connection Machine which is a family of parallel architectures currently marketed by the Thinking Machine Corporation.

Prefix problem is a special case of the linear first-order recurrence

$$x_i = a_i x_{i-1} + d_i.$$

Hence, all the methods for solving this class of recurrence can be readily adapted to computing prefixes. Also, refer to Section 1.2.4, wherein the notion of prefix computation is used in solving linear recurrences in parallel. For a comprehensive survey of solving recurrences in parallel, refer to Kuck [1980] and Lakshmivarahan and Dhall [1990].

The notion of prefix of a word or a sentence and prefix closure of a language has been the subject of study in Formal Language Theory for some time (Hopcroft and Ullman [1979]). Let Σ be a finite alphabet set and $x \in \Sigma^*$, the set of all finite strings over Σ. Then, $z \in \Sigma^*$ is called a prefix of x if there exists $y \in \Sigma^*$ such that $x = zy$. If $L \subseteq \Sigma^*$, then the *prefix closure PREF* (L) of L is defined as

$$PREF(L) = \{z \mid x = zy,\ x \in L,\ \text{and}\ z, y \in \Sigma^*\}.$$

It is well known that if L is accepted by a deterministic finite automaton, then so is *PREF* (L).

The notion of *prefix reversal* has been successfully used as a basic operation in sorting a sequence of numbers. Let the identity permutation be denoted by 1 2 3 ... N, The set of all $(N-1)$ prefix reversals are: 2 1, 3 2 1, 4 3 2 1, ... , $N (N-1) \cdots 3\,2\,1$. The following is an example of sorting using prefix reversal. Let the input sequence to be sorted be 5 4 2 3 1. Then, consider a sequence of prefix reversals leading to the sorted sequence

$$54231 \xrightarrow{54321} 13245 \xrightarrow{21} 31245 \xrightarrow{321} 21345 \xrightarrow{21} 12345.$$

Sorting by prefix reversal is related to the *pancake problem* (Dweighter [1975]) which may be stated as follows. A sloppy chef prepares a stack of pancakes of different sizes. The waiter, for aesthetic reasons, on the way to the table, rearranges the stack so that the smallest is on the top with the largest at the bottom by simply grabbing several on the top and flipping them over. This process is repeated until the desired arrangement is obtained. The reader can readily see that flipping a set of pancakes from the top is the same as prefix reversals. If N is the number of pancakes, let $f(N)$ denote the number of flips, or prefix reversals, needed to sort the pancakes. Several authors have characterized the function $f(N)$ for small values of N. Garey, Johnson and Lin [1977] describe $f(N)$ for $N \le 7$. Gates and Papadimitriou [1979] have shown that $\dfrac{17}{16}N \le f(N) \le \dfrac{5N+5}{3}$.

In addition, if the pancakes are burnt on one side, it is desired to sort them with the burnt side facing down. If $g(N)$ is the number of flips needed to sort burnt pancakes, then $g(N) \le 2N+3$ (Gates and Papadimitriou [1979]). For further analysis of sorting by prefix reversal, refer to Heydari and Sudborough [1993].

Considering the set of $(N-1)$ prefix reversals as a generator for the symmetric permutation group S_N, Akers and Balakrishnan [1989], introduced a class of interconnection networks based on the notion of Cayley graphs of permutation groups, called the *pancake* or *prefix reversal graphs*. It can be seen that optimal sorting using prefix reversal corresponds to shortest paths in this class of Cayley graphs. Refer to Lakshmivarahan, Jwo and Dhall [1993] for a discussion of Cayley graphs of permutation groups.

Section 1.2: The ranking and packing problem in Section 1.2.1 is discussed in Karp and Ramachandran [1990]. Radix sort based on packing is discussed in Blelloch [1989]. Radix sorting is also known as bucket sorting. Refer to Wagner and Han [1986] for a discussion of bucket sort using prefix computation. Blelloch [1989], using the **scan** operation has given efficient parallel implementation of Quick-sort, minimum spanning tree, and parallel merge algorithms. He also provides hardware implementation of the **scan** operation at the logic level. Section 1.2.2 is adapted from Brent and Kung [1982], Section 1.2.3 from Ladner and Fischer [1980], Section 1.2.4 from Fich [1983], and Section 1.2.5 from a series of papers by Eğecioğlu, Gallopoulos and Koç [1989a], [1989b], and [1990]. Section 1.2.6 is adapted from Tarjan and Vishkin [1985], Vishkin [1985], JáJá [1992], and Chen and Das [1990], [1992]. Section 1.2.7 follows from Karp and Rabin [1987].

Section 1.3: The notion of *addition chain* for an integer N (Exercise 1.13) was first discussed by A. Scholz in 1937 (Brauer [1939]), and has been extensively analyzed by Brauer [1939], Knuth [1969], Schonhage [1975], and Volger [1985].

Chapter 2

Parallel Machines And Models — An Overview

This chapter provides an overview of many issues related to the analysis of parallel algorithms in general. Starting with a discussion of the need for parallelism, a classification of parallel architectures, the need and the use of parallel models in algorithm development and various measures for quantifying the performance of parallel algorithms are presented. The definition, the role, and the properties of the key parallel complexity class called *NC* (Nick's Class) are then described. This chapter concludes with a discussion of a basic result called Brent's inequality and the derivation of a simple lower bound on the parallel time complexity.

2.1 The Need for Parallelism

The conventional approach to engineering design critically depends on laboratory testing of scaled models — witness wind tunnel testing of models of aircraft and its parts. While such an approach has resulted in considerable success, it often involves destructive testing and is time consuming. It is said that it took nearly ten years and approximately three billion dollars to develop the now commercially successful Boeing 747 aircraft used in long-haul commercial flights. Computer simulation provides a convenient and economically attractive alternative. In simulation, the physical processes of interest are represented by a system of non-linear partial differential equations involving the three space dimensions and the time. These model equations are solved numerically using the finite difference or finite element methods. The behavior of the solution of these model equations provides insight on the effectiveness of the model in describing the physical phenomenon of interest, be it a model of an aircraft or a model of a weather phenomenon, etc. This approach, based on computer simulations has several inherent advantages. It is certainly non-destructive and easily allows for the analysis of the quality of the model for various combinations of initial and boundary conditions and the values of many key parameters of interest.

The time required to complete a model run is a direct function of a number of factors. The number of grid points in space and time, the nature of the discretization scheme, such as, finite difference, finite elements, etc., the non-linearity and the coupling between the variables in the models. Many of the real world problems of interest require weeks, months and sometimes years of uninterrupted computing when performed on even the fastest of serial machines. Refer to Massey [1993] and Rheinboldt [1984] for a description of several examples of such computationally demanding problems. Several problems arise. How would one ensure the reliability of computations? Perhaps, there was an error in computation resulting from an unforeseen change in the voltage of the power supply resulting from a thunderstorm. Then, there is the question of hardware reliability, uninterrupted power supply, temperature control of the ambience, and many more. Most importantly, the very reason for turning to computer simulation is to reduce the turnaround time in the analysis of models. All of this reasoning points clearly to the fact that, while we cannot change the computational demands of the model, the effectiveness of computer simulation critically depends on the availability of a new generation of powerful computers capable of performing massive computations in a short time.

The raw power of a computer is often measured by the number of floating point operations (such as add, multiply) performed per second, measured in units of million operations, called the megaflops (millions of floating point operations per second). There are principally two ways of increasing the computing power — *technology* and *architecture*. Until recently, we have depended solely on the progression of technology —

vacuum tubes, transistors, integrated circuits, VLSI, etc., to gain power through increased speed of the hardware. There are now indications that we may be reaching the physical limits as far as the speed of the underlying hardware is concerned. Thanks to the same technology, large-scale production of computer chips results in a continuous decline of the cost of computer hardware. The computer architects and engineers recognizing this trend, turned to replication of hardware to increase the computing power. In other words, parallelism in the underlying hardware is a natural engineering solution to producing powerful computers of the future.

Today, parallelism in computers is introduced at various levels. Since the megaflop rating depends on the speed with which the basic arithmetic operations are performed, often parallelism is introduced at the *bit/byte level*. The pipelined vector arithmetic processors, as in CRAY Research machines, and Alliant FX/8, for example, have greatly enhanced the power. Availability of inexpensive hardware promoted the use of more than one functional unit, such as separate floating point adders, multipliers, comparators, integer adders and multipliers, etc., in a single computer. To exploit parallelism, resulting from the use of multifunctional units, there is a need for *compiler level* parallelism. To exploit the *problem level* parallelism at the highest level, one can bring together several stand-alone computers, each with its own memory, multifunctional units, and pipeline vector arithmetic processors, such as CRY X-MP, Alliant FX-8, Intel hypercube, CM-5, to mention a few.

Availability of powerful computers is only a beginning and not an end. The end consists in the efficient use of these machines. Tremendous increase in raw computational power often does not directly translate into comparable increase in performance. The disparity between the *available* computing power and the *achievable* performance can be related to a number of factors. Obviously, for maximum performance, one must keep as many processors busy (performing useful work) as possible. However, the length of time the processors are active depends on the chosen algorithm. Perhaps, the problem is very stubborn and does not admit efficient parallel algorithm, the type of algorithm chosen does not *match the underlying architecture,* or the processors are active, but the algorithm performs *redundant* calculations. Further, when more than one processor *cooperates* in solving a given problem, there will be a definite need for *communication, coordination,* and/or *synchronization* between them. Communication and synchronization are inevitable, and often hinder progress of computation. Analysis of the nature and extent to which these and other factors affect the *gap,* separating the available computing power and the achievable performance constitutes one of the primary goals of the theory of parallel computation.

2.2 A Classification of Parallel Computers

Most commercially available parallel computers may be broadly divided into two groups — *shared memory* machines (such as, CRAY Research machines, Alliant FX/8, Butterfly, Multimax, etc.) and *non-shared* or *distributed memory* machines (such as, Intel's Hypercube, Ncube, CM-5, etc.). Refer to Figure 1 for a schematic representation of the organization of the two types of machines. In a shared memory machine, all the processors have *equal* access rights to all the memory modules and the processors *communicate* indirectly by *reading from,* and *writing into,* the shared memory. *Dynamic, multistage* interconnection

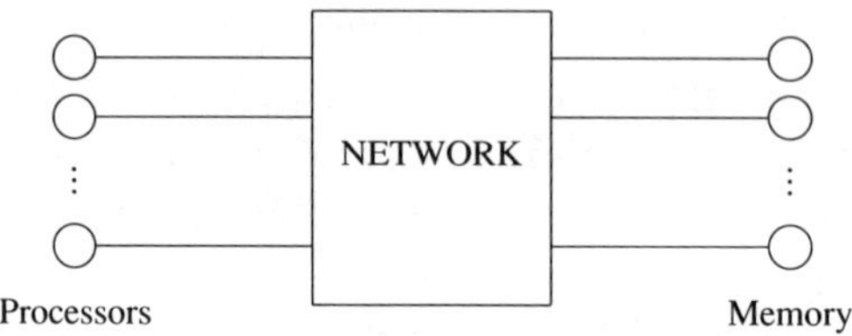

(a) Organization of shared memory machines.

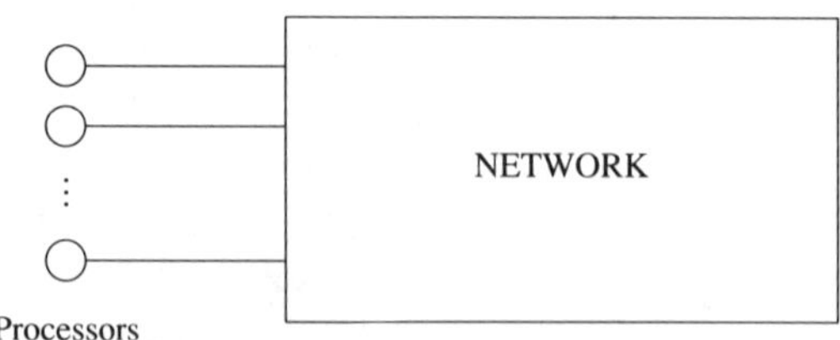

(b) Organization of distributed memory machines.

Figure 1. Two basic organizations of parallel computers.

networks built-out of small, complete *cross-bar* switches are often used to interconnect processors and memory modules, and communication is *via circuit switching*, much like in telephone networks. An example of dynamic networks is given in Figure 2. In a distributed memory machine, a collection of processors are interconnected using a static network, such as a binary hypercube, or shuffle/exchange, to mention only two of the many possibilities. Refer to Figure 3. In this latter organization, processors directly communicate using some form of a handshake protocol based on send/receive commands. This direct communication is realized using *packet switching,* much like communication through the postal or any other courier service.

While the above characterization is based on the architectural/organizational aspects of the machines, there is another useful classification based on the mode of operations. In most of the linear models of interest in science and engineering, the underlying set of computations can be rewritten as component-wise operations on large vectors — such as vector addition, product of a vector by a constant, component-wise product of vectors, etc. In such a case, the same operation is performed on the corresponding elements of a vector. This type of parallelism is embodied in a class called *single instruction stream* operating on a *multiple data stream,* known as a SIMD type. In this terminology, the now classic serial computation may be viewed as the interaction of a single instruction stream on a single data stream, called a

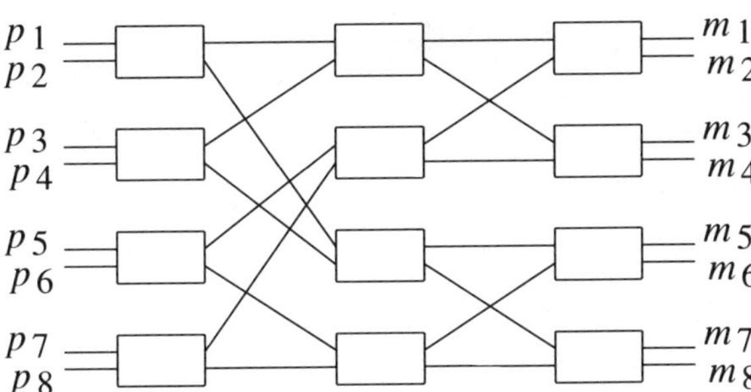

Figure 2: An example of 3-stage 8-input and 8-output network, made up of 2×2 switches called the baseline network.

SISD type. The other mode occurs when multiple (different) instruction streams operate on multiple (different) data streams, called the MIMD type. In a SIMD type of parallelism, computations are performed in a synchronous mode, whereas, MIMD computations are performed either synchronously or asynchronously.

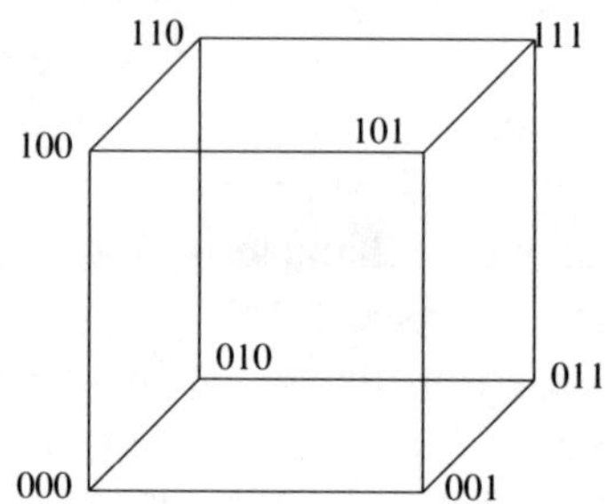

(a) An example of a static network based on binary hypercube.

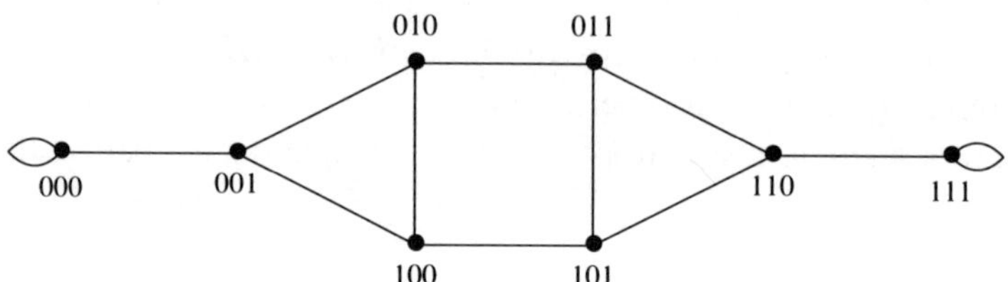

(b) An example of a static network based
on   shuffle-exchange connection.

Figure 3. Examples of static networks.

2.3 Parallel Models

Parallel models provide a framework for the design and development of parallel algorithms that are independent of the idiosynchracies of any specific architecture. In this book, we are particularly interested in two basic types of models, namely *shared memory* (also called PRAM for parallel random access) models and *circuit* models.

2.3.1 Shared Memory Model

The shared memory model is an abstraction of an assemblage of stand-alone processors connected to a common bank of memory modules. It is assumed that each processor has enough local memory, which, in addition to holding the programs and data, also acts as a scratch pad for local computations. The processors *interact* by *writing into,* or *reading from,* the shared memory. In a given step, each processor performs either a local computation, or reads from, or writes to, the shared memory. Depending on the way in which the processors are allowed to perform the read/write operations in the shared memory, *three* different types of shared memory models are usually identified.

(a) EREW (Exclusive Read, Exclusive Write) Model: This is a realistic model. In this model, at one time, only one processor can either read from or write into a given memory location, that is, simultaneous read from or write to a given memory cell is not allowed.

(b) CREW (Concurrent Read, Exclusive Write) Model: This model permits simultaneous read but does not have the simultaneous write capability.

(c) CRCW (Concurrent Read and Concurrent Write) Model: In this case, it is assumed that any sub-collection of processors can simultaneously write into and read from a given location in the shared memory. This is the strongest of the three models and clearly unrealistic. Nevertheless, it provides a useful framework that enables us to concentrate on the sequence of computations without having to worry about the technicalities of *synchronization* and *communication.* From the point of view of proving correctness of algorithms, this model is further subdivided, depending on the way in which the write conflict is resolved. When simultaneous writes occur, one way to solve the conflict is to let, for example, the processor with the least index write. This is called the *priority write* CRCW model. Another way is to require that all processors involved in the simultaneous write, write the *same* quantity. This restriction is called the *common write* rule. In this book, unless specified otherwise, we will use the CRCW model with the common write rule.

A number of observations are in order: (a) by further restricting the read/write access for distinct pairs of processors to disjoint collection of shared memory cells, we can easily simulate the *unidirectional* links in the non-shared or distributed memory architectures, such as the hypercube; (b) a concurrent read/write step of p processors can be simulated in $O(\log p)$ exclusive read/write steps using p processors. Conceptually, this is done by picking a *leader* using a *tournament* tree. Let the processors be numbered from 1 to p. Refer to Figure 1 for an illustration. At the lowest level, processors i and $i+1$, for odd i, compare their labels and declare the one with the smaller label as the winner. In turn, the winners play the same game repeatedly until one winner is obtained. This winning processor then performs the read operation and *broadcasts* the value read to all the other processors using the same tournament tree top down. For details of this simulation, refer to Chapter 1 in Lakshmivarahan and Dhall [1990]. Thus, an algorithm that requires $T(N)$ steps on a CRCW or CREW model would only require $O(T(N)\log N)$ steps when implemented on an EREW model.

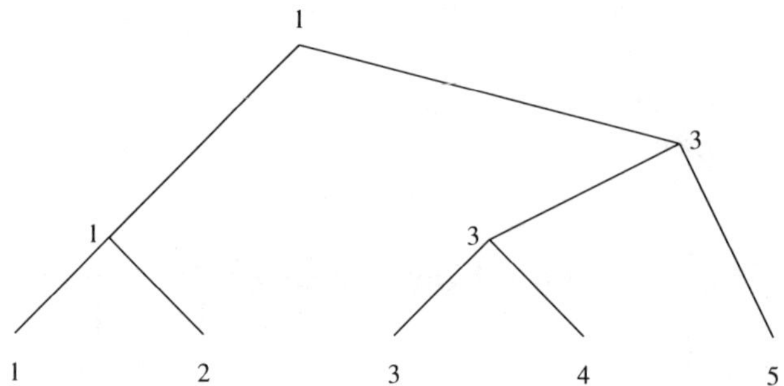

Figure 1. An example of a tournament tree.

2.3.2 Circuit Model

An *arithmetic* circuit $C(N)$ over a field (for example, the field of real numbers) is a *directed acyclic graph* with

(a)   a list of N *input nodes* with in-degree (fan-in) zero;

(b)   a collection of nodes called the *constant nodes* of in-degree zero labeled with elements from the field (for example, 0, 1, π, e, etc.);

(c)   *internal* or *operation nodes* of in-degree two, labeled with one of the four *arithmetic* operators $\{\ +, -, \times, \div\ \}$; and

(d)   a list of *M* distinguished *output nodes* of out-degree (fan-out) zero. Refer to Figure 1 for an example of an arithmetic circuit.

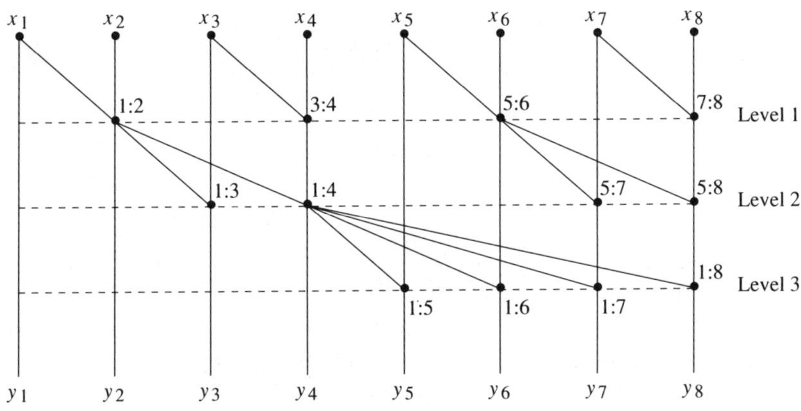

Figure 1. An example of a circuit for $i \leq j$.
$i:j$ denotes the sum $\sum_{k=i}^{j} x_k$.

A *Boolean circuit* is defined along similar lines with the input and constants properly restricted to the Boolean domain and the internal operations to appropriate Boolean operations. In view of this similarity, the following discussion relating to arithmetic circuits carries over to Boolean Circuits.

Let R denote the set of real numbers and R^k denote the set of k-tuples over R. A uniform family $C = < C(N) >$ of arithmetic circuits is said to compute the family $f = < f_N >$ of functions if $C(N)$ computes the function f_N, where

$$f_N : R^N \rightarrow R^M$$

if given N inputs $\mathbf{x} = (x_1, x_2, \cdots, x_N)$, the circuit computes the M outputs $\mathbf{y} = (y_1, y_2, \cdots, y_M)$, where $f_N(\mathbf{x}) = \mathbf{y}$.

The *depth $d(N)$* of $C(N)$ is the *length* of the *longest path* from any one of the input to output nodes. Clearly, the depth relates to the parallel time taken by the algorithm corresponding to the circuit. The *size $s(N)$* of $C(N)$ is the *total number* of operation nodes. Let w_i be the number of operations performed by the circuit $C(N)$ at time step i, where

$i = 1, 2, \cdots d(N)$. Then, we have

$$s(N) = \sum_{i=1}^{d(N)} w_i. \tag{1}$$

The *width* $w(N)$ of the circuit $C(N)$ is defined to be the *maximum* of the number of operations performed in any step. Thus,

$$w(N) = \max_{1 \le i \le d(N)} \{ w_i \}, \tag{2}$$

and

$$s(N) \le d(N)\, w(N). \tag{3}$$

It is also useful to characterize the notion of a *level* in a circuit. It is assumed that the inputs are available at level 0. Level i consists of all those operations that are performed in step i, for $i = 1, 2, \cdots , d(N)$. It follows from the definition that at least one of the two inputs to an operation at level i comes from the output of an operation at level $i - 1$ and the other may come from an output of an operation at level $j < i$. Also, note that the various components of the output are available at or above the level $d(N)$.

The three-level circuit in Figure 1 is of depth 3, size 12, and width 4. All the operation nodes are of *constant* in-degree two and variable out-degree. The operation nodes perform the addition operation and the output $y_i = \sum_{j=1}^{i} x_j$, for $1 \le i \le N$. This is an example of a parallel prefix circuit. Figure 2 is an example of a serial circuit with $d(4) = 3$, $s(4) = 3$ and $w(4) = 1$.

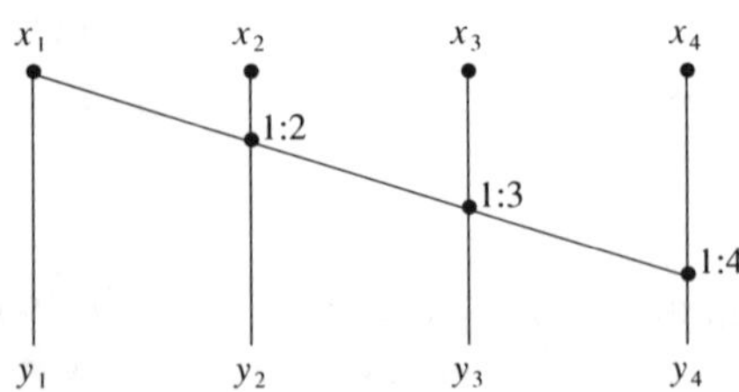

Figure 2. A serial circuit.

A circuit $C(N)$ computing the function $f : R^N \rightarrow R^M$, is said to be *d-optimal (s-optimal)* if, among the class of circuits considered, there exists no other circuit of lesser depth (size) for computing f. Often circuits exhibit *trade-off* between size and depth. In addition, for certain problems, one may be able to prove a *lower bound*, such as

$$s(N) + d(N) \geq B(N) \tag{4}$$

where $B(N)$ is a known function of N. For these problems, we can define the concept of (s, d)-*optimality* as follows. A circuit $C(N)$ is said to be (s, d)-*optimal* for the function f, if indeed

$$s(N) + d(N) = B(N). \tag{5}$$

For the prefix problem, it has been shown by Snir [1986] that $B(N) = 2N - 2$.

Since $y_8 = \sum_{j=1}^{8} x_j$ cannot be computed in less than three steps (refer to Section 2.7 for an argument), the circuit in Figure 1 is d-optimal, but not (s, d)-optimal. The serial circuit in Figure 2 is not d-optimal, but (s, d)-optimal. Define

$$DEF(N) = [s(N) + d(N)] - B(N) \tag{6}$$

as the *deficiency* which is a measure of how far a given circuit is away from (s, d)-optimality. A circuit $C(N)$ is said to be *almost* (s, d)-optimal if $DEF(N)$ is a *constant*. Sometimes (Chapters 5 and 6), to simplify notation we use $s(C(N))$, $d(C(N))$, $DEF(C(N))$ to denote, the size, depth, and deficiency of the circuit $C(N)$.

Another set of parameters of interest are *fan-in* and *fan-out* of a circuit. Respectively, the *fan-in* and *fan-out* of a circuit is the maximum of the fan-in and fan-out of all of its nodes. It turns out that there is an intimate relation between the uniform family of Boolean circuits (with fixed fan-in) and the CREW model on the one hand, and Boolean circuits with unbounded fan-in and CRCW models on the other.

Theorem 1. Let $C = \ $ <C_N> be a uniform family of Boolean circuits computing $f = \ $ <f_N> . Let s_N and d_N be the size and depth of C_N. Then, there exists a CREW algorithm for computing f_N in $O(d_N)$ steps using $p = \left\lceil \dfrac{s_N}{d_N} \right\rceil$ processors.

Proof: The proof consists in simulating the circuit by a CREW model with p processors. (In fact, most of the proofs in the complexity theory relating to the equivalence of various models rely on simulation.) Assume that the N inputs are stored in the first N cells in the shared memory.

Let N_i be the number of gates (nodes) in $C(N)$ at depth i, where

$$\sum_{i=1}^{d_N} N_i = s_N.$$

Simulating a gate with two inputs consists in *reading* the relevant pair of data from the shared memory (in at most two steps), performing the gate operation (in one step), and writing the result into a distinct cell in the shared memory (in one step). To understand the need for the concurrent read, let $u_1, u_2, \cdots, u_k$ be a set of nodes at depth $i + 1$, one of whose inputs is the output of a node v at depth i. Then, in simulating the nodes at depth $i + 1$, processors corresponding to the nodes $u_1, u_2, \cdots, u_k$ simultaneously read the memory cell containing the result of node v. Thus, using p processors, the gates at depth i can be simulated in at most $k \lceil N_i/p \rceil$ steps, where $k \le 4$. If T is the total time for the entire simulation, then

$$T \le \sum_{i=1}^{d_N} k \left\lceil \frac{N_i}{p} \right\rceil.$$

Since $\lceil x \rceil < x + 1$ and $p = \left\lceil s_N/d_N \right\rceil$, we obtain $T = O(d_N)$, and the proof is complete.

The properties of the Boolean circuits are not quite symmetric with respect to the fan-in and fan-out of gates. From the practical point of view, both the fan-in and fan-out must be a small constant. Hoover, Klawe, and Pippenger [1984] showed that, from the complexity theory point of view, restricting the fan-out to be a small constant has an inconsequential effect of increasing the size and depth by only a constant factor. (Refer to Chapter 7 for details.) However, the story with fan-in is quite different. It has been shown by Furst, Saxe, and Sipser [1981] that Boolean circuits with *unbounded* fan-in constitute the *correct* circuit analog of CRCW models. In developing this correspondence between CRCW models and circuits with unbounded fan-in, the *number of edges* (as opposed to the number of nodes) is defined to be the size of the circuit. The following theorem is immediate.

Theorem 2. Let s_N and d_N be the size (number of edges) and depth of an unbounded fan-in circuit computing a Boolean function f_N of N Boolean variables. Then, there exists a CRCW algorithm that computes f_N in d_N steps using s_N processors.

Proof: First, associate one processor with each edge and one memory cell for each gate in the circuit. These latter memory cells are distinguishable from the ones that carry the N inputs. All the cells corresponding to the AND gates are initialized to 1, and those corresponding to OR gates are initialized to 0. As in Theorem 1, the proof is by simulation through the levels.

Let a node u at level i be connected to v_{j_k}, a node at level j_k by an edge e_k, where $j_k < i$, for $k = 1, 2, , \cdots , m$, that is, the m inputs of node u are the outputs of the m nodes v_{j_k}, $k = 1, 2, \cdots , m$. If u is an AND (respectively OR) gate, then the processor corresponding to the edge e_k writes 0 (respectively 1) into the cell corresponding to u if, and only if, it reads a 0 (respectively 1) at the cell v_{j_k}, $k = 1, 2, \cdots , m$ (recall that simultaneous write with common write is permitted in the CRCW model). Clearly, the entire simulation takes d_N steps and the theorem is complete.

The proof of the converse of Theorem 2 is conceptually simple but tedious, and we refer the reader to the paper by Stockmeyer and Vishkin [1984]. For a characterization of the parallel complexity classes based on unbounded fan-in circuits, refer to the papers by Furst, Saxe, and Sipser [1981], Chandra, Stockmeyer, and Vishkin [1984], and Wegener [1987].

It may be tempting to discount the usefulness of CREW and CRCW models and circuits with unbounded fan-in as being impractical. Admittedly, they are impractical, but their real usefulness stems from the fact that they provide a framework for deriving a number of interesting lower bounds on parallel time. It must be realized that lower bounds based on these *euphoric* models still continue to hold for more realistic models. For example, using the circuit model with unbounded fan-in, one can prove that the parity function (given N bits $x_1, x_2, \cdots , x_N$, checking if the sum $\sum_{i=1}^{N} x_i$ is divisible by 2) *cannot* be computed by circuits with polynomial size and constant depth (Furst, Saxe, and Sipser [1981]). Second, there are two components to every parallel algorithm: the computational component and the communication component. By assuming that the processors are powerful enough to compute any function in *one* step, we could often isolate the communication overhead involved in a parallel algorithm.

2.4 Performance Measures

Let π be a problem and $T(N)$ be the time required to solve it by the *best* known serial algorithm. Let $T_p(N)$ be the time required to solve the same problem on a p-processor shared memory model, using a parallel algorithm that is not necessarily the same as the serial algorithm. Now, we introduce a number of measures that characterize the performance of parallel algorithms. The *speed-up* $s_p(N)$ is defined as the ratio

$$s_p(N) = \frac{T(N)}{T_p(N)}, \tag{1}$$

and *processor efficiency* $e_p(N)$ as

$$e_p(N) = \frac{s_p(N)}{p}, \tag{2}$$

which is the speed-up per processor. Let $n_p(N)$ denote the number of operations performed by a parallel algorithm using p processors, then

$$n_p(N) \le pT_p(N). \tag{3}$$

Define

$$r_p(N) = \frac{n_p(N)}{T(N)} \ge 1, \tag{4}$$

which is the ratio of the number of operations performed by a parallel algorithm to that of the best known serial algorithm as the *redundancy* factor. Since the redundancy relates to the extra work done by a parallel algorithm, in a sense it is indicative of the inefficiency, namely, the larger the value of $r_p(N)$, the larger the inefficiency. Thus, if $r_p(N) = O(1)$, a constant, the algorithm has constant inefficiency, and if $r_p(N) = O(N^t)$ for some $t > 0$, the algorithm is of polynomial inefficiency, etc.

A parallel algorithm is said to have *optimal speed-up* if

$$pT_p(N) = O(T(N)), \tag{5}$$

that is, when

$$s_p(N) = \Omega(p). \tag{6}$$

The notion of optimal speed-up relates to the (processor) efficiency of parallel algorithms. Exercises 2.1 and 2.2 elaborate on factors affecting the speed-up.

We conclude this subsection with yet another useful and perhaps more practical measure of performance. Let $T_p(N)$ be such that

$$T_p(N) = O(T(N^{\varepsilon})), \tag{7}$$

for some $0 < \varepsilon < 1$, where $T(N)$ is the best known serial time. Then, since

$$s_p(N) = \frac{T(N)}{O(T(N^{\varepsilon}))} = O(N^t), \tag{8}$$

for some $0 < t$, a parallel algorithm satisfying (7) is said to achieve *polynomial speed-up*.

We can now combine many of the above measures to create many different classifications of parallel algorithms and problems. A parallel algorithm is said to be *optimal* if, (a) $T_p(N) = O((\log N)^r)$ and (b) $pT_p(N) = O(T(N))$, that is, the algorithm takes polylog time and has optimal speed-up. A parallel algorithm is said to be *efficient* if $T_p(N) = O((\log N)^r)$ and $pT_p(N) = O(T(N)(\log N)^r)$. Since the time taken by an algorithm on the three shared memory models differs, at most, by a factor of $\log N$, this notion of problems with efficient parallel algorithms remains invariant across CRCW, CREW and EREW models.

2.5 A Parallel Complexity Class

While it is a challenge in itself to design parallel algorithms achieving optimal speed-up, theoretically it is desirable to find how fast one can solve a problem in parallel. To capture this note of a "fast" parallel algorithm, complexity theorists have isolated an interesting class of problems, called *NC* (for *Nick Class,* named after Nick Pippenger).

Following Cook [1985], we define *NC* as follows:

$$NC = \bigcup_{r \geq 1} NC^{(r)},$$

where $NC^{(r)}$ is the set of all problems solvable by uniform Boolean circuit family $C = \;<C(N)>\;$, where the size $s(N)$ and the depth $d(N)$

of the Nth circuit $C(N)$ are such that for some $t \geq 1$

$$s(N) = O(N^t)$$

and

$$d(N) = O((\log N)^r).$$

Stated in words, NC consists of a class of problems solvable (using fixed fan-in) Boolean circuits of polylog depth[1] and polynomial size. Since $O(N^t)/O((\log N)^r) = O(N^k)$ for some k, using Theorem 1 of Section 2.3.2, we can also view NC as a class of problems solvable in polylog time using polynomial number of processors.

A related class is called AC, where

$$AC = \bigcup_{r \geq 1} AC^{(r)},$$

and $AC^{(r)}$ consists of problems solvable by a uniform family of circuits with *unbounded fan-in, polylog depth and polynomial size*.

To understand the relation between $AC^{(r)}$ and $NC^{(r)}$, the following result is useful.

Lemma 1. A M-way fan-in can be realized by a circuit using, at most, $(M-1)/(k-1)+1$ components with only k-way fan-in, for $2 \leq k \leq M$, where the length of the longest path in the circuit does not contain more than $\lceil \log_k M \rceil$ components.

Proof: Clearly one component can use k inputs, two components $k+(k-1)$ inputs, and in general, r components can use a total of $k+(r-1)(k-1)$ inputs. Choose r, such that

$$M \leq k + (r-1)(k-1) < M + k - 1.$$

From the second inequality, we obtain

$$\frac{M-1}{k-1} \leq r \leq \frac{M-1}{k-1} + 1.$$

Trivially, the length of the longest path is $\lceil \log_k M \rceil$. Refer to Figure 1 for an illustration of $k = 2$ and $M = 7$.

---

[1] Polylog refers to a polynomial in the logarithm of N such as $c_1(\log N)^2 + c_2(\log N) + c_3$.

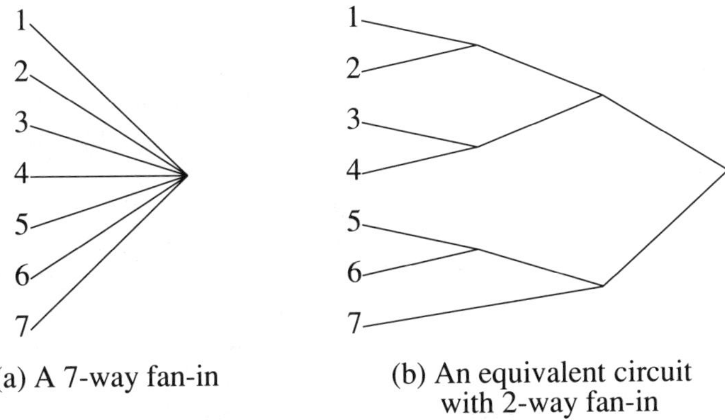

(a) A 7-way fan-in

(b) An equivalent circuit
with 2-way fan-in

Figure 1. An illustration of Lemma 1.

As a corollary, when $k = 2$, we need $M - 1$ components with fixed fan-in of 2 to realize a M-way fan-in in the form of a binary tree of depth $\lceil \log_2 M \rceil$. Also, refer to Exercise 2.3.

Turning to the class of circuits defined by $AC^{(r)}$, it follows that a node in $AC^{(r)}$ may have a $p(N)$ fan-in for some polynomial $p(\cdot)$. Now, replacing each node by a tree of components of fixed fan-in and of depth $O(\log_k p(N)) = O(\log_k N)$, it follows from Lemma 1 that

$$AC^{(r)} \subseteq NC^{(1+r)}.$$

Since $NC^{(r)} \subseteq AC^{(r)}$ by definition, we can readily conclude that the class of problems defined by NC and AC are one and the same, that is $NC = AC$.

The interest in NC stems from a number of facts:

(a)   If π is in NC, then π is in P (P is the now-classic set of problems known to be solvable serially in polynomial time).[2] It is now widely believed that not every problem in P is in NC. In fact, the aspect of the complexity theory dealing with the relation between P and NC parallels that between NP and P. For details, refer to Parberry [1987].

---

[2] There exist problems in P that are not known to be NC. To understand the relation between P and NC, the notion of P-complete problems has been introduced. The question, "is $P = NC$" is unresolved. See Karp and Ramachandran [1990] for details.

(b)   The notion of *NC* remains robust across various parallel models.

(c)   There are many basic problems (such as the summation problem) which are *not* known to be solvable in less than log$N$ steps. (Refer to Section 2.7.) Hence, the interest in problems solvable in polylog time.

(d)   Requiring exponential amount of resources — be it time, space or hardware — is unrealistic and practically infeasible. Using polynomial time as the yardstick, the class P of problems representing the "feasible" serial computation has successfully been isolated. Thus, it is but natural to limit the amount of hardware needed in a parallel computation by a polynomial in the size of the problem. With the advances in VLSI technology, we can now pack enormous computing power occupying very little space at very affordable cost, the notion of polynomial bound on the hardware could become a reality in the foreseeable future.

In closing, consider a problem π admitting a serial algorithm of complexity, for example, $\sqrt{N}$, and a parallel algorithm of complexity, for example, $(\log N)^3$. It can be verified that

$$\sqrt{N} < (\log N)^3 \quad \text{for} \quad N \le 2^{29.2} = 6.17 \times 10^8,$$

that is, for problems of size up to $N = 6.17 \times 10^8$, the serial algorithm is better. In other words, for a parallel algorithm to be useful, we must seek algorithms with parallel time complexity of $O((\log N)^r)$ with r as low as possible. (Refer to Exercise 2.4.)

2.6 BRENT'S INEQUALITY

Assume that we have a parallel algorithm **A** taking T_p units of steps using p processors to solve a problem Π, but only $q < p$ processors are available. If T_q is the number of steps required to implement the same algorithm using q processors, the question is: how large T_q is compared to T_p?

Let N be the total *number of operations* performed by the algorithm A in solving Π. That is, N denotes the *total work done* in terms of the number of operations performed by algorithm **A**. Furthermore, let N_i be the number of operations performed using p processors at stage i, for $1 \le i \le T_p$, where $\sum_{i=1}^{T_p} N_i = N$. Now, using only q processors, step i of algorithm **A** will take $\left\lceil \dfrac{N_i}{q} \right\rceil$ steps. Thus, the total time required to complete all N operations using q processors

$$T_q \le \sum_{i=1}^{T_p} \left\lceil \frac{N_i}{p} \right\rceil. \tag{1}$$

Using the standard inequality

$$\frac{x}{y} \le \left\lceil \frac{x}{y} \right\rceil \le \frac{x-1}{y} + 1, \tag{2}$$

it follows that

$$\sum_{i=1}^{T_p} \frac{N_i}{q} \le T_q \le \sum_{i=1}^{T_p} \left[1 + \frac{N_i - 1}{q} \right],$$

that is,

$$\frac{N}{q} \le T_q \le T_p + \frac{N - T_p}{q}. \tag{3}$$

Inequality (3) is called *Brent's inequality* and relates to the extra time needed when the available degree of parallelism is smaller. Note that if the number N of operations performed by the parallel algorithm **A** is not excessively large, then this extra time resulting from the decrease in parallelism could be quite reasonable. Thus, in developing parallel algorithms, it is not necessary to constrain oneself to fixed parallelism as long as one can contain the total work to be done.

2.7 A Simple Lower Bound

Understanding the intrinsic complexity of problems constitutes one of the challenges facing the computational complexity theory. A useful approach to this characterization is to derive a lower bound on the resources, such as time needed to solve the problem. In this section, we derive a general bound that throws light on the intrinsic complexity of the problems related to the prefix computation.

To this end, we introduce the notion of a *p-computation* where p denotes the number of processors. It is assumed that each processor is capable of performing the standard arithmetic operations in unit time. Let I_0 be a set of real numbers corresponding to a set of input. A *p*-computation from I_0 consists of a sequence of sets $I_0, I_1, I_2, \cdots$, where

$$I_{i+1} = I_i \cup \{\, Z_{i1}, Z_{i2}, \cdots, Z_{ip} \,\},$$

where

$$Z_{ij} = \{\, x \text{ o } y \mid x, y \in I_i \text{ and o is a binary arithmetic operation} \,\}.$$

That is, I_{i+1} consists of I_i and all the results of the p arithmetic operations performed on p pairs of numbers taken from I_i.

A set I is said to be p-computable from I_0 in t steps if $I \subseteq I_t$. Note that the notion of p-computation formalizes the sequence of computations performed by a set of p identical processors without regard to any architectural issues relating to interconnection networks, memory access, conflict resolution, etc. Thus, the notion of p-computation is an abstraction for the type of computations that are feasible using a p-processor parallelism.

We now state and prove a very basic result from Munro and Patterson [1973].

Theorem 1. Assume that the serial computation of a quantity, for example, Q, takes M binary arithmetic operations. If $t = T_p(N)$ is the time taken by the shortest p-computation of Q, then

$$t \geq \left\lceil \frac{M + 1 - 2^{\lceil \log p \rceil}}{p} \right\rceil + \lceil \log p \rceil \qquad \text{if } M \geq 2^{\lceil \log p \rceil},$$

and

$$t \geq \lceil \log (1 + n) \rceil, \qquad \textit{otherwise.}$$

Proof: A little reflection reveals that at time t, only one processor is useful in computing Q. At time $t - 1$, at most, 2 processors are needed, and, for $j > 0$, at time $t - j$, at most, $\min\{\, p, 2^j \,\}$ processors are needed. Thus, in $\lceil \log p \rceil$ steps, a total of

$$\sum_{i=1}^{\lceil \log p \rceil} 2^{i-1} = 2^{\lceil \log p \rceil} - 1$$

operations are performed. Two cases arise.

Case A: $M > 2^{\lceil \log p \rceil} - 1$, and $t > \lceil \log p \rceil - 1$, and $t > \lceil \log p \rceil$. In this case, in $\lceil \log p \rceil$ steps a total of $2^{\lceil \log p \rceil} - 1$ operations are performed. In the rest of the $(t - \lceil \log p \rceil)$ steps, a total of $p(t - \log p)$ operations are performed. Thus,

$$M < p(t - \lceil \log p \rceil) + 2^{\lceil \log p \rceil} - 1,$$

from which the first inequality follows. Refer to Figure 1, for an illustration.

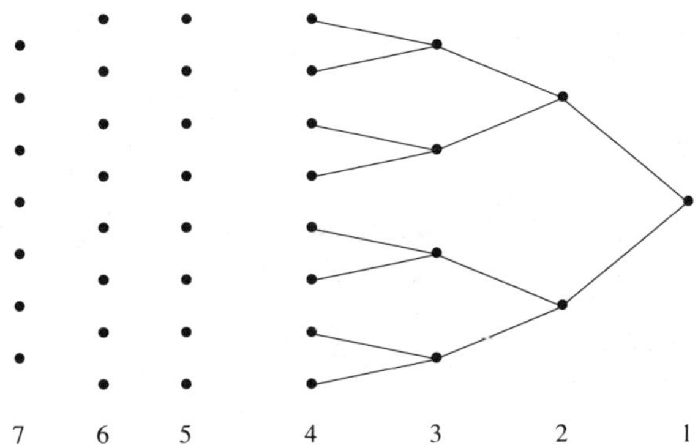

Figure 1. Illustration with $p = 2^3 = 8, N = 38, t = 7$.

Case B: If $M \le 2^{\lceil \log p \rceil} - 1$, then $t \le \lceil \log p \rceil$. In t steps a total of $\sum_{i=1}^{t} 2^{i-1} = 2^t - 1$ operations are performed. Thus,

$$M \le 2^t - 1,$$

and the second inequality follows.

Hence, the theorem.

Since the computation of the sum of N numbers requires a total of $M = N - 1$ operations, it follows from the above theorem that we cannot calculate the sum of N numbers in less than $\log N$ steps irrespective of the number of processors. This is called an *associative fan-in* algorithm. Refer to Figure 2. Recall that the sum $d_1 + d_2 + \cdots + d_N$ is one of the N prefixes. Since one of the prefixes cannot be computed in less than $\log N$ time, an algorithm for computing prefixes would be time optimal up to a multiplicative constant. In fact, Chapters 3 through 6 are replete with such time optimal algorithms.

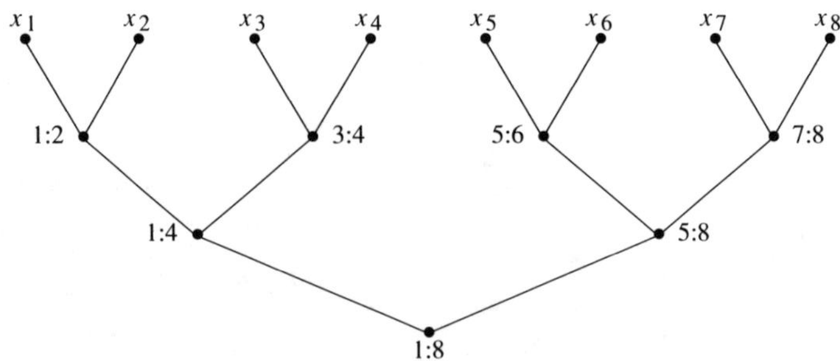

Figure 2. Associative fan-in algorithm.

$$i:j = x_i + x_{i+1} + \cdots + x_j, \text{ for } j \geq i.$$

2.8 Exercises

2.1 Amdahl's Law (Amdahl [1967]). Consider a computer that operates in two modes — the high speed mode and the low speed mode. (The high speed may correspond to performing computations on the attached parallel processor with p processors, and the low speed to the main serial processor.) Given an algorithm, let f_h and f_l be the fraction of the computation performed at high speed and low speed, respectively, where $f_h + f_l = 1$. Let T denote the elapsed time when the algorithm is executed in the low speed mode. Clearly, the speed-up

$$S_p = \frac{T}{Tf_l + \dfrac{Tf_h}{p}} = \frac{p}{pf_l + f_h} = \frac{p}{f_l(p-1) + 1}.$$

(a) Analyze the behavior of S_p vs. f_l for $0 \le f_l \le 1$.

Note: To exploit the heterogeneity in computations such as the low speed *vs.* high speed, researchers are currently investigating the use of a suite of heterogeneous architectures to improve the overall speed-up. A discussion of this topic is beyond our scope and the reader is referred to the special issue of IEEE Computer on *Heterogeneous Processing*, edited by Freund and Siegel [1993].

2.2 Gustafson [1988]. In the derivation of Exercise 2.1 leading to speed-up, it was tacitly assumed that the problem size is fixed. However, with the increase in the processor size, it is natural to increase the problem size as well. Thus if T is the time taken by an algorithm using p processors, then $Tf_l + Tf_h p$ would be the time required to implement it on a serial machine, where f_h and f_l have the same meaning as in Exercise 2.1. Clearly, the speed-up then is

$$S_p = \frac{Tf_l + Tf_h p}{Tf_l + Tf_h} = p + (1-p)f_l.$$

(a) Analyze the behavior of this speed-up as a function of f_l, for $0 \le f_l \le 1$.

(b) Compare the implications of the speed-up computations in Exercises 2.1 and 2.2.

2.3 If E is an arithmetic expression with N atoms (an atom is a constant or a variable), then the time $T(N)$ for evaluating E satisfies the following inequalities:

$$\left\lceil \log_2 N \right\rceil \leq T(N) \leq N - 1.$$

2.4 Plot $\sqrt{N}$, $\log N$, $(\log N)^2$, $(\log N)^3$, and compare the behavior of the rate of growth of these functions.

2.9 Notes And References

Section 2.1: An eloquent testimony for the need of parallel computing to solve large-scale problems of interest in science and engineering is contained in the National Research Council report of a Committee chaired by Rheinboldt [1984], on "Computational Modeling and Mathematics Applied to the Physical Sciences". Also, refer to a more recent National Science Foundation report of a Committee chaired by Massey [1993] on "Grand Challenges 1993: High Performance Computing and Communications".

For an introduction to finite difference methods, refer to Anderson *et al* [1984], and to Strange and Fix [1973] for finite element methods. A discussion of pipelined arithmetic processors is contained in Hwang and Briggs [1984]. To explore compiler level parallelism, refer to Banerjee [1988], and Zima and Chapman [1990]. Also, refer to Hwang and DeGroot [1989] and Lakshmivarahan and Dhall [1990], Akl [1989], Almasi and Gottlieb [1989], Bertsekas and Tsitsiklis [1989], JáJá [1992], Krishnamurthy [1989], Kuck [1978], Kung [1980], and Quinn [1987] for various aspects of parallel processing.

For an account of parallelism in numerical problems, refer to Golub and Van Loan [1989], Lakshmivarahan and Dhall [1990], Heller [1978], Miranker [1971], and Ortega [1988].

Section 2.2: For a succinct introduction to the properties of static and dynamic networks, refer to Lakshmivarahan and Dhall [1990], and Siegel [1985]. The SIMD/MIMD characterization is from Flynn [1972].

Section 2.3: The contents of this Section are now standard. Refer to Karp and Ramachandran [1990], Balcazar, Diaz and Gabarro [1988][1990], and Parberry [1987]. Circuit models are discussed extensively in Wegener [1987], Dunne [1988], and Savage [1976]. For a general discussion of trade-off analyses, refer to Savage [1976]. The Handbook of Theoretical Computer Science, Volumes A and B, edited by Leeuwen [1990] contains survey articles on virtually every topic relating to theoretical computer science.

Section 2.4-2.5: For further discussions, of performance measures and parallel complexity classes, refer to Karp and Ramachandran [1990],

Cook [1985], Parberry [1987], Balcazar, Diaz and Gabarro [1988], [1990], and Hockney and Jesshope [1981].

Section 2.6: This section follows from Brent [1974]. Also, refer to JáJá [1992].

Section 2.7: The notion of p-computation is due to Munro and Patterson [1973], and the results in this section are taken from this paper. Also, refer to Heller [1978]. For an introduction to different techniques for proving lower bound, refer to Reingold [1972].

Part Two

Algorithms For Shared Memory Models

Chapter 3

Parallel Prefix Algorithms On Arrays

In the parlance of the design and analysis of algorithms, it is now common knowledge that the type of operations used and the overall efficiency of an algorithm critically depend on the organization of the input data for the given problem. Most of the parallel algorithms for prefix computations exploit one of two different types of data organizations, namely, *arrays* and *linked lists*. This chapter examines parallel prefix algorithms based on the shared memory models when the input data is in an array. Corresponding algorithms for linked lists are described in Chapter 4.

3.1 Methods of Cyclic Elimination and Reduction

Let $N = 2^n$, for some $n \geq 1$. For definiteness, consider the semigroup of real numbers with the usual addition operation. The problem is to compute

$$x_i = x_{i-1} + d_i, \qquad (1)$$

where $\mathbf{d} = (d_1, d_2, \cdots, d_N)$ is the given input, and $x_1 = d_1$. Let $d_i^{(0)} = d_i$, for $1 \leq i \leq N$. Rewrite (1) as

$$x_i = x_{i-1} + d_i^{(0)}. \tag{2}$$

Now, iterating (2) once and substituting back

$$x_i = x_{i-2} + d_i^{(1)}, \tag{3}$$

where

$$d_i^{(1)} = d_i^{(0)} + d_{i-1}^{(0)}.$$

All the quantities with subscripts outside the range 1 to N are taken to be zero. Proceeding in this way, it follows that

$$x_i = x_{i-2^j} + d_i^{(j)}, \tag{4}$$

where

$$d_i^{(j)} = d_i^{(j-1)} + d_{i-2^{j-1}}^{(j-1)}. \tag{5}$$

Now, if $j = n = \log N$, since $x_i = 0$, for $i \leq 0$, from (4) it follows that

$$x_i = d_i^{(n)} \tag{6}$$

is the solution to the prefix problem. In other words, computing $x_i's$ is equivalent to computing $d_i^{(j)}$, for $i = 1$ to N and $j = 1$ to n. From (5), it follows that, for a given j, computation of $d_i^{(j)}$, for all i can be done in parallel, as shown in the algorithm in Figure 1.

```
for j = 1 to n
    for i ∈ {1, 2, ··· , N} do in parallel
        h = 2^(j-1)
        d_i ← d_i + d_(i-h)
    end
end
```

Figure 1. Cyclic elimination algorithm, $n = \log N$.

Graphical representations of these computations for $N = 8$ and $N = 16$ are given in Figure 2. Node i in these graphs corresponds to the computation of $d_i^{(j)}$. An edge labeled j refers to the interaction of the variables at the jth step of the computation. Thus, when $j = 1$, there are edges labeled 1 connecting i to $i + 1$, for all $i = 1$ to $N - 1$. For $j = 2$, there are edges labeled 2 connecting nodes i to $i + 2$, for all $i = 1$ to $N - 2$ and so on. Note that the number of x_i's computed *doubles* after each step, and hence, all the x_i's, for $1 \leq i \leq N$, can be computed in no more than $\log N$ steps. This *doubling effect* is an important characteristic of this algorithm. Since these graphs depict the logical interaction between various computations, they are called *communication graphs* of this algorithm. Analysis of these graphs is crucial to the mapping of this algorithm on any parallel architecture.

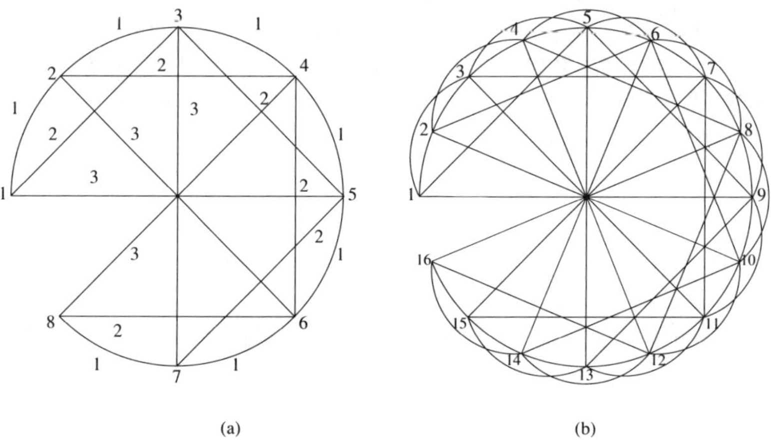

(a)   (b)

Figure 2. Communication graph for cyclic elimination.

This class of algorithms is well suited for implementation on vector machines. To this end, define a right shift operation on an N-vector as follows. If $y = (y_1, y_2, \cdots, y_N)$, then

$$\mathbf{shiftr}(y, \alpha) = (0, 0, ..., 0, y_1, y_2, \cdots, y_{N-\alpha}).$$

Thus, $\mathbf{shiftr}(\mathbf{y}, \alpha)$ is a vector $\mathbf{y}$ obtained by shifting $\mathbf{y}$ to the right by α positions and filling the left-most α positions with zeros. The Cyclic Elimination Algorithm — Vector Version, given in Figure 3, computes all the partial sums.

/* x and d are two arrays. x is initialized and contains
the input vector ($d_1, d_2, ..., d_N$) */

```
x = d
for i = 1 to n
      x = x + shiftr (x, 2^(i-1));
end
```

Figure 3. Cyclic elimination algorithm —
A vector version. $n = \log N$.

An example of this latter version of the algorithm is given in Figure 4. It is readily seen from this algorithm that each trip through the for-loop involves component-wise addition of vectors. If N processors are available, the addition of two N-vectors can be completed in a unit step. Hence, the computations in the algorithm take $n = \log N$ units of time. That is,

$$T_N(N) = \log N.$$

	$i = 1$		$i = 2$		$i = 3$	
x Initialized	**shiftr**$(x, 1)$	$x = x+$ **shiftr**$(x, 1)$	**shiftr**$(x, 2)$	$x = x+$ **shiftr**$(x, 2)$	**shiftr**$(x, 4)$	$x = x +$ **shiftr**$(x, 4)$
x_1	0	x_1	0	x_1	0	x_1
x_2	x_1	$x_1 + x_2$	0	$x_1 + x_2$	0	$x_1 + x_2$
x_3	x_2	$x_2 + x_3$	x_1	$x_1 + .. + x_3$	0	$x_1 + .. + x_3$
x_4	x_3	$x_3 + x_4$	$x_1 + x_2$	$x_1 + .. + x_4$	0	$x_1 + .. + x_4$
x_5	x_4	$x_4 + x_5$	$x_2 + x_3$	$x_2 + .. + x_5$	x_1	$x_1 + .. + x_5$
x_6	x_5	$x_5 + x_6$	$x_3 + x_4$	$x_3 + .. + x_6$	$x_1 + x_2$	$x_1 + .. + x_6$
x_7	x_6	$x_6 + x_7$	$x_4 + x_5$	$x_4 + .. + x_7$	$x_1 + .. + x_3$	$x_1 + .. + x_7$
x_8	x_7	$x_7 + x_8$	$x_5 + x_6$	$x_5 + .. + x_8$	$x_1 + .. + x_4$	$x_1 + .. + x_8$

Figure 4. An illustration of algorithm in Figure 3 with $N = 8$.

While this algorithm is clearly time optimal (why?), it has a large redundancy factor as shown below. At the ith step, the algorithm involves addition of $N - 2^{i-1}$ non-zero quantities, and the total number of scalar operations is bounded by

$$\sum_{i=1}^{\log N} (N - 2^{i-1}) = N \log N - (2^0 + 2^1 + \cdots + 2^{\log N - 1})$$

$$= N \log N - (2^{\log N} - 1)$$

$$= N \log N - N + 1.$$

Thus, the redundancy factor (Refer to Chapter 2)

$$r_N \geq \log N - 1.$$

Herein lies the basic disadvantage of this method. Thus, if only p processors are available, it follows from the first principles that

$$T_p(N) \geq \frac{N \log N - N}{p}.$$

In other words, unless $p \geq \log N$, the above algorithm using p processors takes a longer time compared to the serial algorithm.

The above class of cyclic elimination (also called *odd-even elimination*) based algorithms are well suited for implementation on pipelined architectures, such as Cray Research machines, Alliant FX/8, etc.

A variation of the cyclic elimination algorithm in Figure 1 is called *cyclic (odd-even) reduction* and is given in Figure 5.

An example of the algorithm in Figure 5 is given in Figure 6. The analysis of the properties of this algorithm is the content of Exercise 3.1. Since the total scalar operations required by this algorithm are $O(N)$, this version of the algorithm is preferred when the available parallelism is small and independent of the size of the problem.

The communication graph of the two phases of the cyclic reduction algorithm for $N = 16$ is given in Figure 7. The edge marked nF indicates communication during the nth step of the forward elimination phase, while the label nB indicates communication during the nth step of the backward substitution phase.

/* Forward-Elimination Phase */

for $j = 1$ **to** n **do**
   for $i \in \{2^j, 2 \times 2^j, 3 \times 2^j, \cdots, 2^n\}$ **do in parallel**
     $h = 2^{j-1}$
     $d_i = d_i + d_{i-h}$
   end
end

/* Backward Substitution Phase */

for $j = n - 1$ **to** 1 **step** -1
   for $i \in \{3 \times 2^{j-1}, 5 \times 2^{j-1}, \cdots, 2^n - 2^{j-1}\}$ **do in parallel**
     $h = 2^{j-1}$
     $d_i = d_i + d_{i-h}$
   end
end

Figure 5. The cyclic (odd-even) reduction.

Initial Data	Forward Elimination				Backward Substitution		
x_1	x_1	x_1	x_1	x_1	x_1	x_1	x_1
x_2	$x_1{:}x_2$	$x_1{:}x_2$	$x_1{:}x_2$	$x_1{:}x_2$	$x_1{:}x_2$	$x_1{:}x_2$	$x_1{:}x_2$
x_3	x_3	x_3	x_3	x_3	x_3	x_3	$x_1{:}x_3$
x_4	$x_3{:}x_4$	$x_1{:}x_4$	$x_1{:}x_4$	$x_1{:}x_4$	$x_1{:}x_4$	$x_1{:}x_4$	$x_1{:}x_4$
x_5	x_5	x_5	x_5	x_5	x_5	x_5	$x_1{:}x_5$
x_6	$x_5{:}x_6$	$x_5{:}x_6$	$x_5{:}x_6$	$x_5{:}x_6$	$x_5{:}x_6$	$x_1{:}x_6$	$x_1{:}x_6$
x_7	x_7	x_7	x_7	x_7	x_7	x_7	$x_1{:}x_7$
x_8	$x_7{:}x_8$	$x_5{:}x_8$	$x_1{:}x_8$	$x_1{:}x_8$	$x_1{:}x_8$	$x_1{:}x_8$	$x_1{:}x_8$
x_9	x_9	x_9	x_9	x_9	x_9	x_9	$x_1{:}x_9$
x_{10}	$x_9{:}x_{10}$	$x_9{:}x_{10}$	$x_9{:}x_{10}$	$x_9{:}x_{10}$	$x_9{:}x_{10}$	$x_1{:}x_{10}$	$x_1{:}x_{10}$
x_{11}	x_{11}	x_{11}	x_{11}	x_{11}	x_{11}	x_{11}	$x_1{:}x_{11}$
x_{12}	$x_{11}{:}x_{12}$	$x_9{:}x_{12}$	$x_9{:}x_{12}$	$x_9{:}x_{12}$	$x_1{:}x_{12}$	$x_1{:}x_{12}$	$x_1{:}x_{12}$
x_{13}	x_{13}	x_{13}	x_{13}	x_{13}	x_{13}	x_{13}	$x_1{:}x_{13}$
x_{14}	$x_{13}{:}x_{14}$	$x_{13}{:}x_{14}$	$x_{13}{:}x_{14}$	$x_{13}{:}x_{14}$	$x_{13}{:}x_{14}$	$x_1{:}x_{14}$	$x_1{:}x_{14}$
x_{15}	x_{15}	x_{15}	x_{15}	x_{15}	x_{15}	x_{15}	$x_1{:}x_{15}$
x_{16}	$x_{15}{:}x_{16}$	$x_{13}{:}x_{16}$	$x_9{:}x_{16}$	$x_1{:}x_{16}$	$x_1{:}x_{16}$	$x_1{:}x_{16}$	$x_1{:}x_{16}$

Figure 6. An illustration of the algorithm in Figure 5.

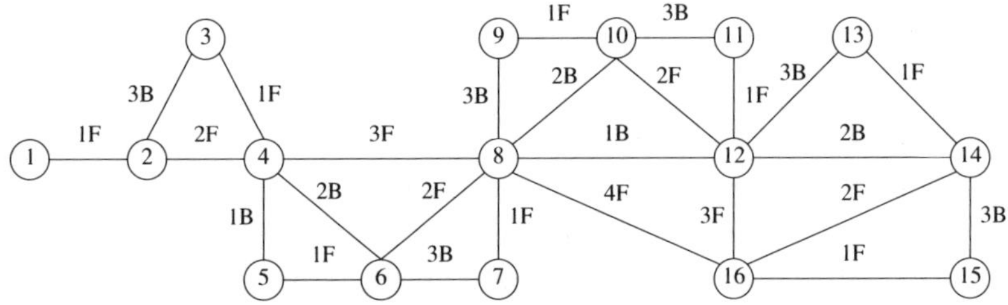

Figure 7. Communication graph of cyclic reduction.

Prefix circuits $CR\,(N)$ based on cyclic reduction play a crucial role in the design of $(s,\ d)$-optimal circuits described in Chapter 6.

A. Asynchronous Recursive Doubling

In the algorithm in Figure 1 of Section 3.1, processor i accesses elements d_i and d_{i-h}, adds them together and stores the result in location d_i. For the correct functioning of this algorithm, it is essential that the values needed for addition are accessed before they are overwritten. Therefore, it is assumed that all the processors are synchronized in their access to the memory. This is possible in a SIMD machine where all processors are synchronized in their functioning. In a MIMD machine where each processor works independently, it is necessary to ensure that the processor writing the information does not do so until the value needed by the reading processor has been accessed. This requirement can be fulfilled by introducing appropriate synchronization primitives in the algorithm. The following algorithm from Lubachevsky and Greenberg [1987] can be used on a MIMD machine.

First, assume that the system contains an instruction *save_and_add*(x, y) which returns the value x and updates x as $x := x + y$ and these operations are performed in an uninterruptible manner. We use this instruction to solve the reader-writer problem where a number of processes access shared data either for reading or writing. It is desirable that the readers/writers access data in a mutually exclusive fashion. That is, when a reader is accessing data the writer should be prevented from accessing the data, and *vice versa*. However, more than one reader may be allowed to access the data simultaneously. A number of solutions have been proposed for this problem from time to time, refer to the book by Maekawa, Oldehoeft,

Oldehoeft [1987]. The solution in Figure 8 (Lubachevsky and Greenberg[1987]) is suitable for the case where there is only one writer and a number of readers. The solution ensures that the readers and writers are never locked out for a long time. When a new writer arrives and some readers are in the process of accessing the data, this writer is allowed to access data when the active readers are done. The readers that arrive after the writer must wait until the writer is done. Similarly, the readers arriving during the time that a process is writing will have priority over the next request of the writer.

/* *turn*, *rdr_cnt* [0..1], *wrtr_cnt*, and *sem* are shared variables, with
   initial values as *turn* = *wrtr_cnt* = *sem* = *rdr_cnt* [0] = *rdr_cnt* [1] = 0 */

procedure *reader_entry*;
    Step 1. *my_turn*:=*turn* ; *save_and_add* (*rdr_cnt* [*my_turn*], 1);
    Step 2. wait until ((*wrtr_cnt* = 0) **or** (*my_turn* $\neq$ *turn*));
    Step 3. if (*save_and_add* (*sem*, 1) < C) **then**
        save_and_add (*sem*, −1) and **goto** Step 2;

procedure *reader_end*;
    Step 1. *save_and_add* (*sem*, −1);
    Step 2. *save_and_add* (*rdr_cnt* [*my_turn*], −1);

procedure *writer_entry*;
    Step 1. *wrtr_cnt* = 1;
    Step 2. wait until (*rdr_cnt* [(*turn* + 1) *mod* 2] = 0)
    Step 3. if (*save_and_add* (*sem*, C) $\neq$ 0) **then**
        save_and_add (*sem*, − C) and **goto** Step 2;

procedure *writer_end*;
    Step 1. *save_and_add* (*sem*, − C);
    Step 2. *turn* = *turn* + 1 *mod* 2;
    Step 3. *wrtr_cnt* = 0;

Figure 8. Solution to readers-and-one-writer problem.

Before performing a read operation, a process will invoke the procedure *reader_entry*, and after the read operation is completed, it will invoke the procedure *reader_end*. Similarly, a writer process will call procedures *writer_entry* and *writer_end* before and after the write operation, respectively.

If the readers and writers follow the above protocol, the solution in Figure 8 guarantees that, (a) if a process is writing at any time no process will be reading at that time, (b) if a process invokes a *read_entry*/*write_entry* procedure at time t, some process will be performing a read/write operation at a time $t' > t$, and (c) if a process invokes an *entry* procedure, it will perform the corresponding operation within a finite interval of time.

The algorithm for computing prefixes is given in Figure 9. The algorithm uses N processors. Processor i contains the value d_i and is responsible for computing $\sum_{j=1}^{i} d_j$. Two shared arrays, $x[1..N]$ and $p[1..N]$ are used. There are N copies of these arrays. Initially, $x[i] = d_i$ and $p[i] = i - 1$, for $1 \leq i \leq N$. The procedures *reader_entry*, *writer_entry*, *reader_end* and *writer_end* when invoked are passed on a variable i, and these procedures access the ith copy of $x[i]$ and $p[i]$. Since each processor invokes synchronization primitives before performing the read or write operation, it is possible that a processor will sometimes be blocked for a time. However, the blocked processor will eventually unblock because of the properties of the algorithm in Figure 8.

```
/* Initially shared variables x[i] = dᵢ,  p[i] = i − 1,   for 1 ≤ i ≤ N. */

        /* next_x, next_p, and next_prefix are local variables. */


    function prefix;
        while (p[i] > 0) do {
            reader_entry(p[i]);
                next_x := x[p[i]]; next_p := p[p[i]];
            reader_end(p[i]);

            next_prefix := next_x + x[i];

            writer_entry(i);
                x[i] := next_prefix; p[i] := next_p;
            writer_end(i); }

        prefix := x[i];
```

Figure 9. Asynchronous algorithm for computing prefixes.

The synchronous algorithm in Figure 1 of Section 3.1 produces the prefixes in increasing order or i. Since the processors in a MIMD machine work independently, the order in which the prefixes will be computed by the algorithm in Figure 9 is completely arbitrary.

In the above algorithm, we assumed N processors for computing the prefixes of N items. For details of algorithms when a fixed number of processors are available, refer to the paper by Lubachevsky and Greenberg [1987].

3.2 Schwartz's Method

We begin by introducing some notations. Let $x \in\ <N>\ = \{0, 1, 2, \cdots, N-1\}$, where $N = 2^n$, and $x = b_{n-1}b_{n-2} \cdots b_1 b_0$ in binary. Define

$$\sigma:\ <N>\ \rightarrow\ <N>$$

as

$$\sigma(x) = \begin{cases} 2x, & \text{if} \quad 0 \le x < \dfrac{N}{2} \\[2ex] 2x - N + 1, & \text{if} \quad \dfrac{N}{2} \le x < N. \end{cases}$$

This is called the *perfect shuffle* (Stone [1971]) permutation. Stated in binary notation, it is readily seen that

$$\sigma(b_{n-1}b_{n-2} \cdots b_1 b_0) = b_{n-2}b_{n-3} \cdots b_1 b_0 b_{n-1},$$

that is, $\sigma(x)$ in binary is obtained by the unit left circular shift of the binary value of x. The inverse of perfect shuffle (σ), called *unshuffle* (σ^{-1}), is given by

$$\sigma^{-1}(x) = \begin{cases} \dfrac{x}{2}, & \text{if } x \text{ is even} \\[2ex] \dfrac{x-1}{2} + \dfrac{N}{2}, & \text{if } x \text{ is odd.} \end{cases}$$

Expressed in binary

$$\sigma^{-1}(b_{n-1}b_{n-2} \cdots b_1 b_0) = b_0 b_{n-1} b_{n-2} \cdots b_2 b_1,$$

that is, it corresponds to the unit right circular shift.

Let

$$\varepsilon(x) = b_{n-1} \, b_{n-2} \cdots b_1 \, \overline{b_0},$$

where $x = b_{n-1} \, b_{n-2} \cdots b_1 \, b_0$. $\varepsilon(x)$ is called the *exchange permutation*.

The Schwartz's [1980] algorithm is developed for a *paracomputer*, which is essentially a shared memory machine with N processors operating in the exclusive-read and exclusive-write (EREW) mode of operation. (Refer to Chapter 2 for the definition of EREW model.) The processors are numbered p_0 through p_{N-1}. In the following, it is assumed that the processors communicate with each other according to two *distinct* patterns. First, for each i, processor p_i can communicate in unit step with processor $p_{\varepsilon(i)}$. Second, processor p_i can communicate with processor $p_{\sigma(i)}$ in unit step. Refer to Figure 1 for an example of this communication pattern with $N = 8$. It is assumed that each processor has a set of registers, and let the input x_i be stored in a distinguished register R of processor p_i, $i = 0, 1, \cdots, N-1$. The problem is to compute $y_i = \sum_{j=1}^{i} x_j$ and store it in register R of processor p_i.

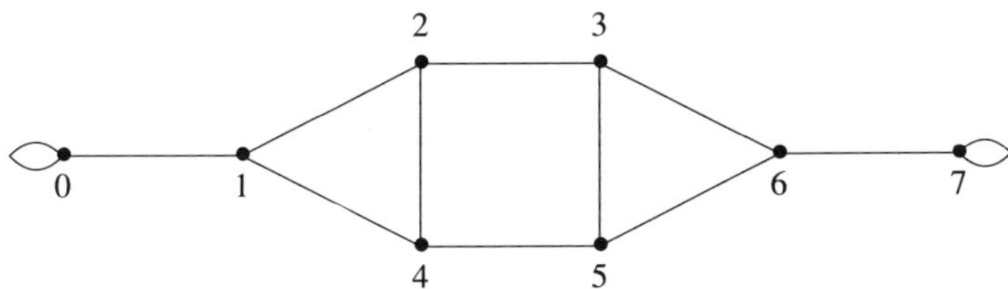

Figure 1. Shuffle-exchange interconnection.

The algorithm uses four procedures called **addodd, addeven, shuffle** and **unshuffle**.

1. **addodd** (*low, high*) lets each processor p_i, for i odd and $low \le i \le high$, fetch the contents of register R of p_{i-1} and add them to the contents of its own R-register.

2. **addeven** (*low, high*) lets each processor p_i, for i even and $low < i \le high$, fetch the contents of R-register of p_{i-1} and add them to the contents of its own R-register.

3. **unshuffle** (*low, high*) permutes the contents of R-registers of processor p_i, for $low \le i \le high$, according to the unshuffle permutation.

4. **shuffle** (*low, high*) is the inverse of **unshuffle**.

Note that using the assumed interconnection scheme, all of the above procedures can be executed in parallel, in one step.

In its entirety, the Schwartz's algorithm is given in Figure 2. An example illustrating Schwartz's algorithm for $N = 16$ is contained in Figure 3.

/* It is assumed $N = 2^n$ and $n \geq 2$, since $n = 1$ is trivial */

```
low = 0;
high = N - 1;
inc = N
for i = 1 to n - 1 do in parallel
        addodd (low, high)
        unshuffle (low, high)
        inc = inc /2; low = low + inc
end

addodd (low, high)

low = 4;
for i = 1 to n - 1 do in parallel
        shuffle (N - low, high)
        addeven (N - low, high)
        low = 2*low
end
```

Figure 2. Schwartz's algorithm.

Since **addodd, addeven, shuffle** and **unshuffle** operations can be performed in parallel, each in suitably defined unit step, it is readily seen that Schwartz's algorithm takes $O(log\ N)$ units of time. The algorithm is a SIMD type synchronous algorithm with very low granularity and very cleverly exploits the chosen interconnection scheme. Counting the number of operations performed by this algorithm is Exercise 3.3.

		addodd	σ^{-1}	addodd	σ^{-1}	addodd	σ^{-1}	addodd
p_0	x_0	x_0	x_0	x_0	x_0	x_0	x_0	x_0
p_1	x_1	$x_0{:}x_1$	x_2	x_2	x_2	x_2	x_2	x_2
p_2	x_2	x_2	x_4	x_4	x_4	x_4	x_4	x_4
p_3	x_3	$x_2{:}x_3$	x_6	x_6	x_6	x_6	x_6	x_6
p_4	x_4	x_4	x_8	x_8	x_8	x_8	x_8	x_8
p_5	x_5	$x_4{:}x_5$	x_{10}	x_{10}	x_{10}	x_{10}	x_{10}	x_{10}
p_6	x_6	x_6	x_{12}	x_{12}	x_{12}	x_{12}	x_{12}	x_{12}
p_7	x_7	$x_6{:}x_7$	x_{14}	x_{14}	x_{14}	x_{14}	x_{14}	x_{14}
p_8	x_8	x_8	$x_0{:}x_1$	$x_0{:}x_1$	$x_0{:}x_1$	$x_0{:}x_1$	$x_0{:}x_1$	$x_0{:}x_1$
p_9	x_9	$x_8{:}x_9$	$x_2{:}x_3$	$x_0{:}x_3$	$x_4{:}x_5$	$x_4{:}x_5$	$x_4{:}x_5$	$x_4{:}x_5$
p_{10}	x_{10}	x_{10}	$x_4{:}x_5$	$x_4{:}x_5$	$x_8{:}x_9$	$x_8{:}x_9$	$x_8{:}x_9$	$x_8{:}x_9$
p_{11}	x_{11}	$x_{10}{:}x_{11}$	$x_6{:}x_7$	$x_4{:}x_7$	$x_{12}{:}x_{13}$	$x_{12}{:}x_{13}$	$x_{12}{:}x_{13}$	$x_{12}{:}x_{13}$
p_{12}	x_{12}	x_{12}	$x_8{:}x_9$	$x_8{:}x_9$	$x_0{:}x_3$	$x_0{:}x_3$	$x_0{:}x_3$	$x_0{:}x_3$
p_{13}	x_{13}	$x_{12}{:}x_{13}$	$x_{10}{:}x_{11}$	$x_8{:}x_{11}$	$x_4{:}x_7$	$x_0{:}x_7$	$x_8{:}x_{11}$	$x_8{:}x_{11}$
p_{14}	x_{14}	x_{14}	$x_{12}{:}x_{13}$	$x_{12}{:}x_{13}$	$x_8{:}x_{11}$	$x_8{:}x_{11}$	$x_0{:}x_7$	$x_0{:}x_7$
p_{15}	x_{15}	$x_{14}{:}x_{15}$	$x_{14}{:}x_{15}$	$x_{12}{:}x_{15}$	$x_{12}{:}x_{15}$	$x_8{:}x_{15}$	$x_8{:}x_{15}$	$x_0{:}x_{15}$

Figure 3. (a) Example of Schwartz's algorithm, $N = 16$ — first half.

	σ	addeven	σ	addeven	σ	addeven
x_0	x_0	x_0	x_0	x_0	x_0	x_0
x_2	x_2	x_2	x_2	x_2	$x_0{:}x_1$	$x_0{:}x_1$
x_4	x_4	x_4	x_4	x_4	x_2	$x_0{:}x_2$
x_6	x_6	x_6	x_6	x_6	$x_0{:}x_3$	$x_0{:}x_3$
x_8	x_8	x_8	x_8	x_8	x_4	$x_0{:}x_4$
x_{10}	x_{10}	x_{10}	x_{10}	x_{10}	$x_0{:}x_5$	$x_0{:}x_5$
x_{12}	x_{12}	x_{12}	x_{12}	x_{12}	x_6	$x_0{:}x_6$
x_{14}	x_{14}	x_{14}	x_{14}	x_{14}	$x_0{:}x_7$	$x_0{:}x_7$
$x_0{:}x_1$	$x_0{:}x_1$	$x_0{:}x_1$	$x_0{:}x_1$	$x_0{:}x_1$	x_8	$x_0{:}x_8$
$x_4{:}x_5$	$x_4{:}x_5$	$x_4{:}x_5$	$x_0{:}x_3$	$x_0{:}x_3$	$x_0{:}x_9$	$x_0{:}x_9$
$x_8{:}x_9$	$x_8{:}x_9$	$x_8{:}x_9$	$x_4{:}x_5$	$x_0{:}x_5$	x_{10}	$x_0{:}x_{10}$
$x_{12}{:}x_{13}$	$x_{12}{:}x_{13}$	$x_{12}{:}x_{13}$	$x_0{:}x_7$	$x_0{:}x_7$	$x_0{:}x_{11}$	$x_0{:}x_{11}$
$x_0{:}x_3$	$x_0{:}x_3$	$x_0{:}x_3$	$x_8{:}x_9$	$x_0{:}x_9$	x_{12}	$x_0{:}x_{12}$
$x_8{:}x_{11}$	$x_0{:}x_7$	$x_0{:}x_7$	$x_0{:}x_{11}$	$x_0{:}x_{11}$	$x_0{:}x_{13}$	$x_0{:}x_{13}$
$x_0{:}x_7$	$x_8{:}x_{11}$	$x_8{:}x_{11}$	$x_{12}{:}x_{13}$	$x_0{:}x_{13}$	x_{14}	$x_0{:}x_{14}$
$x_0{:}x_{15}$	$x_0{:}x_{15}$	$x_0{:}x_{15}$	$x_0{:}x_{15}$	$x_0{:}x_{15}$	$x_0{:}x_{15}$	$x_0{:}x_{15}$

Figure 3. (b) Example of Schwartz's algorithm, $N = 16,$ — second half.

3.3 An Algorithm for Fixed Parallelism

Schwartz's algorithm needs a number of processors equal to the size of the data and the odd-even elimination based algorithm requires $\Omega(log\ N)$ processors to perform at least as well as the serial algorithm. In this section, we describe a class of algorithms that attain effective speed-up for as low as two processors. This algorithm matches the performance of the above two algorithms when, in fact, a large number of processors are available. Furthermore, this algorithm is amenable for implementation on multi-vector architectures such as Cray-XMP or ALLIANT FX/8, as well as the non-shared memory machines, such as the Hypercube.

Define

$$C[s, t] = \sum_{j=s}^{t} d_j.$$

Clearly,

$$C[s, t] = 0 \quad \text{for} \quad s > t,$$

$$C[s, s] = d_s,$$

$$C[s, t+i] = C[s, t]+C[t+1, t+i], \quad \text{for} \quad i \geq 0,$$

and

$$C[1, t] = x_t = \sum_{j=1}^{t} d_j.$$

Let $N = mp$ and $p = 2^k$; $m > 1$ is even, and $k \geq 1$. Let $P_0, P_1, \cdots, P_{p-1}$ be the p processors. The above properties of $C[., .]$ immediately suggest a parallel algorithm for computing $C[1, t]$, $1 \leq t \leq n$ described in Figure 1. An example of the various stages are given in Figure 2.

In stage 1, each processor P_i computes the sum of m data items serially. Hence, this stage takes $m\ (= \dfrac{N}{p})$ units of time. In stage 2, for each value of s, the p processors are divided into 2^{k-s} groups, each with 2^s processors. Since each processor group handles $m2^{s-1}$ number of data items, each processor for any value of s simply handles $m/2$ data items.

Thus, the entire stage 2 takes $\dfrac{mk}{2}(=\dfrac{N}{2p}\log p)$ units. Hence, the entire algorithm on a CREW model takes (why?)

$$T_p(N) = \frac{N}{2p}[2 + \log p].$$

For $p = 2$,

$$T_2(N) = \frac{3}{4}N < T(N) = N.$$

Also, for $p = \dfrac{N}{2}$,

$$T_{\frac{N}{2}}(N) = \log N + 1,$$

which is close to optimal. An improvement of this algorithm is given in Exercise 3.5.

Stage 1:

Each processor $P_i, 0 \le i \le p-1$ computes the following:

```
for j = 0 to m − 1 do
        for i ∈ { 0, 1, 2,  ···  , p − 1 } do in parallel
                compute C [im + 1, im + 1 + j]
        end
end.
```

Stage 2:

```
for s = 1 to k do
        for g ∈ { 0, 1, 2,  ···  , 2^{k−s}−1 } do in parallel
                for j = 1 to m 2^{s−1} do
                        compute C [2^s mg + 1, m2^{s−1}(1+2g) + j]
                end
        end
end
```

Figure 1. A parallel algorithm for all partial sums.

Stage 1	Stage 2	
$0 \le j \le 3$	$s = 1$ $1 \le j \le 4$	$s = 2$ $1 \le j \le 8$
$P_0 : C[1, 1+j]$		
$P_1 : C[5, 5+j]$	$P_0 - P_1 : C[1, 4+j]$	
$P_2 : C[9, 9+j]$		$P_0 - P_3 : C[1, 8+j]$
$P_3 : C[13, 13+j]$	$P_2 - P_3 : C[9, 12+j]$	

Figure 2. An illustration of the algorithm in
Figure 1 with $N = 16$, $m = 4$, $p = 4$.

3.4 A Balanced Binary Tree Algorithm

Let $N = 2^n$. Consider a balanced binary tree of $n + 1$ levels, with the
root at level n and the leaves at level 0. The nodes at level k are labeled
(k, j), $1 \le j \le 2^{n-k}$, and $0 \le k \le n$. Refer to Figure 1 for an example.

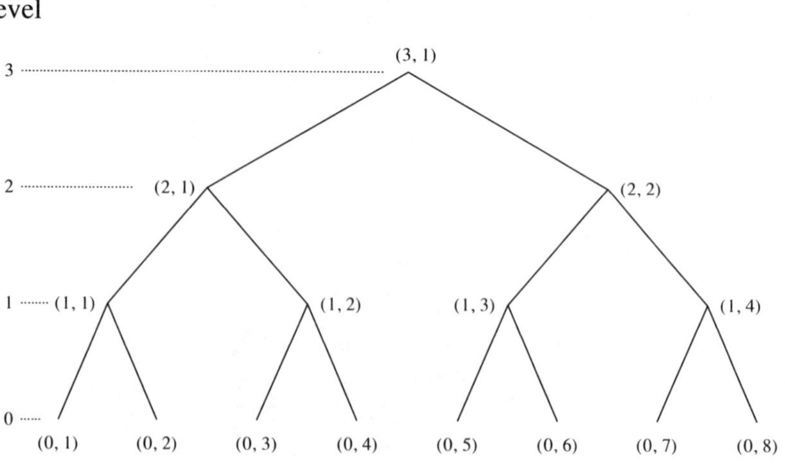

Figure 1. An illustration of a balanced binary tree.

This algorithm consists of two parts — the *up-sweep* (Figure 2a), and the *down-sweep* (Figure 2b). The up-sweep is essentially the parallel summation process, also known as the *associative fan-in* algorithm (Heller [1978]). It can be verified that when up-sweep terminates, $A[n, 1]$ contains the sum $\sum_{i=1}^{N} x_i$, and at the end of the down-sweep

$$B[0, i] = \sum_{j=1}^{i} x_j, \quad \text{for} \quad 1 \le i \le N.$$

It can also be verified that this algorithm performs a total of $O(N)$ operations and can be implemented in an EREW model in $O(\log N)$ time steps.

$/* N = 2^n.$ Input is contained in $A[0, i] = x_i, \quad 1 \le i \le N.$ $*/$

for $i = 1$ to n **do**
    for $j \in \{1, 2, \cdots, 2^{n-i}\}$ **do in parallel**
        $A[i, j] = A[i-1, 2j-1] + A[i-1, 2j]$
    end
end

Figure 2a. Algorithm up-sweep.

$/* B[i, j] = 0$ for $0 \le i \le n, \quad 1 \le j \le 2^{n-i}$ $*/$

for $i = n - 1$ downto 0 **do**
    for $j \in \{1, 2, \cdots, 2^{n-i}\}$ **do in parallel**
        $B[i, j] = B[i+1, \frac{j+1}{2}],$ if j is odd
        $B[i, j] = B[i+1, \frac{j}{2}] + A[i, j-1],$ if j is even
    end
end

for $i \in \{1, 2, \cdots, N\}$ **do in parallel**
    $B[0, i] = B[0, i] + A[0, i]$
end

Figure 2b. Algorithm down-sweep.

3.5 Cole-Vishkin Algorithm

In this section we present a new class of fast algorithms for computing prefixes. More specifically, this algorithm computes the prefixes of N input numbers, each $(\log N)$-bit long, in $O(\frac{\log N}{\log \log N})$ time by performing $O(N)$ operations using $\frac{N \log \log N}{\log N}$ processors on a CRCW model. In the following, it is assumed that the processors can operate on $O(\log N)$ bit numbers in constant time. We begin by describing several building blocks of this algorithm, the first of which is called a *preprocessing* phase.

Given a set of m numbers, each m-bit long, the idea is to build a *table* of prefixes. Clearly, there are m^2 bits, and 2^{m^2} possible configurations. By allocating m processors to each of these 2^{m^2} configurations, compute the prefixes of m numbers in a given configuration using a standard algorithm, such as the one in Section 3.4. The following lemma summarizes the activities of this phase.

Lemma 1. Given a set of m input numbers, each m-bit long, the table of prefixes for all 2^{m^2} configurations of this input can be computed using $m2^{m^2}$ processors in $O(\log m)$ time.

In the development that follows, it is assumed that such a table is available for consultation, hence, the cost of computing this table will *not* be charged to the algorithm under development. The next lemma describes the use of this table.

Lemma 2. Given a set of m numbers, each m-bit long, using $m2^{m^2}$ processors, the required prefixes can be computed using a table look-up in constant time and performing $m2^{m^2}$ operations.

Proof: Each of the 2^{m^2} groups of m processors will compare the input with the 2^{m^2} configurations of m, m-bit numbers in parallel. Clearly, the input will match with only one of these 2^{m^2} configurations. While the processors corresponding to the unmatched group stop functioning, the ith processor corresponding to the matched group goes on to read the ith prefix from the table, for $1 \leq i \leq m$, and the lemma follows.

The second building block relates to computing the prefixes of small numbers — in particular, prefixes of n numbers each of size $m = \log^{1/3} n$ bits.[1]

---

[1] Recall that $\log^{(2)} x = \log\log x$ and $\log^2 x = (\log x)^2$.

Let $\{x_1, x_2, \cdots, x_n\}$ be the set of n input numbers. Define, for $1 \leq i \leq \dfrac{n}{m}$,

$$A_i = \{\ x_j\ \mid\ (i-1)m + 1 \leq j \leq im\ \}.$$

Let

$$z_i = \sum_{j=(i-1)m+1}^{im} x_j, \quad 1 \leq i \leq \frac{n}{m},$$

that is, A_i, $1 \leq i \leq \dfrac{n}{m}$, defines a partition of the input numbers, with z_i being the sum of the numbers in the ith partition. Since each x_i is m-bit long, clearly, z_i is the sum of m numbers each m-bit long, and hence size of z_i is $m + \log m < 2m$ bits.

Step 1: By allocating $m2^{m^2}$ processors to each group A_i, $1 \leq i \leq \dfrac{n}{m}$, the prefixes of numbers in each group are computed by the table look-up procedure described in Lemmas 1 and 2. (It is assumed that each group A_i, is endowed with the required table.) Refer to Figure 1 for an illustration.

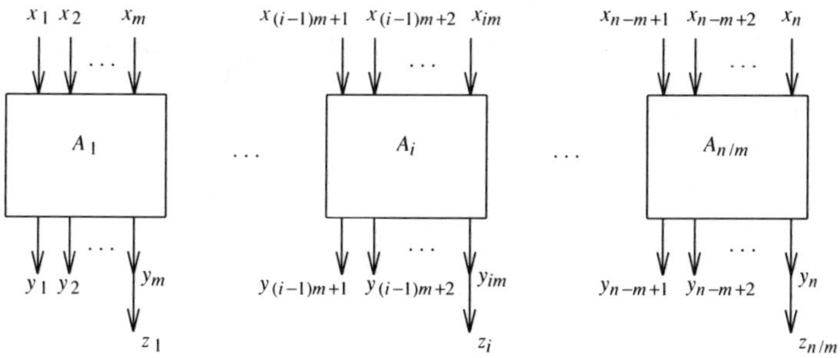

Figure 1: Illustration of step 1. $y_{(i-1)m+j}$ is the jth prefix which is the sum of the first j inputs to A_i, for $1 \leq j \leq m$ and $1 \leq i \leq \dfrac{n}{m}$. Clearly, $z_i = y_{im}$, for $1 \leq i \leq \dfrac{n}{m}$.

This step requires a total of $n2^{m^2}$ processors and takes constant time. Note that z_i is the last output which is the sum of all the inputs to the ith group, A_i, $1 \leq i \leq \dfrac{n}{m}$.

Step 2: Recursively compute the prefixes $z_1 + z_2 + \cdots + z_i$, for $1 \le i \le \dfrac{n}{m}$.

Step 3: Adding $(z_1 + z_2 + \cdots + z_{i-1})$ to the output prefixes $y_{(i-1)m + j}$, for $1 \le j \le m$ of group A_i, obtain the required prefixes of the input $x_1, x_2, \cdots, x_n$. This process is called *backtracking*.

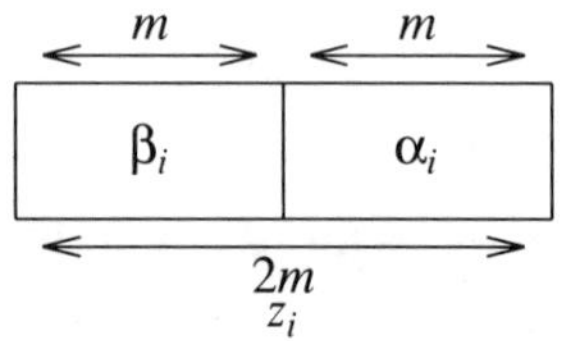

Figure 2: A splitting of z_i used in the recursive step 2.

We now move on to describe the details of the recursive step. Since z_i is, at most, $2m$-bit long, express z_i as

$$z_i = 2^{m-1}\beta_i + \alpha_i,$$

where α_i and β_i are two *m–bit* numbers corresponding to the trailing (least-significant) m bits and leading (most-significant) m bits of z_i (refer to Figure 2), respectively. From

$$\sum_{j=1}^{i} z_j = 2^{m-1} \sum_{j=1}^{i} \beta_j + \sum_{j=1}^{i} \alpha_j,$$

it follows that the required prefix $\sum_{j=1}^{i} z_j$, can be obtained by first computing the prefixes $\sum_{j=1}^{i} \beta_j$ and $\sum_{j=1}^{i} \alpha_j$, and then combining the latter two prefixes. Thus, consider the set $\{ \alpha_1, \alpha_2, \cdots, \alpha_{n/m} \}$. Define, for $1 \le k \le \dfrac{n}{m^2}$,

$$B_k = \{ \alpha_j \mid (k-1)m + 1 \le j \le km \}.$$

Clearly, each B_k consists of m, m-bit numbers. By allocating $m2^{m^2}$ processors, the required prefix is read off from the tables (refer to Lemmas 1 and 2) in constant time. Similarly, define for $1 \le k \le \dfrac{n}{m^2}$,

$$C_k = \{ \beta_j \mid (k-1)m + 1 \le j \le km \},$$

a set consisting of m m-bit numbers. By allocating another set of $m2^{m^2}$ processors, the prefixes of C_k, $1 \le k \le \dfrac{n}{m^2}$ can be read off from the table in constant time. Since $m = \log^{1/3} n$, from

$$2m2^{m^2} < n2^{m^2} = \text{number of available processors,}$$

it follows that the prefixes $\sum\limits_{j=1}^{i} \alpha_j$ and $\sum\limits_{j=1}^{i} \beta_j$ can be computed in parallel.

Given $\sum\limits_{j=1}^{i} \alpha_j$ and $\sum\limits_{j=1}^{i} \beta_j$, since $O(\log n)$-bit numbers can be added in constant time, z_i can be computed in constant time.

To compute the depth of recursion, recall that after each step, the size of the input reduces by a factor of m. Thus, if r is the number of calls needed, then

$$\frac{n}{m^r} = \frac{n}{\log^{r/3} n} \approx m,$$

that is,

$$r = O\left(\frac{\log n}{\log \log n}\right).$$

Using $n2^{\log^{2/3} n}$ processors, since each step can be completed in constant time, we readily have the following.

Lemma 3. The prefix of n numbers, each $(\log^{1/3} n)$-bit long, can be computed in $O\left(\dfrac{\log n}{\log \log n}\right)$ time using $n2^{\log^{2/3} n}$ processors.

We now move on to describe a new class of algorithms from Cole and Vishkin [1989] for computing the prefixes of N numbers, each of size $\log N$ bits, using $p = \dfrac{N \log \log N}{\log N}$ processors. Since the sum of N numbers, each $(\log N)$-bit long is, at most, $2 \log N$ bits, the size of each prefix is at most $2\log N$ bits.

Divide the N inputs into p groups $G_1, G_2, \cdots, G_p$, each consisting of $q = \dfrac{N}{p} = \dfrac{\log N}{\log \log N}$ elements.

Step 1: Allocate one processor to each group G_i, $1 \le i \le p$, and compute the prefixes serially in $O(\dfrac{\log N}{\log \log N})$ time. Refer to Figure 3. The output $y_{(i-1)q+j}$ are the prefixes of the input $x_{(i-1)q+j}$, $1 \le j \le q$, and $1 \le i \le p$. Let $y_{jq} = z_j$, $1 \le j \le p$. Since each z_i is the sum of q numbers, each $(\log N)$-bit long, z_i's have sizes, at most, $(\log N + \log q) < 2 \log N$ bits.

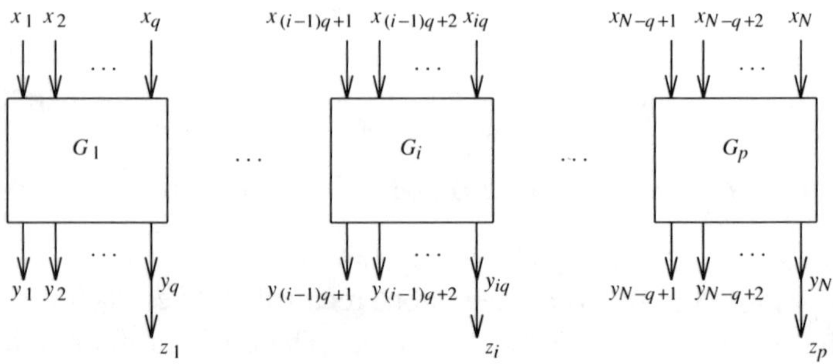

Figure 3: Illustration of step 1.

Step 2: Consider the collection $\{z_1, z_2, \cdots, z_p\}$ of the last outputs of G_i, $1 \le i \le p$. Divide these p numbers in $\frac{p}{r}$ groups $H_1, H_2, \cdots, H_{p/r}$, where each group H_i consists of $r = 4M^2 2^{M^2}$ elements, where $M = \log^{1/3} N$. Now, allocate the total of p processors at the rate of r processors to each of the $\frac{p}{r}$ groups, and compute the prefixes of each group in $O(\log r) = O(\log^{2/3} N)$ time using a standard prefix algorithm (such as the one in Section 3.4). Let η_i be the last output of H_i, $1 \le i \le \frac{p}{r}$, and the size of each η_i is, at most, $2 \log N$ bits. Refer to Figure 4. Let

$$s = \frac{p}{r} = \frac{N \log \log N}{4 \log^{5/3} N \, 2^{\log^{2/3} N}}.$$

Thus,

$$\log 4s = \log N + \log^{(3)} N - \frac{5}{3} \log^{(2)} N - \log^{2/3} N \tag{1}$$

and, for $N \ge 4$,

$$\log N - 3 \log^{2/3} N \le (2 + \log s). \tag{2}$$

Applying the standard approximation $(1 \pm x)^k \approx 1 \pm kx$, when $|x| < 1$, to inequality (2), it follows that

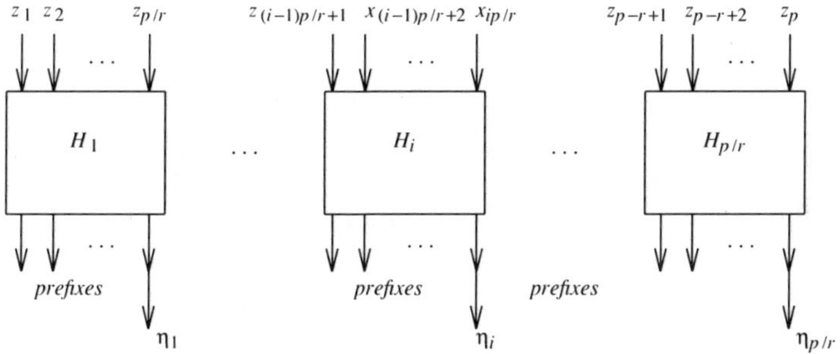

Figure 4: Illustration of step 2.

$$\log^{1/3} N - 1 \leq (1 + \frac{2}{3 \log s}) \log^{1/3} s. \tag{3}$$

Thus, for large N,

$$\log^{1/3} N \leq 2 \log^{1/3} s. \tag{4}$$

Now, using (4), we obtain that

$$\frac{2 \log N}{\log^{1/3} s} \leq 4 \log^{2/3} N.$$

Step 3: Let $t = 4 \log^{2/3} N = 4M^2$. Divide each η_i into t pieces, each consisting $\log^{1/3} s$ bits. Referring to Figure 5, a_{i1} consists of the trailing bits, a_{i2} the next set of trailing bits, and so on. Clearly,

$$\eta_i = \sum_{k=1}^{t} 2^{(k-1)M} a_{ik}. \tag{6}$$

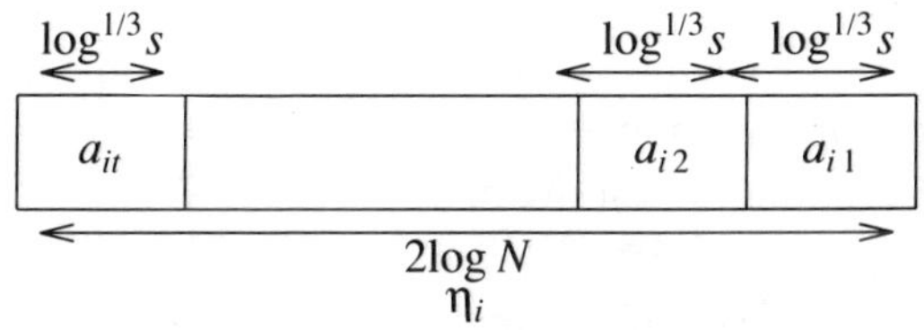

Figure 5: A partition of η_i.

From

$$\sum_{i=1}^{j} \eta_i = \sum_{k=1}^{t} 2^{(k-1)M} \sum_{i=1}^{j} a_{ik}, \quad \text{for } 1 \le j \le \frac{p}{r}, \tag{7}$$

it follows that the prefixes of η_i can be obtained by combining the prefixes $\sum_{i=1}^{j} a_{ik}$ of $\{ a_{1k}, a_{2k}, \cdots, a_{sk} \}$, for $1 \le k \le t$. In other words, we create t subproblems, each consisting of s numbers and size $\log^{1/3} s$ bits. Using the algorithm leading to Lemma 3, we now allocate $s2^{\log^{2/3} s}$ processors to each of the t subproblems and compute their prefixes in parallel in $O(\frac{\log s}{\log \log s}) = O(\frac{\log N}{\log \log N})$ time. The total number of processors needed is given by

$$ts2^{\log^{2/3} s} = \frac{N \log \log N}{\log N} \times \frac{2^{\log^{2/3} s}}{2^{\log^{2/3} N}} \le p,$$

since $s < N$.

Step 4: Compute $\sum_{i=1}^{j} \eta_i$, using (7) as the sum of t prefixes in $t = O(\log^{2/3} N)$ steps using $\frac{p}{r}$ processors. Using $\sum_{i=1}^{j} \eta_i$, we can readily compute the prefixes of $(z_1, z_2, \cdots, z_{p/r})$, hence, the prefixes of $(x_1, x_2, \cdots, x_N)$ in constant time using the idea of *backtracking* used earlier.

The following is the summary of the above development. (See Exercise 3.8.)

Theorem 4. The prefixes of N numbers, each $(\log N)$-bit long, can be computed in $O(\frac{\log N}{\log \log N})$ steps by performing $O(N)$ operations using $O(\frac{N \log \log N}{\log N})$ processors.

This algorithm can be extended to handle N numbers each of size $c \log N$ bits for some integer $c > 1$. In this case, by partitioning the input numbers into c pieces, each $(\log N)$-bit long, we can repeatedly apply the above procedure for each piece and later combine the prefixes of the c pieces. Thus, we obtain the following:

Corollary 5. The prefixes of N numbers, each $O(\log N)$-bit long, can be computed in $O(\frac{\log N}{\log \log N})$ steps by performing $O(N)$ operations using $O(\frac{N \log \log N}{\log N})$ processors.

3.6 A Comparison

Table 1 provides a comparison of the six different methods illustrated in this Chapter. While all of these algorithms have desirable time complexity, they differ widely in the number of operations performed. Only three algorithms — odd-even reduction, balanced binary tree algorithms, and the Cole-Vishkin algorithm — require $O(N)$ operations. Accordingly, these algorithms are amenable for implementation on a p processor machine, even if p is small. (Exercises 3.6 and 3.7.)

Method	Model	No. of Processors	Parallel Time	No. of Operations
Odd-even Elimination (Section 3.1)	EREW	$O(N)$	$O(\log N)$	$O(N\log N)$
Odd-even Reduction (Section 3.1)	EREW	$O(N)$	$O(\log N)$	$O(N)$
Schwartz's Method (Section 3.2)	EREW	$O(N)$	$O(\log N)$	$O(N\log N)$
Fixed Parallelism (Section 3.3)	CREW	p	$\dfrac{N}{2p}(2 + \log p)$	$O(N\log p)$
Balanced Binary Tree (Section 3.4)	EREW	$O(N)$	$O(\log N)$	$O(N)$
Cole-Vishkin (Section 3.5)	CREW	$\dfrac{N \log \log N}{\log N}$	$O\left(\dfrac{\log N}{\log \log N}\right)$	$O(N)$

3.7 Exercises

3.1   Prove the following properties of the algorithm in Figure 5 of Section 3.1.

(a) Show that the algorithm requires $2N - 2 - \log N$ scalar operations and that it takes $2 \log N - 1$ units of time for completion.

(b) Compute the redundancy factor.

3.2   Show that $\sigma^{-1} = \sigma^{N-1}$, where $\sigma^{i+1} = \sigma^i.\sigma$, for $i \geq 1$.

3.3   Compute the number of operations performed by Schwartz's algorithm. Also, compute the redundancy factor of this algorithm.

3.4   Illustrate the sequence of computations of the Algorithm in Figure 1 of Section 3.3, for $p = \dfrac{N}{2}$.

3.5   In this exercise we provide a strategy that modifies the algorithm in Figure 1 of Section 3.3. Note that the output of stage 1 of this algorithm consists of p partial sums, $C[im + 1, (i + 1)m]$. Now, compute the prefixes of the partial sums $C[im + 1, (i + 1)m]$, $0 \leq i \leq p - 1$, using p processors. Then compute the required prefixes by combining these prefixes with the partial sums obtained in stage 1.

(a) Compute the complexity and the implementation of this strategy. Does this require concurrent read?

(b) Compare this strategy with that of the algorithm in Figure 1 of Section 3.3.

3.6   Compare the mechanics of cyclic reduction (Section 3.1) and the balanced binary tree algorithm (Section 3.4).

3.7   Using the Brent's Lemma described in Chapter 2, develop an implementation of, (a) cyclic reduction (Section 3.1), and (b) balanced binary tree algorithm (Section 3.4), using p processors. Derive an upper bound on the time and number of operations performed when $p = \dfrac{N}{\log N}$.

3.8   Carefully compute the total number of operations performed by the algorithm leading to Theorem 4 in Section 3.5.

3.9   Cole and Vishkin [1989]. In this exercise we describe a parallel algorithm for sorting N (small) integers, $\{ x_1, x_2, \cdots , x_N \}$, each in the range $[0, \dfrac{\log N}{\log \log N} - 1]$. Using $p = \dfrac{N \log \log N}{\log N}$ processors, it takes $O(\dfrac{\log N}{\log \log N})$ time. The core of this algorithm is the new parallel prefix algorithm from Cole and Vishkin [1989] described in Section 3.5. Let $q = \dfrac{\log N}{\log \log N} = \dfrac{N}{p}$.

Step 1:   Divide the N input integers into p groups, each consisting of $\dfrac{N}{p}$ integers. Define

$$A_k = \{ \, x_j \mid (k-1)\frac{N}{p} \le j \le k\frac{N}{p} \, \}, \quad 1 \le k \le p.$$

Now, by allocating one processor to each A_k, $1 \le k \le p$, compute $\mid I_{ki} \mid$, where

$$I_{ki} = \{ \, x_j \in A_k \mid x_j = i \, \},$$

that is, compute the number of x_j's in A_k which are equal to i, for $0 \le i < q$, and $1 \le k \le p$, (parallel in k and serial in i).

Clearly, this step takes q time units using p processors.

Step 2:   Define $r_i = \displaystyle\sum_{k=1}^{p} \mid I_{ki} \mid$, for $0 \le i < q$.

Clearly, each $\mid I_{ki} \mid$ is at most $(\log N)$-bit long. Thus, altogether we have N values of $\mid I_{ki} \mid$, each of size $(\log N)$ bits. Hence, by applying the new prefix algorithm of Section 3.5, we can compute r_i, $0 \le i < q$, in $O\left\lceil \dfrac{\log N}{\log \log N} \right\rceil$ steps using p processors.

Step 3:   Use a *sequential prefix algorithm* to compute the prefixes of $\{ r_0, r_1, \cdots , r_{q-1} \}$, that is, $r_0 + r_1 + \cdots + r_j$, for $0 \le j \le q - 1$. This takes $\dfrac{\log N}{\log \log N}$ time units.

Thus, the number of elements in the input that are less than i is given by $r_0 + r_1 + \cdots + r_{i-1}$.

While in principle, Step 3 gives the sorted list, in some special applications one may be interested in computing the ranks of the input elements. This can be accomplished as follows.

Step 4:   For each x_i, we can obtain its rank, denoted by $rank(x_i)$, as follows:

$rank(x_i) = ($number of elements that are less than $x_i) +$

(number of elements whose value is equal to
that of x_i and appears before x_i in the input list).

The first item on the right hand side is available in Step 3 and the second is available from Step 1. Clearly, no two x_i's have the *same* rank.

The computations in Step 4 take constant time for each x_i. Again, by dividing the N inputs into $\dfrac{N}{p}$ groups and allocating p processors to each group repeatedly, q times, this step can be completed in $O(q)$ time.

In summary, this algorithm takes $O(\dfrac{\log N}{\log \log N})$ time using $\dfrac{N \log \log N}{\log N}$ processors.

(a) A sorting algorithm is said to be *stable* if the relative order among the input integers that are equal, is preserved at the output. In other words, if $x_i = x_j$, with $i < j$, then x_i is to the left of x_i in the sorted list as well. Prove that the above sorting algorithm is stable.

(b) Show that a set of N integers, each of size $2 \log N$ bits, can be sorted in $O(\dfrac{\log N}{\log \log N})$ time using $\dfrac{N \log \log N}{\log N}$ processors, first, by applying the above integer sorting algorithm to the leading $\log N$ bits and then to the trailing $\log N$ bits.

(c) Extend this method to sorting N integers, each of size $k \log N$ bits in $O(\dfrac{\log N}{\log \log N})$ time using $\dfrac{N \log \log N}{\log N}$ processors by applying it to chunks of $\log N$ bits starting from the leading to the trailing bits.

3.8 Notes And References

Section 3.1: The methods of cyclic elimination and cyclic reduction are now classic in parallel algorithm design. The method of cyclic reduction was originally proposed by Hockney in 1967 to solve linear tridiagonal systems. Since then, it has been widely studied and extended in a number of directions. It is similar in spirit to the method of *recursive doubling* where the number of answers doubles after each step. Refer to Stone [1973], [1975] for a description of recursive doubling. Refer to Hockney and Jesshope [1981], Lakshmivarahan and Dhall [1985], [1986] and [1990] for additional details. The asynchronous algorithm is from Lubachevsky and Greenberg [1987].

Section 3.2: Schwartz's method is taken from Schwartz [1980].

Section 3.3: This section is adapted from Lakshmivarahan and Dhall [1985]. Recently, Eğecioğlu and Koç [1992] have analyzed the arithmetic and communication complexity of computing prefixes on a distributed memory machine with p processors. Also, refer to Eğecioğlu and Srinivasan [1992].

Section 3.4: Balanced binary tree approach to parallel algorithm design is quite basic and our treatment follows from Vishkin [1984]. Also, refer to Mejier and Akl [1987].

Section 3.5: This section is derived from Cole and Vishkin [1986].
Exercise 3.9 describes an integer sorting algorithm using the notion of parallel prefix computation. Reif [1985] was the first to report an optimal algorithm for sorting N numbers each of $O(\log N)$ bits in $O(\log N)$ time using $\dfrac{N}{\log N}$ processors. While the algorithm for sorting small integers from Reif [1985] and Cole and Vishkin [1989] are quite similar, the difference in their performances is primarily due to the prefix algorithm used as a part of the sorting process. Reif [1985] uses the standard prefix algorithm that takes $O(\log N)$ time using $\dfrac{N}{\log N}$ processors, but Cole and Vishkin [1989] use the new prefix algorithm that takes $O\left(\dfrac{\log N}{\log \log N}\right)$ time using $\dfrac{N \log \log N}{\log N}$ processors, described in Section 3.5. Reif [1985] also presents sublogarithmic time algorithms for prefix computation and integer sorting. Also, refer to Reif [1986].

Chapter 4

Parallel Prefix Algorithms On Linked Lists

This Chapter describes algorithms for computing prefixes/suffixes in parallel when the input data is in the form of a linked list. Developments in this Chapter complement those in Chapter 3. We begin by defining a version of the prefix problem called the *list ranking problem.*

Let $< N > = \{1, 2, \cdots , N\}$ and **L** be a list of size N. For each $i \in < N >$, the node i in **L** contains two *types* of information: the *value* $v(i)$ of node i, and the *successor* $s(i)$ of node i. Clearly, $s(N) = 0$. A linked list may conveniently be represented as a directed, labeled graph $G(V, E)$, where $V = < N >$ and

$$E = \{ (i, j) \mid j = s(i), \quad i, j \in V \},$$

and $v(i)$ denotes the value for node i. Let

$$R(i) = \sum_{j = N - i}^{N} v(s(j)), \quad \text{for } 1 \le i \le N.$$

If $v(i) = 1$, for $1 \le i < N$ and $v(N) = 0$, then $R(i)$ denotes the *rank* of node i, which is the *distance*[1] of the node i from the (right) end of L. The problem of computing $R(i)$ is known as the *list ranking problem*. If $v(i) = a_i$, the $R(i)$ denotes the *suffix sum*. Instead of the successor, $s(i)$, if we use the predecessor, $p(i)$, we can likewise consider the prefix sum and the ranking from the left end of the list. For definiteness in the following, we consider the list ranking problem.

4.1 Basic Pointer-Jumping

Given a list L, initially each node points to its successor, which is at distance one from it. By computing the *successor of successor,* it can be verified that a node now points to another node which is at a distance *two* from it. By repeating this successor of successor k times, it is seen that a node points to a node at a *distance* 2^k from it. Thus, given a list with N nodes, in no more than $\lceil \log N \rceil$ steps, we should cover the entire list. In other words, information from one end of the list **L** can be passed on to the other end in no more than $O(\log N)$ steps.

A list ranking algorithm based principally on this idea of pointer-jumping is given in Figure 1, with an illustration in Figure 2. It can be verified that this algorithm can be implemented on an EREW model and requires $O(\log N)$ steps by performing $O(N \log N)$ operations.

Given the list $\mathbf{L} = (v(i), s(i)), \quad 1 \le i \le N$
with $v(i) = 1$, for $1 \le i < N$, and $v(N) = 0$.

for $i = 1$ to N **do in parallel**
    $b(i) = s(i)$
end
while $(b(i) \ne 0$ and $b(b(i)) \ne 0)$ **do in parallel**
    $v(i) = v(i) + v(b(i))$
    $b(i) = b(b(i))$
end

Figure 1. The basic pointer-jumping algorithm.

---

[1]The distance between two nodes x and y in a graph is defined to be the length (measured in terms of the number of edges) of the shortest path from x to y.

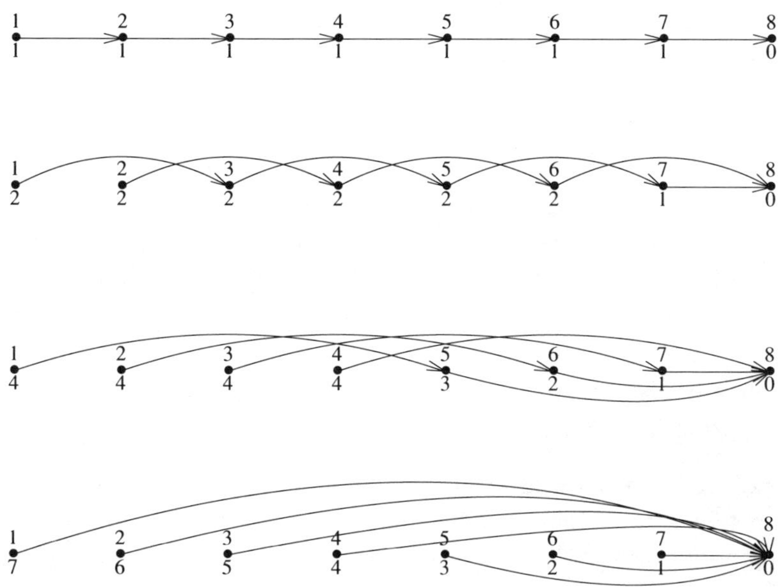

Figure 2. Illustration of pointer-jumping.

This algorithm is the linked list counterpart of the cyclic elimination algorithm given in Section 3.1. Much like cyclic elimination, this algorithm is *time optimal* but does *not* have optimal speed up.

4.2 A Strategy for Optimal List Ranking

An optimal list ranking algorithm is one that takes $O(\log N)$ time and performs $O(N)$ operations. The basic idea that underlies the design of optimal list ranking algorithms may be described as follows. It is assumed that the list is doubly linked, where each node i, in addition to $v(i)$ and $s(i)$, now also has the predecessor $p(i)$. Clearly, $s(N) = p(1) = 0$. (See Exercise 4.1.) Let $\mathbf{I} \subseteq\ <N>$ and $|\mathbf{I}| < N$.

Step 1: Given a list $\mathbf{L}$ of size N, create a list $\mathbf{L'}$ of length $O(\dfrac{N}{\log N})$ by deleting the nodes in the set $\mathbf{I}$.

Step 2: Solve the list ranking problem for the list $\mathbf{L'}$ using the pointer-jumping algorithm of Section 4.1. Since $\mathbf{L'}$ is of length $O(\frac{N}{\log N})$, this step requires $O(N)$ operations, and takes $O(\log N)$ steps.

Step 3: Insert the nodes in **I** into **L'**, and recompute the rank of all nodes in **L**.

Clearly, step 2 is obvious and step 3 is the reverse of step 1. We first examine a strategy for implementing step 1. For reasons that will become apparent the subset **I** is selected with the following property, namely, if $i \in$ **I**, then $s(i) \notin$ **I**, that is, nodes in **I** are *not* adjacent in **L**. Such a set of nodes is called an *independent set*[2] for **L**. Thus, step 1 consists of two parts — (a) choose an independent set **I** large enough such that **L'** is of length $O(\frac{N}{\log N})$, and (b) given an independent set, extract information sufficient enough to recompute the ranks of the nodes in **I** in step 3, then contract the list by deleting the nodes in **I**. An algorithm for this list contraction is given in Figure 1 with an illustration in Figure 2.

/* The list **L** is given with $v(i) = 1$, for $1 \le i < N$ and $v(N) = 0$. $s(i)$ and $p(i)$ are the successor and the predecessor of node i. $\mathbf{I} = \{\, i_1, i_2, \cdots, i_k \,\}$ is the independent set.*/

$$\textbf{for } i_j \in \mathbf{I} \textbf{ do in parallel}$$
$$A(j) = (i_j,\ s(i_j),\ v(i_j))$$
$$v(p(i_j)) = v(p(i_j)) + v(i_j)$$
$$s(p(i_j)) = s(i_j)$$
$$p(s(i_j)) = p(i_j)$$
$$\textbf{end}$$

Figure 1. Algorithm for deleting an independent set.

This algorithm clearly takes constant time and performs $O(N)$ operations.

---

[2] Let $G = (V, E)$ be a graph. The subset $\mathbf{I} \subseteq V$ is called an independent set if, and only if, $(i, j) \notin E$ when $i, j \in \mathbf{I}$.

An algorithm for step 3 is given in Figure 3 which consists of computing the ranks of the members of the independent set, given the ranking of the contracted list L'. Again, this takes constant time and performs $O(N)$ operations.

(a) The given doubly linked list, with ■ denoting the independent set.

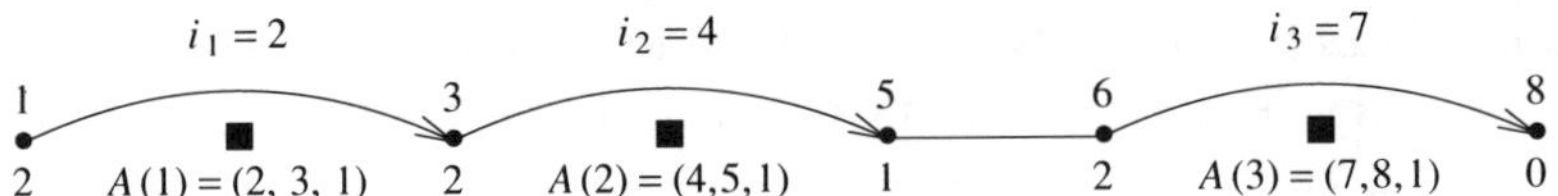

(b) Contracted list.

Figure 2. Deletion of independent set from a list.

In summary, excluding the cost of extracting a large enough independent set **I**, all the other tasks, namely, the deletion of the independent set to obtain L' from **L**, list ranking of L' using pointer-jumping, and computing the ranks of the members of **I** together take a total time of $O(\log N)$ and require $O(N)$ operations. Thus, the overall strategy is optimal only if we can find a large independent set **I** in $O(\log N)$ time using $O(N)$ operations.

```
/* Let  A(j) = (i_j, s(i_j), v(i_j)), for all i_j ∈ I be given. */


        for i_j ∈ I do in parallel
            v(i_j) = v(i_j) + v(s(i_j)),        p(i_j) = p(s(i_j))
            s(p(i_j)) = i_j,                    p(s(i_j)) = i_j.
        end
```

Figure 3. Algorithm for computing the ranks of nodes in **I**.

In the following section, we turn to the problem of finding such an independent set for a given list.

4.3. Independent Set *via* Coloring

In this section, we first describe an algorithm for 3-coloring a directed cycle. Based on this coloring, we then extract an independent set that could be used in the list ranking algorithm.

A *directed cycle* is a graph $G = (V, E)$ in which both the *in-degree* and the *out-degree* of each node is one and there is a *directed path* connecting any two nodes. If $|V| = N$, then it is called a N-cycle. Let $< n > = \{ 1, 2, \cdots, n \}$ be a set of *colors*. A function $f : V \rightarrow < n >$ is called a *n-coloring* of G, if $f(a) \neq f(b)$ when $(a, b) \in E$. Examples of 3-coloring of a 3-cycle and a 2-coloring of a 4-cycle are given in Figure 1.

Figure 1. Examples of coloring odd and even cycles,
where the labels denote colors.

It can be verified that while an *even* cycle needs only *two* colors, an *odd* cycle needs a minimum of three colors. Hence, our interests are in the three-coloring of a directed cycle.

Starting from an arbitrary node, a serial algorithm will successively assign colors 1 and 2 as it traverses through the cycle, using the third color only when needed (for an odd cycle).

Parallel algorithms for coloring are a bit more tricky. Conceptually, it involves *partitioning* the nodes in such a way that the nodes in a given partition are assigned the same color. But then, since all the nodes look alike, there is the problem of deciding which subset of nodes gets colored first. In other words, there is *symmetry* among nodes and there are potentially many legal possible colorings. Thus, we need an approach that breaks this apparent symmetry in the problem. We begin by describing a simple coloring algorithm.

Assume without loss of generality, that the directed cycle $G = (V, E)$ is given in the form of a linked list. Let $2^{k-1} < N \le 2^k$ and $V = \{ 0, 1, 2, \cdots, N - 1 \}$, and the initial coloring f be such that

$$f(x) = x, \quad \text{for} \quad x \in V. \tag{1}$$

Let $x = x_{k-1} x_{k-2} \cdots x_1 x_0$ in binary. An algorithm for reducing the number of colors is given in Figure 2 and is illustrated in Table 1. Refer to Exercise 4.2 for an algorithm to find the index r required in the simple coloring algorithm.

Table 1. Illustration of the simple coloring algorithm.

x	$s(x) = y$	$f(x)$	$f(y)$	r	$g(x)$	A 3-coloring
1	7	0001	0111	1	2	2
2	4	0010	0100	1	3	2
3	2	0011	0010	0	1	1
4	5	0100	0101	0	0	0
5	6	0101	0110	0	1	1
6	10	0110	1010	2	5	2
7	3	0111	0011	2	5	0
8	1	1000	0001	0	0	0
9	8	1001	1000	0	1	1
10	9	1010	1001	0	0	0

To check if g is indeed a coloring, let $(a, b) \in E$, and $f(a) = x \ne y = f(b)$. Let $g(x) = 2r + x_r$ and $g(y) = 2q + y_q$, where r and q are determined by the algorithm in Figure 2. If $g(x) = g(y)$, then

$$2 \mid (r - q) \mid = \mid y_q - x_r \mid, \tag{2}$$

and the right-hand-side of (2) is either 0 or 1, and the left hand side is even and non-negative. Hence, $r = q$ is the only possibility. But then $x_r = y_r$ contradicts the definition of r. Hence, $g(x) \ne g(y)$.

/* Let $G = (V, E)$ be a directed cycle with f as its initial coloring. For $x \in V$, let $s(x) = y$ denote its *successor*. Let $x = x_{k-1} \, x_{k-2} \, \cdots \, x_1 \, x_0$, and $y = y_{k-1} \, y_{k-2} \, \cdots \, y_1 \, y_0$. Compute a new color g. */

$$\textbf{for } x \in V \textbf{ do in parallel}$$
$$r = \min_{j} \{ \, x_j \neq y_j \, \}$$
$$g(x) = 2r + x_r$$
$$\textbf{end};$$

Figure 2. A simple coloring algorithm.

Clearly, this algorithm takes $O(1)$ (constant) time and performs $O(N)$ operations.

The maximum value of $g(x)$ is $2k - 1$ and there are only $2k$ (0 through $2k - 1$) colors. Starting with $N = 2^k$ colors, the simple coloring algorithm finds a new coloring with only $2k = 2\log N$ colors that need $(1 + \log k)$ bits to represent them. Thus, so long as $1 + \log k < k$, (that is, $k > 3$), the simple algorithm will indeed reduce the number of colors. From this we obtain the following result.

Lemma 1. Given a directed cycle, using the simple coloring algorithm we obtain a $O(\log N)$ coloring in constant time by performing $O(N)$ operations.

By applying this algorithm twice, we can reduce the number of colors to $O(\log \log N)$. In general, by repeatedly applying it j times, we can reduce the colors to $O(\log^{(j)} N)$, where $\log^{(j)} N$ is log iterated j times. Define

$$\log^* N = \min \{ \, i \mid \log^{(i)} N \leq 1 \, \}. \tag{3}$$

It can be verified that for $N \leq 2^{65,536} \approx 10^{19727}$, $\log^* N \leq 5$. Thus, starting with $|V|$ colors and by repeatedly applying the simple coloring algorithm in Figure 2, we can reduce the number of colors until the number of bits needed to represent the colors is $k = 3$. In this case, two successive colors can differ in the 0th, 1st, or the 2nd bit position, resulting in, at most, six colors, 0 through 5; that is, not all 3-bit patterns will arise as a color.

Further reduction from six to three colors can be accomplished as follows. Let $C = \{3, 4, 5\}$. All the nodes with color, for example, $x = 3$ are assigned (in parallel) a new color that is the minimum from the set $\{0, 1, 2\}$ and is different from the color of its successor and predecessor. This requires $O(1)$ steps and $O(N)$ operations. By repeating this procedure no more than $3 = |C|$ times, we can obtain a three coloring. Altogether, this reduction procedure takes $O(1)$ steps and $O(N)$ operations. Refer to Table 1 for an illustration.

The following result summarizes the above discussion.

Lemma 2. Given a directed N-cycle, we can obtain a three coloring in $O(\log^* N)$ steps using $O(N \log^* N)$ operations.

Refer to Exercise 4.3 for an alternate 3-coloring algorithm that performs $O(N)$ operations in $O(\log N)$ time.

We now describe a very natural process by which we can extract an independent set. Given an n-coloring of a cycle, let c_i be the color of node i. Define a subset of nodes

$$\mathbf{I} = \{ i \mid i \in V; \text{ with } c_i < c_{p(i)} \text{ and } c_i < c_{s(i)} \},$$

that is, $\mathbf{I}$ consists of nodes whose colors constitute a *local minimum*.[3] Clearly, if $i, j \in \mathbf{I}$, then $(i, j) \notin E$, and hence, such an $\mathbf{I}$ constitutes an independent set. Since each node can compare its color with that of its successor and predecessor nodes, the set of all local minima can be found in constant time in parallel. To get an idea of the size of the set $\mathbf{I}$, let i and j be two local minima with no other minimum in between. In going from i to j, the colors first increase and then decrease. (Refer to Figure 3 for an illustration.) Thus, the number of nodes between i and j is, at most, $2n - 3$. Thus, the number of independent nodes in a list with N nodes resulting from an n-coloring is at least $\dfrac{N}{2n - 3}$, that is $|\mathbf{I}| = \Omega(\dfrac{N}{n})$. The following is a summary of the above discussion.

Lemma 3. Given an n-coloring of a list, an independent set $\mathbf{I}$ of size $\Omega = (\dfrac{N}{n})$ can be obtained in parallel in constant time using only $O(N)$ operations in parallel.

---

[3] We could have considered the local maximum instead of the minimum.

Figure 3. Local minima denoted by ■. Three colors are used.

Now, combining the Lemmas 2 and 3, we obtain the following.

Theorem 4. Given a linked list of size N, we can find an independent set **I** of size $\Omega(\frac{N}{n}) = \Omega(cN)$, for some $0 < c < 1$ in $O(\log^* N)$ operations in parallel.

If the independent set **I** obtained by the above described process is *not* large enough, we must repeat the procedure until one such set is obtained. This algorithm is described in Figure 4.

/* Given the linked list **L** of size N. */

let $N_0 = N$, $i = 0$;
while $N_i \geq \dfrac{N}{\log N}$ **do**
    (i) Obtain a 3-coloring of the list using the algorithm leading to Lemma 2 and extract the independent set **I**.
    (ii) Delete **I** from **L** using the algorithm in Figure 3 in Section 4.2., and obtain **L'**.
    (iii) $i = i + 1$ and N_i is the length of **L'** and **L** $\leftarrow$ **L'**.
end

Figure 4. An algorithm for finding the required independent set of a list.

By Theorem 4, after each iteration, the size of the list reduces by *at least* cN for some constant $0 < c < 1$. Thus,

$$N_{k+1} = N_k - |\,\mathbf{I}\,|$$

$$\leq N_k - cN_k = (1 - c)N_k \leq (1-c)^k N.$$

Therefore, the number of iterations k required before L' is of length $O(\frac{N}{\log N})$ is given by

$$(1 - c)^k N \le \frac{N}{\log N},$$

from which, we obtain $k = O(\log \log N)$.

The time required by step (i) in Figure 4 is given by (using Theorem 4)

$$\sum_{i=0}^{k} \log^* (1 - c)^i N \le k \log^* N = O((\log\log N)\log^* N).$$

The number of operations performed by step (i) in Figure 4 is given by (again using Theorem 4)

$$\sum_{i=0}^{k} O((1 - c)^i N \log^* (1 - c)^i N)$$

$$\le (\log^* N) \sum_{i=0}^{k} O((1 - c)^i N)$$

$$\le (\log^* N) \alpha N \sum_{i=0}^{k} (1 - c)^i \quad \text{for some constant } \alpha > 0$$

$$< (\alpha N \log^* N) \sum_{i=0}^{\infty} (1 - c)^i$$

$$= O(N \log^* N).$$

Referring to the analysis of the algorithm in Figure 3 of Section 4.2, it follows that step (ii) in Figure 4 requires $O(\log \log N)$ time and $\sum_{i=0}^{k} O((1 - c)^i N) = O(N)$ operations.

As an immediate consequence of this analysis, we obtain the following.

Theorem 5. Using the 3-coloring algorithm leading to Lemma 2, the required independent set can be obtained in $O((\log\log N) \log^* N)$ time performing a total of $O(N \log^* N)$ operations.

Exercise 4.4 describes an alternate approach that delivers the required independent set by performing $O(N)$ operations in $O((\log N) \log \log N)$ time.

First, we look for an algorithm that will deliver the required independent set by performing $O(N)$ operations in $O(\log N)$ time. Clearly, the algorithm leading to Theorem 5 is much faster than the $O(\log N)$ time requirement. Since $\log^* N \leq 5$ for all "earthly" values of N, the number of operations is also "linear" in N, for all practical values of N. However, it is theoretically interesting to obtain an algorithm that performs $O(N)$ operations.

4.4 Cole and Vishkin's Algorithm

The basic difficulty with the method of Section 4.3 is in order to obtain the required independent set we must recursively apply the technique for $O(\log \log N)$ times. In this section we describe a method for reducing the size of the given linked list from N to $\dfrac{N}{\log N}$ in a much shorter time. We begin by introducing some new concepts.

Let $G = (V, E)$ be a directed cycle. A subset U of V is called an *r-ruling set if,* (a) no two vertices of U are adjacent, and (b) for any vertex $x \in V$, there is a *directed* path from x to some vertex $u \in U$ of length at most r.

Thus, every r-ruling set is an *independent* set by condition (a). Condition (b) relates to the relative size of U with respect to V. The reader can readily verify that the set of nodes corresponding to the local minima and maxima resulting from the 3-coloring algorithm of Section 4.3 is indeed a r-ruling set, for $r = \lceil \log N \rceil - 1$. In other words, using $O(N)$ processors, we can obtain a $(\lceil \log N \rceil - 1)$-ruling set in constant time by performing $O(N)$ operations.

We now turn to an algorithm from Cole and Vishkin [1989] for finding the 2-ruling set. This algorithm consists of two stages. In the first stage, by using a new algorithm for finding the $(\log N)$-ruling set and applying it twice, we extract a $(\log \log N)$-ruling set. In the second stage, this latter ruling set is then enhanced to obtain a 2-ruling set.

Let $G = (V, E)$ be the given directed cycle with $V = \{ 0, 1, \cdots, N - 1 \}$. For $x \in V$, let $s(x)$ be its successor. Define an initial labeling $f_0 : V \to V$, such that $f_0(x) = x$. Let $x = x_{n-1} \cdots x_1 x_0$, and $s(x) = y = y_{n-1} \cdots y_1 y_0$, where $n = \lceil \log N \rceil$.

Step 1:   For each $x \in V$, assign, in parallel, a new label $f_1(x) = j$ if $j = \min_i \{ x_i \neq y_i \}$. (See Exercises 4.5 and 4.6.)

Step 2: For each vertex x, in parallel, *select* it as a member of the $(\log N)$-ruling set if the new label $f_1(x)$ is a *local minimum*[4] with respect to its neighbors and either of the following two conditions is true:

(a) neither of the vertices adjacent to x is a local minimum,

(b) the jth bit of $f_0(x)$ is 1, where $j = f_1(x)$.

Thus, at the end of step 2, a vertex x is either *selected* (to be in U) or *unselected*. An unselected vertex x is said to be *available* if neither of its neighbors was selected and $f_1(x)$ is a local maximum with respect to its neighbors.

Step 3: For each available vertex x, in parallel, select it as a member of U if either of the following two conditions is satisfied:

(a) neither of the vertices adjacent to x is available,

(b) the jth bit of $f_0(x) = 1$, where $j = f_1(x)$.

Refer to Figure 1 for an example. The following conclusion is immediate.

Lemma 1. A $(\log N)$-ruling set can be obtained in constant time using N processors.

Now, *deleting* the selected vertices and their neighbors from G, a new directed graph $G' = (V', E')$ is obtained. We distinguish *three* cases.

Case 1: Select $x \in V'$ to be in U' if $degree(x) = 0$.

Case 2: $x \in V'$ is selected to be in U' if $degree(x) = 1$, and either of the following is true:

(a) the degree of the neighbor of x is two,

(b) the neighbor of x is its successor.

Case 3: $degree(x) = 2$. In this case, first compute $f_2(x)$ from $f_1(x)$ using step 1 (just as $f_1(x)$ was computed from $f_0(x)$) and apply steps 2 and 3 to x, if the degree of each of its two neighbors is two, to decide if $x \in U'$.

Now, deleting from G' every vertex x, such that, either x is selected or one of its neighbors has been selected, a new graph $G'' = (V'', E'')$ is obtained. It can be verified that this latter graph consists of simple paths containing, at most, $\log \log N$ nodes.

---

[4] In this Section, we define a vertex to be local minimum, if $c_i \leq c_{p(i)}$ and $c_i \leq c_{s(i)}$. Analogous definition applies for local maximum.

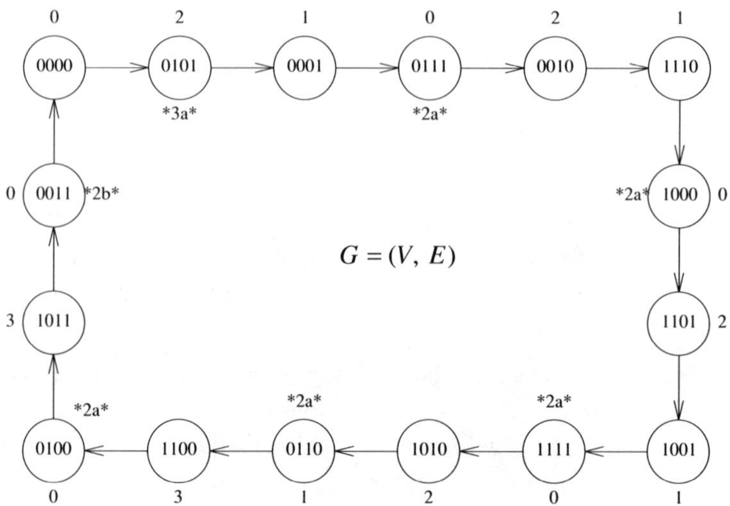

Figure 1: Cole-Vishkin algorithm. Numbers inside the node represent $f_0(x)$, and those outside represent $f_1(x)$. Values between ** indicate the steps when the node is picked up.

The following conclusion is immediate.

Lemma 2. A $(\log \log N)$-ruling set can be obtained in constant time using N processors.

Given a $(\log \log N)$-ruling set, we now describe an algorithm to create a 2-ruling set. First, observe that every $(\log \log N)$-ruling set is also a $\left(\dfrac{\log N}{\log \log N}\right)$-ruling set as well.

This algorithm works with the graph $G'' = (V'', E'')$. All the vertices in this graph are not yet selected to be in the ruling set. Each of the vertices in G'' have been assigned a label $f_2(x)$, where $0 \le f_2(x) < \log \log N$, and it can be verified that no two adjacent vertices have the same label. Based on these labels, we now describe a method for creating the required 2-ruling set.

Step 1:   For each $0 \le i < q$, first identify the set of all vertices $x \in V''$, such that $f_2(x) = i$.

This is accomplished by using the *integer sorting* algorithm described in Exercise 3.9. This sorting algorithm gives the rank of each vertex in the sorted list. This process takes $O(\frac{\log N}{\log \log N})$ time using $\frac{N \log \log N}{\log N}$ processors.

Step 2: For each $x \in V''$, if neither of the neighbors of x is in the ruling set, then add x to the ruling set.

We summarize the above development in the following.

Theorem 3. A 2-ruling set can be obtained in $O(\frac{\log N}{\log \log N})$ time using $\frac{N \log \log N}{\log N}$ processors.

4.5 Independent Set *via* Randomization

In this concluding Section, we present a randomized approach to finding an independent set.

Let $G = (V, E)$ be a directed cycle with $V = \{ 1, 2, \cdots, N \}$. An independent set for G can be easily obtained by a very simple randomization. First, consider a collection of N *fair* coins labeled 1 through N. Toss all the coins simultaneously. Now, assign a label H or T to the node $i \in V$, if the ith coin turned up head or tail, respectively, in the toss. Since the labeling process is *independent,* the probability that a succession of k nodes receives the same label H is $(\frac{1}{2})^k$. Thus, if we are looking to create an independent set of nodes receiving the label H, it is necessary to *relabel* some of the nodes. Thus, change the label of node i from H to T if both i and $s(i)$ received the label H. In this way, we succeed in *"isolating"* the nodes with label H, thereby, creating an independent set. The algorithm is given in Figure 1. The set of all possible node labelings resulting from this algorithm, and the corresponding independent set of a 4-node cycle is given in Table 1. Referring to the first row of this table, if all the nodes receive the label H in step (a) of the algorithm, then all these labels will be changed to T in the second step, and, hence, I is empty. But, in the second row, the labels of only nodes 1 and 2 are changed from H to T in step 2, and, hence, node 3 is selected as the independent set. It can be verified that **I** consists of only those nodes i, such that $label[i] = H$ and $label[s(i)] = T$ at the end of the step (a). Thus, the probability that a node is selected to be in **I** is 1/4.

/*Given $G = (V, E)$, a directed cycle with $V = \{ 1, 2, \cdots, N \}$.*/

for $i \in V$ **do in parallel**

    (a) assign label H or T to node i with equal probability;

    (b) if $label[i] = label[s(i)] = H$, then $label[i] = T$;

end;

Figure 1. A randomized algorithm for independent set.

Table 1. Node Labeling

Node labels				Independent
1	2	3	4	Set **I**
$H \to T$	$H \to T$	$H \to T$	$H \to T$	-
$H \to T$	$H \to T$	H	T	3
$H \to T$	H	T	$H \to T$	2
$H \to T$	H	T	T	2
H	T	$H \to T$	$H \to T$	1
H	T	H	T	1, 3
H	T	T	$H \to T$	1
H	T	T	T	1
T	$H \to T$	$H \to T$	H	4
T	$H \to T$	H	T	3
T	H	T	H	2, 4
T	H	T	T	2
T	T	$H \to T$	H	4
T	T	H	T	3
T	T	T	H	4
T	T	T	T	-

Assuming that N is even, the maximum size of $\mathbf{I}$ is such that $0 \le |\mathbf{I}| \le \frac{N}{2}$. Clearly, when $|\mathbf{I}| = \frac{N}{2}$, it consists of all the alternate nodes in the cycle. Let $A \subseteq V$ with $|A| = \frac{N}{2}$ be the set of all alternate nodes. Thus, if i and j are in A, then their minimum distance is two and the event $i \in \mathbf{I}$ is independent of the event $j \in \mathbf{I}$.

The process of selecting the independent set from A using the algorithm in Figure 1 can be modeled using the standard *Bernoulli* distribution. An element of A is selected (identified as success) to be in $\mathbf{I}$ with a probability of 1/4. Thus, the probability with which k elements from A will be selected to be in $\mathbf{I}$ is the same as the probability of obtaining k heads in m successive tosses of a coin that falls heads with a probability of $p = 1/4$. That is,

$$Prob[\,|\mathbf{I}| = k\,] = \binom{m}{k} p^k q^{m-k},$$

and

$$Prob[\,|\mathbf{I}| \ge k\,] = \sum_{j=k}^{m} \binom{m}{j} p^j q^{m-j}.$$

The latter expression is related to the tail of the *binomial* distribution. There are several ways for estimating the tail distribution. For reasons that will become apparent, we invoke the well known *Chernoff* bounds, namely

$$Prob[\,|\mathbf{I}| \le (1 - \varepsilon)mp\,] \le e^{-\varepsilon^2 mp}.$$

Recognizing that $m = \frac{N}{2}$, and $p = 1/4$, it follows that

$$Prob\left[\,|\mathbf{I}| \le \frac{(1-\varepsilon)N}{8}\,\right] \le e^{-\frac{\varepsilon^2 N}{8}},$$

that is, the probability that $|\mathbf{I}|$ is less than a fraction of $\frac{N}{2}$ is exponentially small. In other words, this algorithm in constant time picks up an independent set $\mathbf{I}$, such that $|\mathbf{I}| \ge \alpha N$ with probability close to unity by performing $O(N)$ operations. By repeating the arguments leading to Theorem 5 in Section 4.3, it follows that this randomized algorithm with a very high probability delivers the independent set in $O(\log\log N)$ time by performing $O(N)$ operations.

4.6 Exercises

4.1   Describe a constant time EREW type parallel algorithm requiring $O(N)$ operations for creating a doubly-linked list from a given singly-linked list of size N.

4.2   The simple coloring algorithm in Figure 2 of Section 4.3 requires finding the index $r = \min_j \{ x_j \neq y_j \}$, where $x = x_{k-1} \cdots x_1 x_0$, and $s(x) = y = y_{k-1} \cdots y_1 y_0$. In this exercise, we describe an algorithm to find r. Assume that $x > y$. (Otherwise interchange the values of x and y.) Define

$$\alpha = \alpha_{k-1} \cdots \alpha_1 \alpha_0 = x - y$$

$$\beta = \beta_{k-1} \cdots \beta_1 \beta_0 = \alpha - 1.$$

(a) Verify that $\alpha_r = 1$, $\beta_r = 0$, $\alpha_j = 0$ and $\beta_j = 1$, for $0 \leq j \leq r - 1$, and $\alpha_j = \beta_j$, for $r + 1 \leq j \leq k - 1$.
(b) Compute $\gamma = \alpha \oplus \beta$ (the exclusive-or sum of α and β) and verify that the number of 1 bits in γ denotes the value of $r + 1$. That is, γ is the unary expression for $r + 1$. Subtract 1 from γ and obtain the value of r.
Note: Cole and Vishkin [1986b] attribute this technique to B. Schieber.

4.3   In this exercise, we introduce an alternate 3-coloring algorithm. Let $2^{k-1} < N \leq 2^k$, and $V = \{ 0, 1, \cdots, N - 1 \}$. Let f be an initial coloring, such that $f(x) = x$, for all $x \in V$.

Step 1:   Apply the simple coloring algorithm of Figure 2 in Section 4.3 once.

This step leads to $O(\log N)$ coloring by performing $O(N)$ operations in constant time. (Lemma 1 in Section 4.3.)

Let $C = \{ 3, 4, \cdots, k - 1 \}$, where $k = O(\log N)$, the number of colors obtained in step 1. For each $i \in C$, let n_i be the number of nodes with color i. Clearly, $\sum_{i \in C} n_i < N$.

Step 2:   Let i be the smallest color in C. All nodes with color i are assigned (in parallel) a new color that is the minimum from the set $\{ 0, 1, 2 \}$ and is different from the color of its successor and predecessor. Remove the color i from C and repeat step 2 until C is empty.

For each $i \in C$, step 2 performs n_i operations in constant time. Since $|C| = O(\log N)$, overall, step 2 takes $O(\log N)$ time and performs $\sum_{i \in C} n_i = O(N)$ operations.

Thus, this algorithm performs a total of $O(N)$ operations in $O(\log N)$ time.

Illustrate the above 3-coloring algorithm for $N = 78$.

4.4   By replacing the 3-coloring algorithm in step 1 of the algorithm in Figure 4 of Section 4.3 by the one given in Exercise 4.3, show that the required independent set can be obtained by performing $O(N)$ operations in $O((\log N)\log\log N)$ time.

4.5   Prove or disprove that $f_1(x)$ defined by step 1 of the Algorithm in Section 4.4 is a *legal* coloring.

4.6   With respect to the labeling $f_1(x)$, show that the shortest path from any vertex x to the next local maximum or minimum is at most $\lceil \log N \rceil$.

4.7 Notes And References

Section 4.1: For a historic perspective on the development of various list ranking algorithms, refer to Cole and Vishkin [1989]. Also, refer to Cole and Vishkin [1986a] and [1988] for other approaches to list ranking. The notion of pointer-jumping was introduced by Wyllie [1979].

Sections 4.2-4.4: The deterministic algorithms for symmetry breaking based on k-coloring are analyzed in Anderson and Miller [1986], Cole and Vishkin [1986b] [1989], and Goldberg, Plotkin and Shannon [1987]. The method used in Section 4.4 is also called the *deterministic coin tossing* method in Cole and Vishkin [1986]. For a comprehensive survey of parallel algorithms for linked list ranking, refer to Halverson and Das [1993].

Section 4.5: Randomized algorithms for independent sets are described in Vishkin [1984]. Also, refer to JáJá [1992]. Vishkin [1984] contains a discussion of randomized list ranking algorithms. Cormen, Leiserson and Rivest [1992] contains an excellent introduction to Bernoulli and binomial distributions along with a derivation of the Chernoff bounds.

Han [1991], Ryu and JáJá [1989], Kruskal, Rudolph, and Snir [1985], Lubachevsky and Greenberg [1987], Snir [1985], Kruskal, Madej and Rudolph [1986] describe the implementation of several list ranking algorithms on several different types of parallel architectures, such as hypercube, fully connected networks, PRAM models with p processors and p-shared memory cells.

Part Three

Algorithms For Circuit Models

Chapter 5

Parallel Prefix Circuits

This chapter presents a survey of parallel algorithms for computing the prefixes using circuit models. The circuits considered in this Chapter are constrained by the *fixed fan-in* (equal to two) but are allowed to have *arbitrary or unbounded fan-out*. Prefix circuits with fixed fan-in and fan-out are described in Chapter 7, and those with *unbounded* fan-in in Chapter 8. The characteristics of algorithms described in this Chapter are judged according to a number of measures including the size, depth, and fan-out. (Refer to Chapter 2 for definitions.)

5.1 Serial Circuit

The layout of the serial circuit, $S(N)$, is given in Figure 1. Clearly, the size, $s(N)$, of this circuit is $(N-1)$, and the depth, $d(N)$, is $(N-1)$. The sum of the size and depth for this circuit is

$$s(N) + d(N) = 2N - 2. \tag{1}$$

Each node has a constant fan-out. In Chapter 6, it is shown that the sum of the size and depth of any prefix circuit is lower-bounded by $2N - 2$.

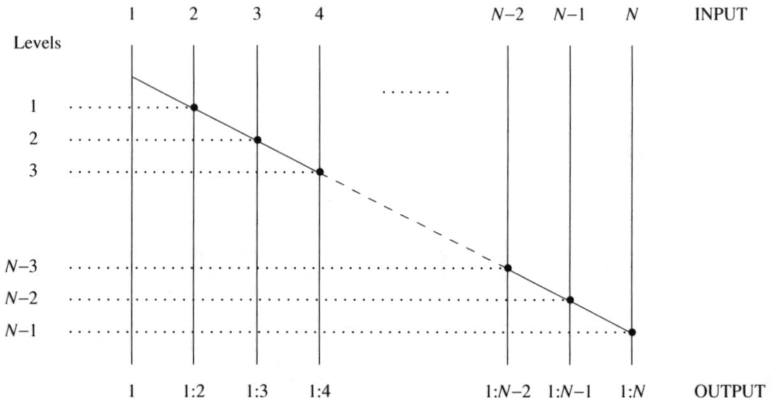

Figure 1. The serial circuit, $S(N)$, for computing all prefixes.

From this, it follows that the serial circuit is optimal. Thus, any circuit that computes all prefixes in less than serial time must have sizes larger than $(N - 1)$.

5.2 A Simple Parallel Prefix Circuit

Perhaps an easy approach to the design of a parallel prefix circuit is to invoke the well known *divide-conquer* strategy. Let $N = 2^n$. According to this strategy, if $DC(N)$ is a circuit that computes the prefixes of N elements, then $DC(N)$ can be designed according to the principle illustrated in Figure 1. The following recurrences for the size and depth of this circuit are immediate:

$$s(N) = 2\,s(\frac{N}{2}) + \frac{N}{2} \qquad \text{and} \qquad d(N) = d(\frac{N}{2}) + 1,$$

where $s(2) = 1$ and $d(2) = 1$. From these relations, we obtain

$$s(N) = \frac{N}{2}\log N \qquad \text{and} \qquad d(N) = \log N.$$

Clearly, $s(N) + d(N) = (\frac{N}{2} + 1)\log N \geq 2N - 2$.

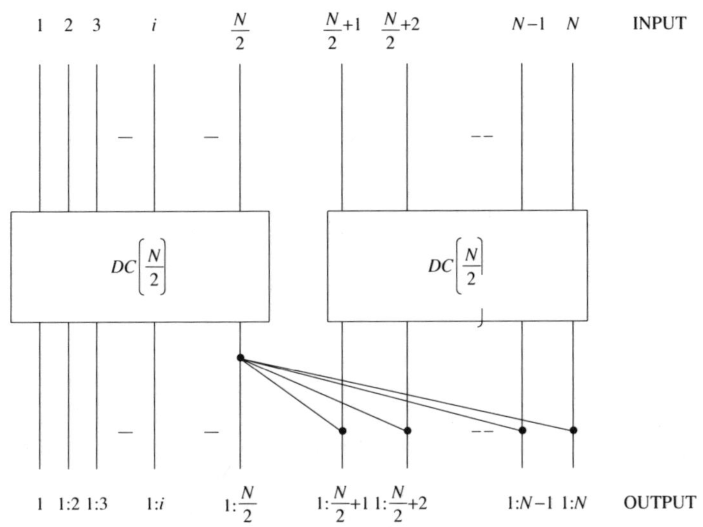

Figure 1. A parallel prefix circuit, $DC(N)$, based on simple divide-conquer strategy for $N = 2$, for some $n \geq 1$.

The ensuing observations are immediate.

The last output of this circuit is available in $\log N$ units of time. (See Exercise 5.1.) In fact, all the prefixes are also available in $\log N$ units of time. Hence, this circuit is clearly *depth optimal (d-optimal* for simplicity). However, $s(N) + d(N) = O(N \log N)$, and the fan-out is $N/2$, occurs at the output node computing $1: N/2$.

An important question now is if circuits exist for computing prefixes in parallel in $O(\log N)$ depth and $O(N)$ size. This question is answered in the affirmative by a parallel prefix circuit, $BK(N)$, based again on divide-conquer strategy from Brent and Kung [1982], which is illustrated in Figure 2. It follows from this Figure that if $N = 2^n$, then

$$s(N) = 2N - \log N - 2 \qquad \text{and} \qquad d(N) = 2 \log N - 2,$$

where $d(4) = 2$ and $s(4) = 4$. Thus, for this class of circuits

$$s(N) + d(N) = 2N + \log N - 4.$$

An illustration of this circuit with $N = 8$ is given in Figure 3.

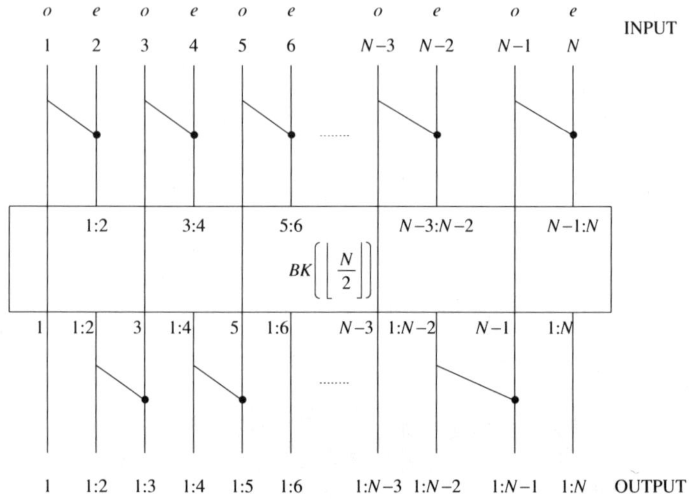

Figure 2. A parallel prefix circuit, $BK(N)$, from Brent and Kung based on divide-conquer strategy($o = odd,\ \ e = even$).

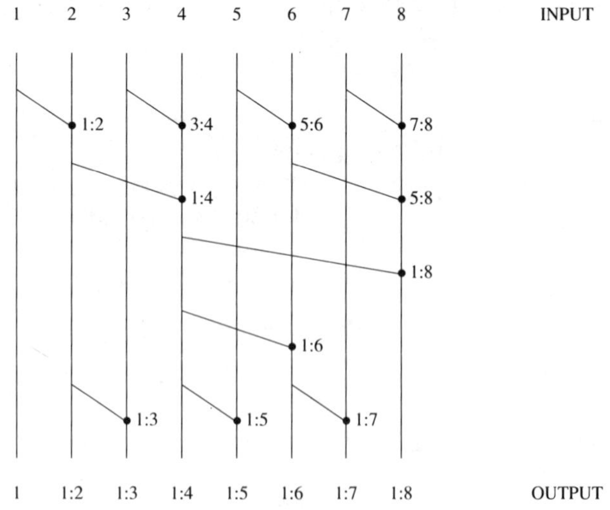

Figure 3. An illustration of the Brent and Kung parallel prefix circuit, $BK(8)$, $s(8) = 11$, $d(8) = 4$.

5.3 Ladner-Fischer Parallel Prefix Circuits

Ladner and Fischer [1980] were the first to quantify the size-depth trade off in parallel prefix circuits. Given N, let k be a parameter in the range, $0 \leq k \leq \lceil \log N \rceil$. Define a family of circuits, $LF_k(N)$, parameterized by k, where k refers to the *extra* depth used to bring about a reduction in the size. This family is defined recursively as follows: $LF_0(N)$ is defined in Figure 1 and $LF_k(N)$, for $k \geq 1$, are defined in Figures 2 and 3 for N odd and N even, respectively. Examples of $LF_k(N)$, for $N = 1$ to 8, are given in Figure 4 (a) through (k) and $LF_3(17)$ in Figure 5.

We begin by characterizing the depth of this class of prefix circuits.

Property 1. The last output of $LF_k(N)$, for all N, is available in $\lceil \log N \rceil$ units of time and is independent of k.

Clearly, when $N = 2$, the claim is true. Assume, that it is true, for $m \leq N - 1$. To see that it is true for $m = N$, first consider $LF_0(N)$. By hypothesis, referring to Figure 1, it is readily seen that the last output in $LF_0(N)$ is available in

$$1 + \log \left\lceil \frac{N}{2} \right\rceil = \lceil \log N \rceil$$

units of time. Now, for $k > 1$, referring to Figures 2 and 3, the property follows by similar arguments.

Any circuit satisfying property 1 is called a *Restricted Parallel Prefix Circuit*. Note that all *d*-optimal parallel prefix circuits are restricted parallel prefix circuits, but *not* conversely.

Let $d_k(N)$, $s_k(N)$ and $f_k(N)$ refer to the depth, size and fan-out of $LF_k(N)$.

Property 2. $\qquad d_k(N) \leq k + \lceil \log N \rceil$ for $k \leq \lceil \log N \rceil$. $\qquad\qquad$ (1)

Consider $LF_0(N)$. In view of property 1, referring to Figure 1, it is readily seen that the last output of $LF_1(\lceil \frac{N}{2} \rceil)$ is available in $\log \lceil \frac{N}{2} \rceil$ units. Clearly,

$$d_0(N) = \max \left[\log \left\lceil \frac{N}{2} \right\rceil, \; d_0(\left\lfloor \frac{N}{2} \right\rfloor) \right] + 1$$

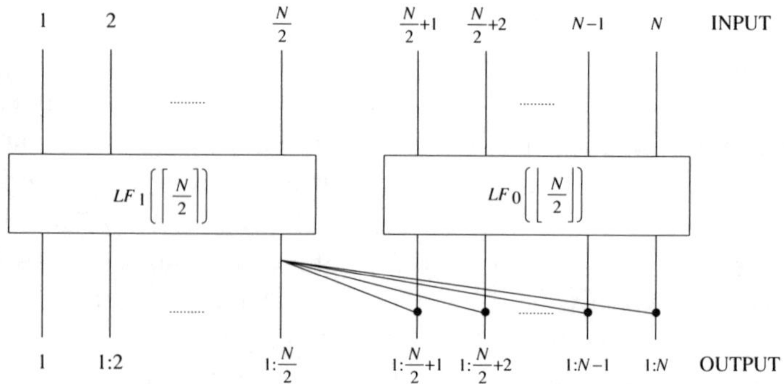

Figure 1. Ladner-Fischer parallel prefix circuit $LF_0(N)$.

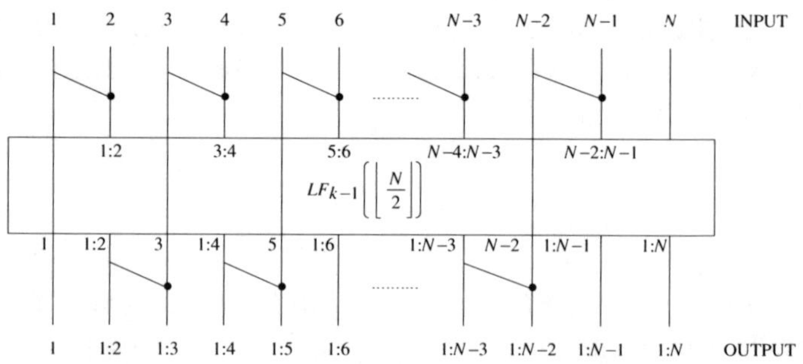

Figure 2. Ladner-Fischer parallel prefix circuit $LF_k(N)$ — N odd.

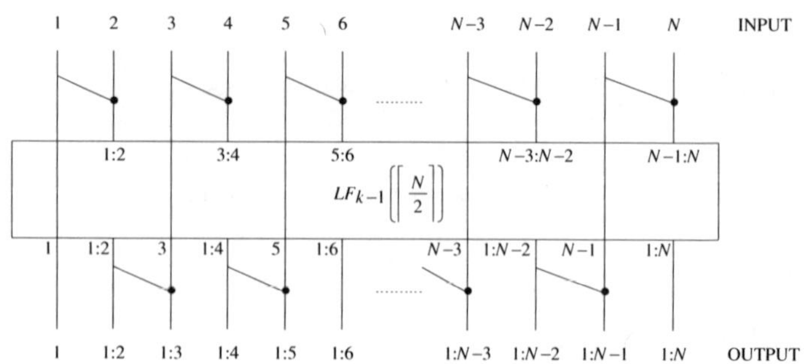

Figure 3. Ladner-Fischer parallel prefix circuit $LF_k(N)$ — N even.

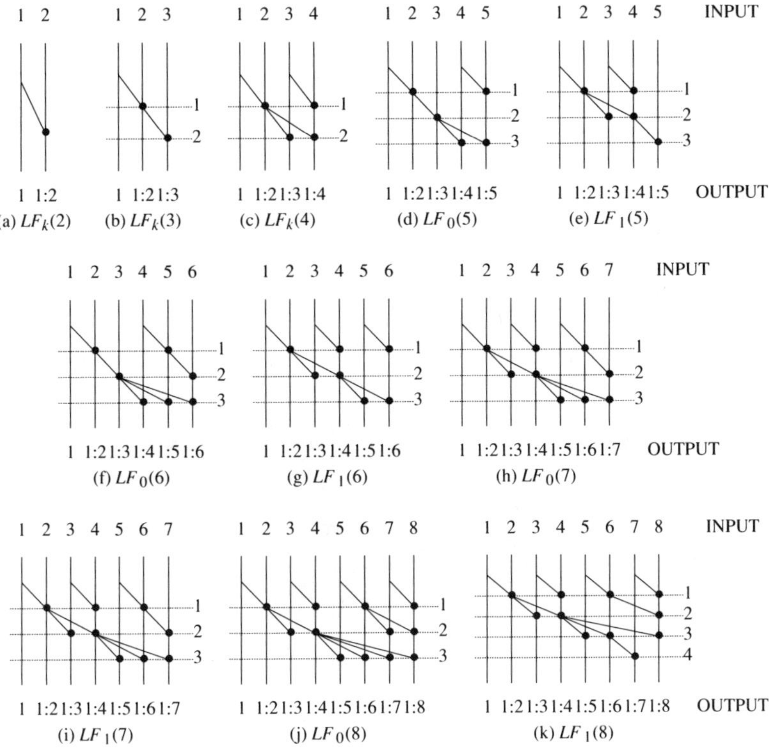

Figure 4. Examples of Ladner-Fischer parallel prefix circuits.

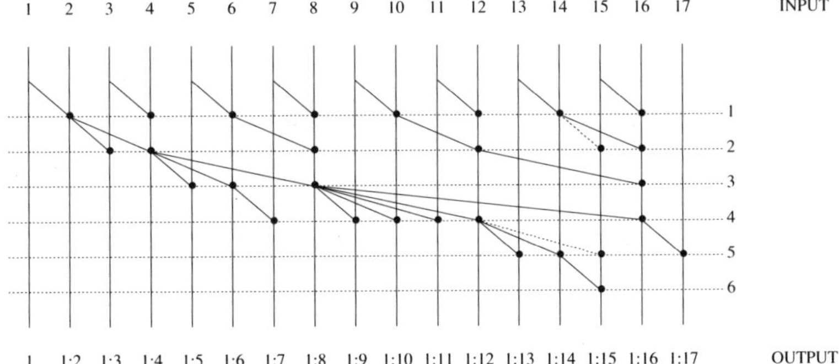

Figure 5: Example of Ladner-Fischer circuit $LF_3(17)$ with size $= 27$, and depth $= 6$. The depth of this circuit can be reduced to 5 if we replace the only connection from level 5 to level 6 by the two dotted connections. This modification results in size 28, but depth 5.

and

$$d_0(N) \le \lceil \log N \rceil.$$

Now, considering $LF_k(N)$, it follows that

$$d_k(N) \le 2 + d_{k-1}\left(\left\lceil \frac{N}{2} \right\rceil\right).$$

Thus,

$$d_k(N) \le 2i + d_{k-i}\left(\left\lceil \frac{N}{2^i} \right\rceil\right)$$

$$= 2k + d_0\left(\left\lceil \frac{N}{2^k} \right\rceil\right)$$

$$= 2k + \left\lceil \log\left(\frac{N}{2^k}\right) \right\rceil$$

$$= \lceil \log N \rceil + k$$

This upper bound is clearly not tight as the examples in Figures 4 and 5 illustrate.

Property 3 quantifies the size $s_k(N)$ of $LF_k(N)$.

Property 3. The following recurrences readily follow from Figures 1, 2, and 3:

$$s_0(N) = s_1\left(\left\lceil \frac{N}{2} \right\rceil\right) + s_0\left(\left\lfloor \frac{N}{2} \right\rfloor\right) + \left\lfloor \frac{N}{2} \right\rfloor, \quad N \ge 2, \tag{2}$$

$$s_k(N) = s_{k-1}\left(\left\lceil \frac{N}{2} \right\rceil\right) + N - 1, \quad \text{if } N \ge 2 \text{ and even, } k \ge 1, \tag{3}$$

$$s_k(N) = s_{k-1}\left(\left\lceil \frac{N}{2} \right\rceil\right) + N - 2, \quad \text{if } N \ge 3 \text{ and odd, } k \ge 1, \tag{4}$$

where

$$s_k(1) = 0, \text{ for } all \ k \ge 0.$$

Since the process of solving these recurrences has some intrinsic interest, we indicate the major steps in the derivation of their solution. Let $N = 2^x$. Then (2) becomes

$$s_0(2^x) = s_1(2^{x-1}) + s_0(2^{x-1}) + 2^{x-1}.$$

Now, using (3), we obtain

$$s_0(2^x) = s_0(2^{x-2}) + s_0(2^{x-1}) + 2^x - 1. \tag{5}$$

Define $s(x) = s_0(2^x)$. Then (5) becomes

$$s(x) = s(x-1) + s(x-2) + (2^x - 1). \tag{6}$$

Using the Fibonacci sequence, defined by

$$F(n) = F(n-1) + F(n-2), \ \ F(0) = 0, \ \ F(1) = 1, \tag{7}$$

$s(x)$ may be expressed as

$$s(x) = F(j+1)\, s(x-j) + F(j)\, s(x-j-1) + \sum_{t=1}^{j} F(t)\, (2^{x-t+1} - 1).$$

Now, setting $j = x - 1$, we obtain (since $s(0) = 0$ and $s(1) = 1$)

$$s(x) = \sum_{t=1}^{x} F(t)\, 2^{x-t+1} - \sum_{t=1}^{x} F(t).$$

Let

$$Z = \sum_{t=1}^{x} F(t)\, 2^{x-t+1}.$$

It can be shown, that

$$Z = (4Z - 2Z - Z)$$

$$= 4N - 4F(x-1) - 6F(x).$$

From Exercise 5.3 it follows, that

$$\sum_{t=1}^{x} F(t) = F(x+2) - 1.$$

Combining these, we get

$$s(x) = 4N - 4F(x-1) - 6F(x) - F(x+2) + 1. \tag{8}$$

Again, from Exercise 5.3, it follows, that

$$4F(x-1) + 6F(x) + F(x+2) \; = \; 5F(x-1) + 8F(x)$$

$$= \; F(5)\,F(x-1) + F(6)\,F(x)$$

$$= \; F(x+5). \tag{9}$$

Combining (8) and (9), it follows, that

$$s_0(N) \; = \; 4N - F(5 + \log N) + 1.$$

From (3), if $N = 2^x$, then it readily follows that

$$s_1(N) \; = \; 3N - F(4 + \log N)$$

and

$$s_k(N) \; = \; s_0(\frac{N}{2^k}) + 2N(1 - \frac{1}{2^k}) - k$$

$$= \; 2N(1 + \frac{1}{2^k}) - F(5 + \log N - k) - k + 1.$$

Solution of the recurrences governing the size $s_k(N)$, when N is not a power of 2, is not exact, although, one can derive a good upper bound. (See Exercises 5.4 — 5.6.)

From the above analysis, it is clear that Ladner-Fischer Parallel Prefix circuits have $O(N)$ size and depth $O(\log N)$. The values of $s_k(N)$ for various N (powers of 2), and k, are given in Table 1. From this Table, it follows that we can reduce the size of the circuit at the expense of only a slight increase in depth.

To further understand this trade-off, rewrite $s_k(N)$ by changing the variable k to $\log N - \varepsilon$. Thus,

$$s_k(N)|_{k = \log N - \varepsilon} \; = \; (2N + 1) - \log N + \phi_N(\varepsilon),$$

where

$$\phi_N(\varepsilon) \; = \; 2^{1+\varepsilon} + \varepsilon - F(5 + \varepsilon).$$

Further, define

$$D_k(N) \; = \; s_k(N) - s_{k+1}(N)$$

$$= \; \phi_N(\varepsilon) - \phi_N(\varepsilon - 1)$$

as the net savings in size resulting from increasing the depth from k to

Table 1. Values of $s_k(N)$ for various k and N.

N	k										
	0	1	2	3	4	5	6	7	8	9	10
1	0									•	
2	1	1									
4	4	4	4								
8	12	11	11	11							
16	31	27	26	26	26						
32	74	62	58	57	57	57					
64	168	137	125	121	120	120	120				
128	369	295	264	252	248	247	247	247			
256	792	624	550	519	507	503	502	502	502		
512	1672	1303	1135	1061	1030	1018	1014	1013	1013	1013	
1024	3487	2695	2326	2158	2084	2053	2041	2037	2036	2036	2036

$k+1$. The values of $\phi_N(\varepsilon)$ and $D_k(N)$ are given in Tables 2 and 3, respectively. Thus, from Table 3, it is clear that in going from $LF_0(1024)$ to $LF_1(1024)$, we obtain a net savings of 792 operations as opposed to 74 operations in going from $LF_3(1024)$ to $LF_4(1024)$. Furthermore, it is clear from this analysis that $LF_k(N) = LF_{k-1}(N)$, for all $k \geq \log N - 2$.

Property 4. A restricted parallel prefix circuit with N inputs contains at least $2N - \log N - 2$ gates, where $N = 2^k$, for some $k \geq 1$.

Recalling property 1, the output $1{:}2^k$ in a restricted parallel prefix circuit is available at depth $k = \log N$. It follows that in such a circuit $1{:}2^{k-1}$ and $2^{k-1}+1{:}2^k$ must be available at depth $k - 1$. Continuing in this way, we can readily identify a complete binary tree of depth $k + 1$ rooted at $1{:}2^k$, with all inputs at its leaves. This tree clearly has $N_1 = 2^k - 1 = N - 1$ internal nodes, each of which perform the associative

Table 2. Table of ε vs. $\Phi_N(\varepsilon)$. $\varepsilon = \log N - k$.

ε	0	1	2	3	4	5	6	7	8	9	10
$\Phi_N(\varepsilon)$	-3	-3	-3	-2	2	14	45	119	287	656	1448

Table 3. Values of $D_k(N)$.

N	k									
	0	1	2	3	4	5	6	7	8	9
2	0									
4	0	0								
8	1	0	0							
16	4	1	0	0						
32	12	4	1	0	0					
64	31	12	4	1	0	0				
128	74	31	12	4	1	0	0			
256	168	74	31	12	4	1	0	0		
512	369	168	74	31	12	4	1	0	0	
1024	792	369	168	74	31	12	4	1	0	0

binary operation. Furthermore, the leftmost path leading from $1\!:\!N$ to the input node 1 contains a total of $\log N + 1$ output nodes, (that is, nodes with labels $1\!:\!2^x$ for $x = 0, 1, \ldots, k$). Since a prefix circuit with N inputs must have N outputs, there must exist $N_2 = (N - \log N - 1)$ output nodes that are not part of the above binary tree. Thus, it follows that any restricted prefix circuit must contain at least $N_1 + N_2 = 2N - \log N - 2$ nodes. Hence, the property.

Combining this lower bound with Exercise 5.7, it follows that the circuits $LF_k(N)$, for $k \geq \lceil \log N \rceil - 2$, have optimal size.

We now characterize the fan-out of these parallel prefix circuits. Let, $g(k, N, i)$ be the fan-out of the ith output of $LF_k(N)$. Then, clearly, $f_k(N) = \max_i g(k, N, i)$ is the fan-out of $LF_k(N)$ (see Exercise 5.8(a)).

Note that the fan-out of any input node is, *at most,* two. Also, recall that in computing the fan-out of output nodes, we do not count the vertical lines which represent the output. The first output node is the first input node itself. Thus,

$$g\,(0, N, 1) \;=\; 1, \quad \text{for } all\ N.$$

All the other output nodes are product nodes. Referring to Figure 1, the following recurrences are immediate.

$$g(0, N, i) = \begin{cases} g\,(1, \left\lceil \dfrac{N}{2} \right\rceil, i), & \text{if } i < \left\lceil \dfrac{N}{2} \right\rceil \\[2em] \left\lfloor \dfrac{N}{2} \right\rfloor, & \text{if } i = \left\lceil \dfrac{N}{2} \right\rceil \\[2em] 0, & \text{if } i > \left\lceil \dfrac{N}{2} \right\rceil. \end{cases} \tag{10}$$

For $k \geq 1$, referring to Figures 2 and 3,

$$g\,(k, N, i) = \begin{cases} 0, & \text{if } i \text{ is odd and } i \neq 1 \\[1.5em] g\,(k-1, \left\lceil \dfrac{N}{2} \right\rceil, \dfrac{i}{2}) + 1, & \text{if } i \text{ is even and } i < N - 1 \\[1.5em] g\,(k-1, \left\lceil \dfrac{N}{2} \right\rceil, \dfrac{i}{2}), & \text{if } i \text{ is even and } i \geq N - 1. \end{cases} \tag{11}$$

Define

$$f_k(N) \;=\; \max_i\ g\,(k, N, i).$$

Then, clearly

$$f_0(N) \;=\; \max_i\ g\,(0, N, i)$$

$$= \max\,[2^{x-1},\ \max_{1 \leq i \leq 2^{x-1}}\ g\,(1, 2^{x-1}, i)].$$

Since the fan-out of any output node in $LF_k(N)$ is, at most, $(N - 1)$ (see Exercise 5.8(b)), it follows, that

$$f_0(N) = \max\left\{2^{x-1},\, 2^{x-1} - 1\right\} = 2^{x-1} = \frac{N}{2}.$$

To quantify $f_k(N)$, define

$$b_k(N) = \left\lfloor \frac{N + 2^k - 1}{2^{k+1}} \right\rfloor + k. \tag{12}$$

It can be shown (see Exercise 5.9), that

$$f_k(N) \leq b_k(N) \quad \text{for } all\ k < \log N - 1. \tag{13}$$

Furthermore, it can be verified that this is the best bound, since, given N and k, there exists $i_k(N)$ given by

$$i_k(N) = \begin{cases} 2^{k-1}\left\lceil \dfrac{N}{2^{k+1}} \right\rceil, & \text{if } 2^{k+1} < N \leq 2^{k+1} + 2^{k-1} \\[4mm] 2^k\left\lceil \dfrac{N}{2^{k+1}} \right\rceil & \text{if } N > 2^{k+1} + 2^{k-1}, \end{cases} \tag{14}$$

such that, $g[k, N, i_k(N)] = f_k(N) = b_K(N)$. Combining these with the property that

$$LF_k(N) = LF_{k-1}(N) \quad \text{if } k \geq \log N - 2$$

completes the analysis of the fan-out of these parallel prefix circuits.

Analysis of a class of modified $LF_k(2^n)$ circuits from Fich [1983] is pursued in Exercise 5.10. The circuits in this family, denoted by $F_k(2^n)$, are of sizes less than those of their $LF_k(2^n)$ counterparts.

5.4 Exercises

5.1 Show that the last output in the circuit in Figure 1 of Section 5.2 is available in $\log N$ units of time.

Hint: Use induction.

5.2 Compute and compare the fan-out for the circuits in Figures 1 and 2 of Section 5.2.

5.3 Show, that

$$\text{(a) } F(n+2) - 1 = \sum_{y=0}^{n} F(y)$$

$$\text{(b) } F(n+m) = F(m) F(n+1) + F(n) F(m-1)$$

$$\text{(c) } F(m) = \frac{1}{\sqrt{5}} (\phi_1^m - \phi_2^m)$$

$$\text{where } \phi_1 = \frac{1+\sqrt{5}}{2} \text{ and } \phi_2 = \frac{1-\sqrt{5}}{2}.$$

5.4 Show, that

$$s_k(N) < 2N(1 + \frac{1}{2^k}) - a_k N^{0.69424}$$

where $a_k > 0$ depends only on k.

5.5 Prove by induction that, for $0 \le k \le \lceil \log_2 N \rceil - 2$,

$$s_k(N) < 2N(1 + \frac{1}{2^k}) - 2.$$

5.6 Show, that

$$s_k(N) - s_{k+1}(N) \approx \frac{N}{2^k} + 1 - 1.8943 \frac{N^{0.69424}}{1.618^k}$$

5.7 Prove that the Ladner-Fischer circuit $LF_k(N)$, is such that, for $N = 2^x$, $x \ge 1$ and $k \ge \log N - 2$,

$$s_k(N) = 2N - \log N - 2.$$

5.8 (a) In $LF_k(N)$, show that the fan-out of any output node is at least as great as an internal node.

(b) Show that no output node has fan-out exceeding $(N-1)$.

5.9   Prove the inequality (13) of Section 5.3 and show that it is the best bound.

5.10   (Fich [1983]) In this exercise, we describe a recursive family of restricted parallel prefix circuits $F_k(N)$, for $N = 2^n$. For values of $k \neq 1$, $F_k(N)$ is defined exactly in the same way as the Ladner-Fischer circuit $LF_k(2^n)$. Likewise, for $n \leq 3$, $F_k(2^n)$ is defined in the same way as $LF_k(2^n)$. For $n \geq 4$, $F_1(2^n)$ is defined in the Figure below.

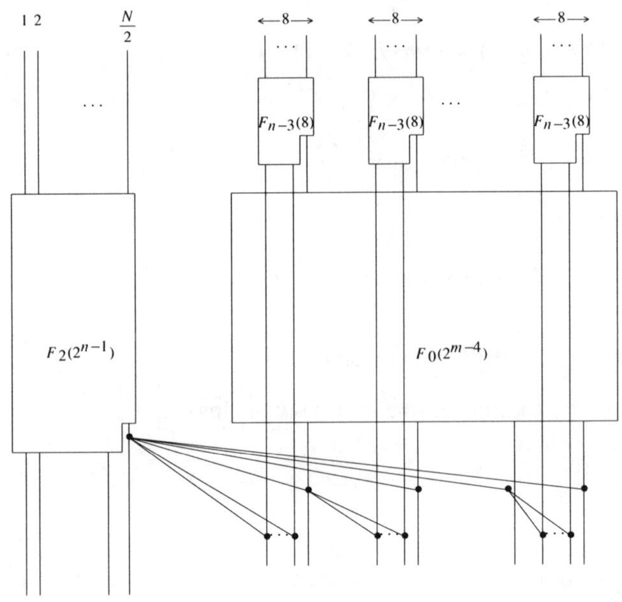

Fich's circuit $F_1(2^n)$.

Note that $F_1(2^n)$ is made up of two halves. The left half of $F_1(2^n)$ is $F_2(2^{n-1})$. The right half of $F_1(2^n)$ is obtained by dividing the input into groups of 8 inputs each and combining circuits $F_{n-3}(8)$ and $F_0(2^{n-4})$.

(a) Draw $F_k(32)$, $F_k(64)$ for various values of k, and compare them with $LF_k(32)$ and $LF_k(64)$.

(b) Let $s_k(2^n)$ denote the size of $F_k(2^n)$. Verify the following, for $k \geq 0$ and $n \geq 4$:

(i) $s_k(1) = 0$; $s_k(2) = 1$; $s_k(4) = 4$; $s_0(8) = 12$; $s_{k+1}(8) = 11$.

(ii) $s_0(2^n) = s_1(2^{n-1}) + s_0(2^{n-1}) + 2^{n-1}$.

(iii) $s_{k+2}(2^n) = s_{k+1}(2^{n-1}) + 2^{n-1}$.

(iv) $s_1(2^n) = s_2(2^{n-1}) + 2^{n-4}s_{n-3}(8) + s_0(2^{n-4}) + 2^{n-1}$
$\qquad = s_1(2^{n-2}) + s_0(2^{n-4}) + 27 \times 2^{n-4} - 1$.

(c) Verify by induction, for $n \geq 0$ and $1 \leq k \leq n - 1$,

(i) $s_0(2^n) < \dfrac{39}{11}2^n + 1$, and

(ii) $s_k(2^n) < (2 + \dfrac{3}{11}2^{2-k})2^n - k + 1$.

(d) Hence, verify, for all $k \geq 0$ and $n \geq 0$, size of $F_k(2^n) \leq$ size of $LF_k(2^n)$.

Note: Another restricted parallel prefix circuit is described in Fich [1983] whose size is less than that of $F_k(2^n)$ described above. We refer the reader to this interesting paper for details.

5.5 Notes And References

Sections 5.1–5.2: Parallel prefix circuits based on the cyclic reduction type strategy (refer to Chapter 2 for details) have been independently developed by Brent and Kung [1982] in the context of design of parallel adders, and by Snir [1986] in the context of design of (s, d)-optimal circuits. (Refer to Chapter 6.)

Sections 5.3: Ladner and Fischer [1980] initiated the (size + depth) trade-off study for parallel prefix circuits. Property 4 in Section 5.3 was first proved by Fich [1983]. Fich [1983] presented an interesting analysis of the structure of parallel prefix circuits of *optimal* size. This analysis culminated in the design of a new family of circuits with depth similar to $LF_k(N)$, but of sizes much smaller than those of $LF_k(N)$. Fich's circuits are developed in Exercise 5.10.

Chapter 6

Size vs. Depth Trade-Off In Parallel Prefix Circuits

Ladner-Fischer [1980] was the first one to demonstrate size *vs.* depth trade-off in parallel prefix circuits. In this Chapter, a lower bound from Snir [1986] on (size + depth) for prefix circuits is first derived. Several designs of parallel prefix circuits with optimal (size + depth) trade-offs are described.

6.1 A Lower Bound On (Size + Depth)

In this section, we derive a lower bound from Snir [1986] on the sum of depth and size of a class of prefix circuits.

Let $\mathbf{x} = \{\, x_1, x_2,\ \cdots\ , x_N \,\}$, be a set of N variables. Let D be the domain over which elements of $\mathbf{x}$ take their values, and let $F_N = \{\, f_1, f_2,\ \cdots\ , f_N \,\}$ be a set of functions satisfying the following conditions:

(SR1) f_i depends only on the variables $x_1, x_2,\ \cdots\ x_i$ and

(SR2) For each variable x_i, $i = 1, 2,\ \cdots\ , N$, there exist values a_i in D, such that, the set of functions

$$f_j \mid_{x_i = a_i} = f_j(x_1, x_2, \; \cdots \; , x_{i-1}, x_i = a_i, x_{i+1}, \; \cdots \; , x_j), \quad j=1, 2, \; \cdots \; , N,$$

contains a family of $(N - 1)$ functions satisfying these conditions.

The family F_N satisfying these two conditions is called a *self-reducible* family of functions. Clearly,

$$f_i(x_1, x_2, \; \cdots \; , x_i) = x_1 \, o \, x_2 \, o \; \cdots \; o \, x_i, \quad 1 \le i \le N,$$

satisfies these conditions.

Following is an example of a self-reducible family of functions.

An associative binary operation θ is said to be non-trivial if the following conditions are satisfied:

(i) Let $z = x \, \theta \, y$. Then z depends on both x and y, that is, θ is not a projection, nor a constant operation, and

(ii) There exists a (right) unit element e of θ, such that, $x = x \, \theta \, e$.

The family of functions

$$f_i(x_1, x_2, \; \cdots \; , x_i) = x_1 \, \theta \, x_2 \, \theta \; \cdots \; \theta \, x_i$$

defining the prefix problem is an example of a self-reducible family. For, setting $x_j = e$, will reduce the family from size N to $N - 1$. It can be verified that the Horner's expression (Hyfil and Kung [1977]) is another example of a self-reducible family of functions. Refer to Exercises 6.1 through 6.4 for other examples.

Formally, a circuit is a labeled directed acyclic graph G with leaves labeled by constants in D or variables in **x**. The internal nodes performing an operation o has in-degree, $k \ge 2$. Each node α is associated with a value $Val(\alpha)$, defined as follows:

(a) If α is a leaf, then $Val(\alpha)$ is equal to its label.

(b) $Val(\alpha) = o(Val(\beta_1), Val(\beta_2), \; \cdots \; , Val(\beta_k))$, where B_i, $i = 1$ to k, are all immediate predecessors of the internal node α with label o.

The circuit is said to compute the family of functions F_N if there exist output nodes $r_1, r_2, \; \cdots \; , r_N$, such that

$$f_i = Val(r_i), \quad i = 1, 2, \; \cdots \; , N.$$

Let G_N be a circuit that computes the self-reducible family F_N. Let s_N and d_N be the size and depth of G_N. The following theorem is fundamental.

Theorem 1. $s_N + d_N \geq 2N - 2$.

Proof: The proof is by induction. For $N = 2$, $s_2 = 1$ and $d_2 = 1$, and the claim is true.

For $N > 2$, assume that the theorem is true for $N - 1$. To prove it for N, recall that for each i there exists a value a_i, such that, assigning a_i to x_i yields a self-reducible family F_{N-1}. Two cases arise.

Case 1. There is at least one input node with out-degree greater than one. If we replace the variable x_i with a_i, and delete all the "trivial" nodes from G_N, then the resulting circuit G_{N-1} has size s_{N-1} and depth d_{N-1}, which by inductive hypothesis satisfies

$$s_{N-1} + d_{N-1} \geq 2(N - 1) - 2.$$

But $s_N - 2 \geq s_{N-1}$ and $d_N \geq d_{N-1}$. Combining these, we obtain

$$s_N + d_N \geq 2N - 2.$$

Case 2. There is no input node with out-degree greater than unity.

Let α be an internal node of G_N with in-degree two, such that, all the nodes below α (i.e. the nodes closer to leaves than α) have in-degree less than or equal to unity. Let x_i and x_j be the variables labeling the two leaves which form the input to node α, with $i < j$. Clearly, $Val(\alpha)$ depends on x_i and x_j, and the values of the output nodes in G_N depend on $Val(\alpha)$, and x_k, where $k \neq i, j$. From this it follows that functions exist in the set $\{f_2, f_3, \cdots f_N\}$ which are dependent on both x_i and x_j, or on neither of these two variables. Since, $i < j$, f_i depends only on x_i and not on x_j. In turn, this implies that $i = 1$, that is, α is the only node at level one of G_N and all the other output nodes depend on $Val(\alpha)$. Assigning a_1 to x_1 and deleting the "trivial" node in G, we obtain a circuit of size, at most, s_{N-1} and depth d_{N-1}. Again, by inductive hypothesis

$$s_N - 1 + d_N - 1 \geq 2(N - 1) - 2,$$

from which the conclusion follows.

This derivation closely resembles that from Hyfil and Kung [1977] relating to size and time for linear first order recurrence.

6.2 A Layered Prefix Circuit CR(N)

Now, we proceed to the design of a layered parallel prefix circuit, called $CR(N)$, and compare its size and depth with the above lower bound. This design follows very closely the cyclic reduction based algorithm described in Chapter 3. (See Exercise 6.7.)

Define a set g_α of pairs of input lines

$$g_\alpha = \left\{ (i, j) \mid a \; node \; at \; level \; \alpha \; is \; fed \; by \; lines \; i \; and \; j \right\}.$$

Now, given N, let $m = \lceil \log N \rceil$. Define a layered circuit as follows:

$$g_t = \left\{ (k2^t - 2^{t-1}, \min(N, k2^t)) \mid k = \left\lfloor \frac{N-1}{2^t} + \frac{1}{2} \right\rfloor, \cdots, 2, 1 \right\},$$

for, $t = 1 \cdots m$, and

$$g_{m+t} = \left\{ (k2^{m-t}, k2^{m-t} + 2^{m-t-1}) \mid k = \left\lfloor \frac{N-1}{2^{m-t}} - \frac{1}{2} \right\rfloor, \cdots, 2, 1 \right\},$$

for, $t = 1 \cdots m-1$.

As an example, connections of $CR(32)$ at different layers are given in Figure 1. Refer to Figure 2 for the actual layout of this circuit.

g_1 {(1, 2), (3, 4), (5, 6), (7, 8), (9, 10), (11, 12), (13, 14), (15, 16), (17, 18), (19, 20), (21, 22), (23, 24), (25, 26), (27, 28), (29, 30), (31, 32)}

g_2 {(2, 4), (6, 8), (10, 12), (14, 16), (18, 20), (22, 24), (26, 28), (30, 32)}

g_3 {(4, 8), (12, 16), (20, 24), (28, 32)}

g_4 {(8, 16), (24, 32)}

g_5 {(16, 32)}

g_6 {(16, 24)}

g_7 {(8, 12), (16, 20), (24, 28)}

g_8 {(4, 6), (8, 10), (12, 14), (16, 18), (20, 22), (24, 26), (28, 30)}

g_9 {(2, 3), (4, 5), (6, 7), (8, 9), (10, 11), (12, 13), (14, 15), (16, 17), (18, 19), (20, 21), (22, 23), (24, 25), (26, 27), (28, 29), (30, 31)}

Figure 1. Connections at various levels of $CR(32)$.

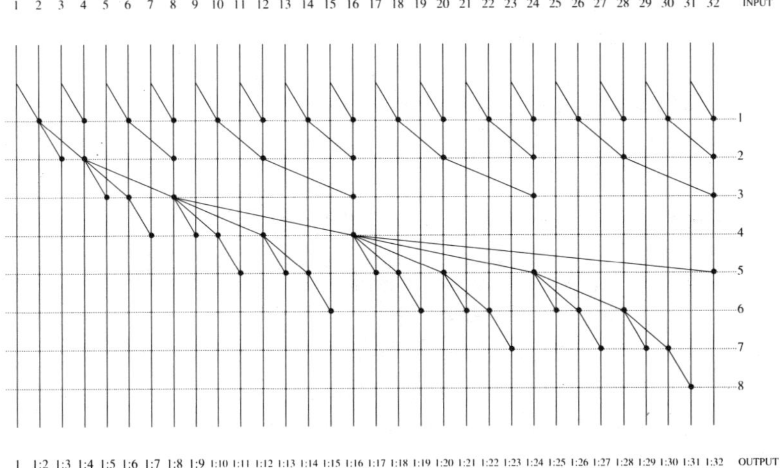

Figure 2. A layout of the circuit *CR* (32).

Property 1. From the definition, it follows that there are $2\lceil \log N \rceil - 1$ levels in *CR*(*N*). Furthermore, the first $\lceil \log N \rceil$ levels have $(N - 1)$ nodes and the remainder of $\lceil \log N \rceil - 1$ levels contain $N - 1 - \lceil \log N \rceil$ nodes, giving a total size $s(N) = 2N - 2 - \lceil \log N \rceil$. (See Exercise 6.8.)

Property 2. The last output of *CR* (*N*), $x_1{:}x_N$, is available in $\lceil \log N \rceil$ steps. That is, the last output of this circuit is available before the last level. (See Exercise 6.9.)

However, the overall depth of *CR* (*N*) can be reduced by suitably overlapping the various node operations. This is done by scheduling each node operation as close to the input side as possible. More specifically, the following result is easily proved (see Exercise 6.10).

Property 3. Let $d(N)$ be the depth of *CR* (*N*), defined above. Then

$$
d(N) = \begin{cases}
\lceil \log N \rceil & \text{if } N \leq 5 \\
2r - 3 & \text{if } r \geq 3 \text{ and } 3 \times 2^{r-2} \leq N < 2^r \\
2r - 2 & \text{if } r \geq 3 \text{ and } 2^r \leq N < 3 \times 2^{r-1}.
\end{cases}
$$

The following examples illustrate this property.

Let $N = 29$. Then $m = \lceil \log N \rceil = 5$, $r = 5$ and $3 \times 2^{r-2} \le N < 2^r$. The circuit is given in Figure 3.

Clearly, g_6 can be overlapped with g_5 and nodes at g_7 can be overlapped with other levels. For example, $(8, 12)$, $(16, 20)$, and $(24, 28)$ can be overlapped with g_4, g_5, and g_8, respectively. Thus, the resulting depth $d(N)$ is $2r - 3 = 7$.

Let $N = 45$. Then $m = 6$, $r = 5$, and the circuit $CR\,(45)$ is given in Figure 4.

In this case, g_7 is empty and g_8 can be overlapped with g_6. Furthermore, as before, nodes at g_9 can be overlapped with nodes at other levels. Thus, the overall depth is $2r - 2 = 8$. We invite the reader to draw these circuits and verify these claims.

To measure the deviation from $(s,\, d)$-optimality, the quantity

$$DEF\,(N) = s(N) + d(N) - (2N - 2),$$

called *deficiency,* is often used (see Section 2.3.2).

Since $2N - 2$ is the lower bound on the sum of the size and depth, clearly, if $DEF\,(N) = 0$, then the circuit is called $(s,\, d)$-*optimal*. Clearly, the serial circuit $S(N)$, described in Section 5.1 is $(s,\, d)$-optimal. In light of this definition, combining properties 1 and 3, we immediately obtain another property as follows.

g_1 $\{(1, 2), (3, 4), (5, 6), (7, 8), (9, 10), (11, 12), (13, 14), (15, 16), (17, 18), (19, 20), (21, 22), (23, 24),$
$(25, 26), (27, 28)\}$

g_2 $\{(2, 4), (6, 8), (10, 12), (14, 16), (18, 20), (22, 24), (26, 28)\}$

g_3 $\{(4, 8), (12, 16), (20, 24), (28, 29)\}$

g_4 $\{(8, 16), (24, 29)\}$

g_5 $\{(16, 29)\}$

g_6 $\{(16, 24)\}$

g_7 $\{(8, 12), (16, 20), (24, 28)\}$

g_8 $\{(4, 6), (8, 10), (12, 14), (16, 18), (20, 22), (24, 26)\}$

g_9 $\{(2, 3), (4, 5), (6, 7), (8, 9), (10, 11), (12, 13), (14, 15), (16, 17), (18, 19), (20, 21), (22, 23), (24, 25),$
$(26, 27)\}$

Figure 3. Specification of $CR\,(29)$.

g_1 {(1, 2), (3, 4), (5, 6), (7, 8), (9, 10), (11, 12), (13, 14), (15, 16), (17, 18), (19, 20), (21, 22), (23, 24), (25, 26), (27, 28), (29, 30), (31, 32), (33, 34), (35, 36), (37, 38), (39, 40), (41, 42), (43, 44)}

g_2 {(2, 4), (6, 8), (10, 12), (14, 16), (18, 20), (22, 24), (26, 28), (30, 32), (34, 36), (38, 40), (42, 44)}

g_3 {(4, 8), (12, 16), (20, 24), (28, 32), (36, 40), (44, 45)}

g_4 {(8, 16), (24, 32), (40, 45)}

g_5 {(16, 32)}

g_6 {(32, 45)}

g_7 ϕ

g_8 {(16, 24), (32, 40)}

g_9 {(8, 12), (16, 20), (24, 28), (32, 36), (40, 44)}

g_{10} {(4, 6), (8, 10), (12, 14), (16, 18), (20, 22), (24, 26), (28, 30), (32, 34), (36, 38), (40, 42)}

g_{11} {(2, 3), (4, 5), (6, 7), (8, 9), (10, 11), (12, 13), (14, 15), (16, 17), (18, 19), (20, 21), (22, 23), (24, 25), (26, 27), (28, 29), (30, 31), (32, 33), (34, 35), (36, 37), (38, 39), (40, 41), (42, 43)}

Figure 4. Specification of $CR(45)$.

Property 4. For the prefix circuit $CR(N)$

$$DEF(N) \geq \lceil \log N - 3 \rceil.$$

In other words, the circuit $CR(N)$ is *not* (s, d)-optimal with respect to this lower bound.

In the following, a framework for the design of (s, d)-optimal prefix circuits is described.

6.3 (s, d)-Optimal Design And Snir's Circuit

Let $G(N)$ and $G(M)$ be two parallel prefix circuits with inputs N and M, respectively. Let $G(N + M - 1) = G(N) \cdot G(M)$ be a circuit obtained by combining $G(N)$ and $G(M)$, as shown in Figure 1, where the last output of $G(N)$ feeds the first input of $G(M)$. (It is assumed that the input/outputs are numbered from the top, down). Clearly,

$$s\,(G(N + M - 1)) = s\,(G(N)) + s\,(G(M))$$

and

$$d(G_{N + M - 1}) = d\,(G(N)) + d\,(G(M)).$$

Thus,

$$DEF\,(G(N){\cdot}G\,(M)) = DEF\,(G(N)) + DEF\,(G(M)).$$

In other words, the composite circuit $G(N + M - 1)$ is (s, d)-optimal if the component circuits $G(N)$ and $G(M)$ are (s, d)-optimal. If the last output of $G\,(N)$ is available before its last level, then it is possible to reduce the depth of the overall circuit, as shown in the following property.

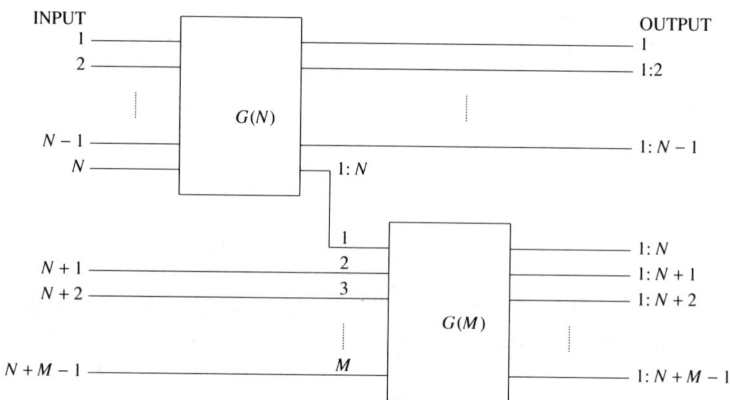

Figure 1. Definition of the composition $G\,(N){\cdot}G\,(M)$
of prefix circuits $G(N)$ and $G(M)$.

Property 1. If $G(N) = CR(N)$, and

$$d\,(CR(N)) \leq \lceil \log N \rceil + d(G(M)) \tag{1}$$

then

$$DEF\,(CR\,(N){\cdot}G(M)) = DEF\,(G(M)).$$

Proof: To prove the claim, using property 2 of Section 6.2, observe that

$$d(G(N + M - 1)) = \max\left\{ d(CR(N)), \lceil \log N \rceil + d(G(M)) \right\}.$$

Combining this with (1), it follows that

$$d(G(N + M - 1)) = \lceil \log N \rceil + d(G(M)).$$

Thus,

$$DEF(CR(N){\cdot}G(M)) = s(CR(N)) + s(G(M)) + d(CR(N){\cdot}G(M))$$

$$- 2(N + M - 1) + 2$$

$$= 2N - 2 - \lceil \log N \rceil + s(G(M)) + \lceil \log N \rceil$$

$$+ d(G(M)) - 2(N + M - 1) + 2$$

$$= s(G(M)) + d(G(M)) - (2M - 2)$$

$$= DEF(G(M)).$$

In other words, property 1 implies that $CR(N){\cdot}G(M)$ is (s, d)-optimal provided (1) is true, and $G(M)$ is (s, d)-optimal. This property is central to the design of (s, d)-optimal circuits. In fact, as will be evident from the algorithm (implicit in Theorem 1) below, the circuit $G(M)$ is invariably chosen as the serial circuit, $S(M)$.

Figures 2 (a) through (n) provide a number of examples of (s, d)-optimal circuits for $N = 2$ to 7. For circuits in these figures, while $s + d = 2N - 2$, for each N, in the range 2 to 7, there are also examples of d-optimal circuits (with minimum depth $d = \lceil \log N \rceil$). But for $N = 8$, while there are (s, d)-optimal circuits, there are, in fact, no (s, d)-optimal circuits with minimum depth. Refer to Figures 3(a) through (g) for examples with $N = 8$.

In light of these examples, we now state the main result which provides an algorithm for the design of (s, d)-optimal circuits.

Theorem 1. For any $N \geq 2$, and any t in the range

$$\max\left\{ 2\lceil \log N \rceil - 2, \lceil \log N \rceil \right\} < t \leq N - 1, \tag{2}$$

there exists a parallel prefix circuit $G(N)$ of depth $d(G(N)) = t$ and $DEF(G(N)) = 0$.

Proof: The proof is by induction. That the theorem is true, for all $N < 9$, follows from the examples given above.

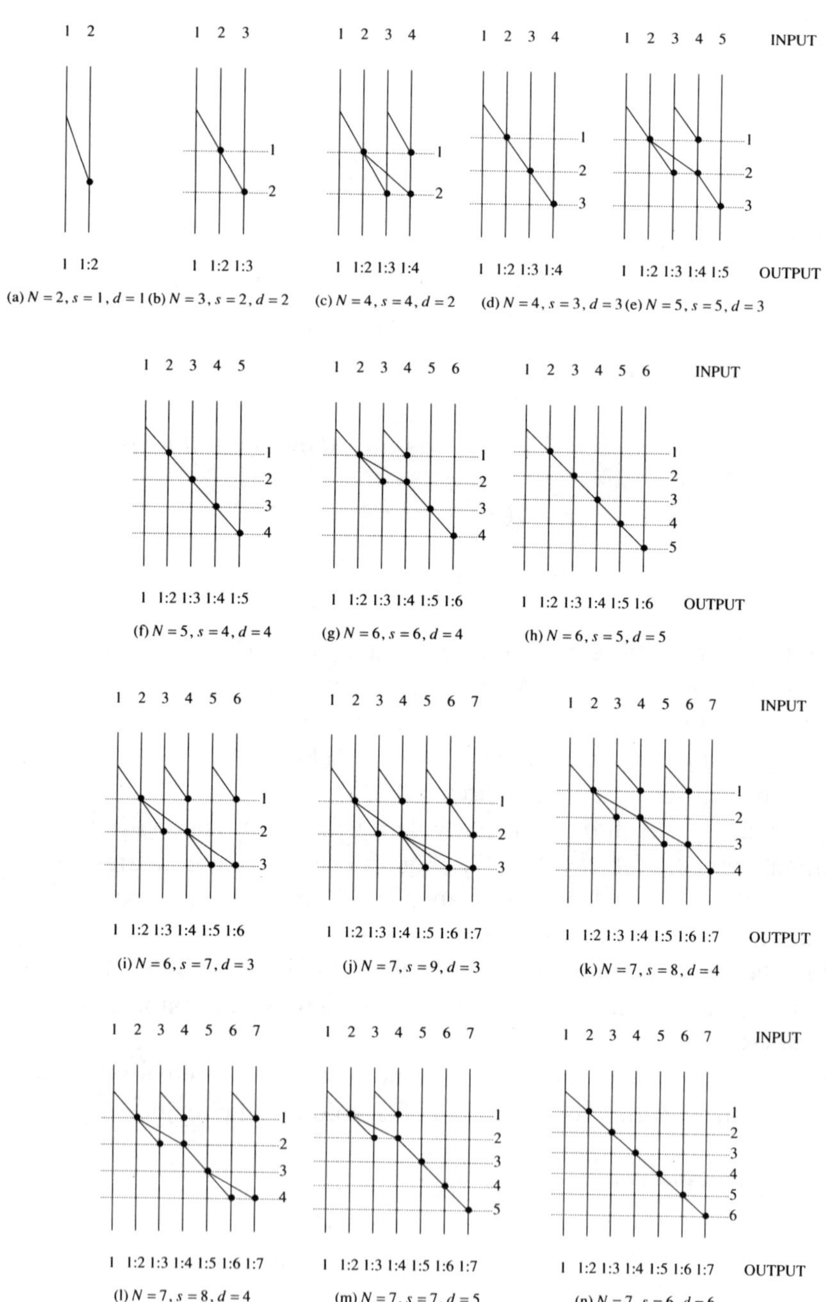

Figure 2. Examples of (s, d)-optimal circuits, for $N = 1$ to $N = 7$.

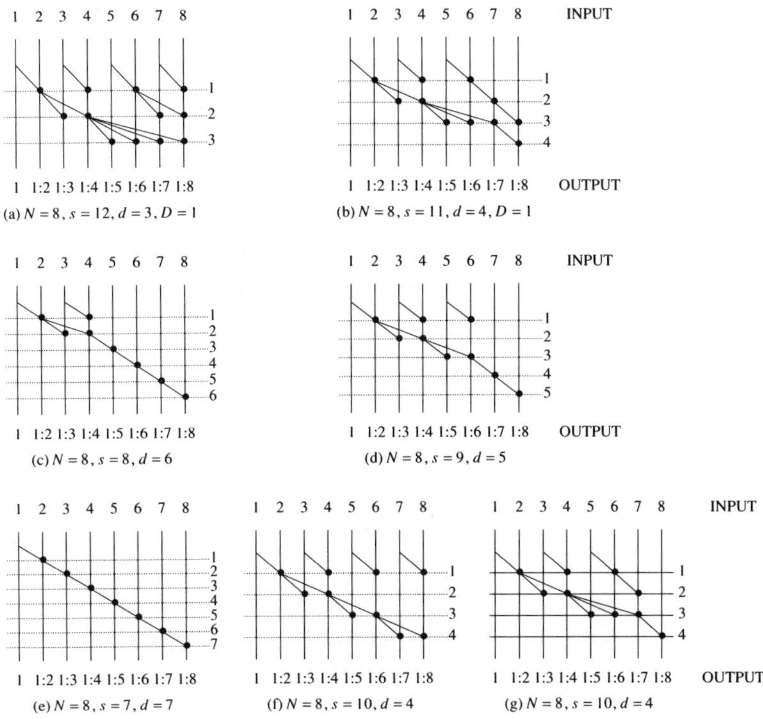

Figure 3. Examples of (s, d)-optimal circuits for $N = 8$.

Let $N > 8$ and let the theorem be true, for all $N' < N$. Two cases arise. If the given N is, such that

$$2\lceil \log N \rceil - 2 \le t < 2\log (N - 1) - 1, \tag{3}$$

then the design recursively defines (s, d)-optimal circuit with depth t. Refer to Table 1 for typical values of N that do not satisfy the inequality (3). If N does not satisfy (3), then a circuit with depth t, where

$$N - 1 \ge t \ge 2\log (N - 1) - 1 \tag{4}$$

is given.

Table 1. Comparison of values of $2\lceil \log N \rceil - 2$ and $2\log(N - 1) - 1$.

N	$2\lceil \log N \rceil - 2$	$2 \log (N - 1) - 1$
9	6	5.0
12	6	5.91886
17	8	7.0
23	8	7.91886
33	10	9.0
46	10	9.98371
65	12	11.0
91	12	11.98371
129	14	13.0
182	14	13.997
257	16	15.0

Case 1. Let N be such that it does not satisfy (3). Define

$$N_2 = 2 \qquad N_1 = N - 1$$

$$t_2 = 1 \qquad t_1 = t - 1,$$

where t satisfies (4). Then

$$t_1 = t - 1 \geq 2 \log (N - 1) - 2 = 2 \log N_1 - 2$$

and

$$N_1 - 1 = N - 2 \geq t - 1 = t_1,$$

that is, N_1 and t_1 satisfy the inequality in (4). Thus, by the induction hypothesis, there exists a $G^*(N_1)$, such that

$$d(G^*(N_1)) = t_1 \quad \text{and} \quad DEF(G^*(N_1)) = 0.$$

Since the serial circuits are (s, d)-optimal, the circuit $G^*(N)$ is obtained by composing $G^*(N_1)$ and $S(2)$, that is

$$G^*(N) = G^*(N_1) \cdot S(2).$$

Case 2. Let N satisfy (3). Then it is easily verified, that

$$t = 2 \lceil \log N \rceil - 2.$$

Choose

$$N_2 = r + 1, \quad \text{if } 2^r < N < 2^r + r$$

$$= r, \qquad \text{if } 2^r + r \leq N \leq 2^{r+1}.$$

Clearly $N > N_2 > 0$. Let $N_1 = N + 1 - N_2$.

Now, $G(N)$ built by composing $CR(N_1)$, and the serial circuit $S(N_2)$, will be (s, d)-optimal (refer to property 1), provided

$$\lceil \log N_1 \rceil + (N_2 - 1) \geq d(CR(N_1)). \tag{5}$$

Let, $2^r < N < 2^r + r$ and $r \geq 3$. Then

$$\lceil \log N_1 \rceil + N_2 - 1 = r + (r + 1) - 1 = 2r.$$

Now, from property 3 of Section 6.2, it follows, that

$$d(CR(N_1)) \leq 2r - 2 < 2r. \tag{6}$$

Combining (5) and (6), it follows that the condition (2) is true.

If, $2^r + r \leq N \leq 2^{r+1}$, then

$$\lceil \log N_1 \rceil + N_2 - 1 = (r + 1) + r = 1 = 2r \tag{7}$$

and

$$d(CR(N_1)) \leq 2r - 2 < 2r. \tag{8}$$

Again, by combining (7) and (8), condition (2) readily follows. Hence, the Theorem.

The circuits designed in this fashion are called Snir's circuits and are denoted by $SN(N)$. An example of an (s, d)-optimal $SN(N)$ circuit, for $N = 33$ is given in Figure 4.

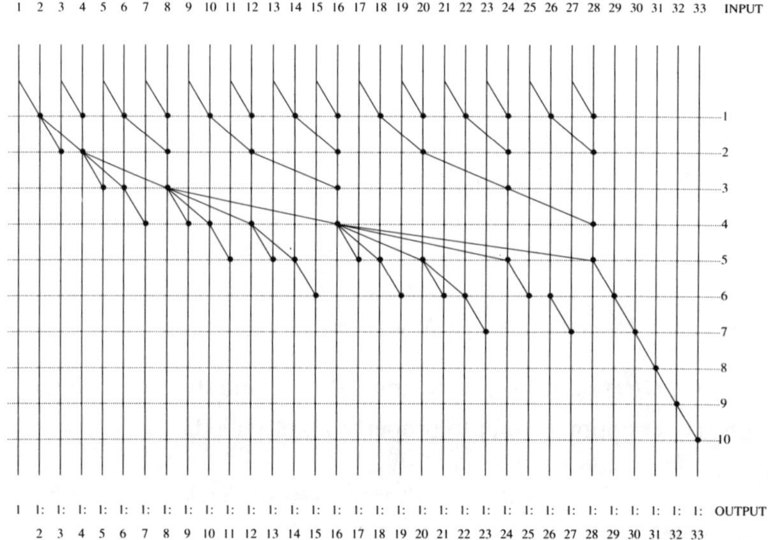

Figure 4. Snir's circuit. $SN(33)$, $size = 54$, $depth = 10$, $DEF(33) = 0$.
(*s*, *d*)-optimal, not-restricted prefix circuit.

6.4 LYD Circuit

Snir's (*s*, *d*)-optimal parallel prefix circuits described in Section 6.3 have depth in the range $\max(\lceil \log N \rceil, 2\lceil \log N \rceil - 2) \le d(N) \le (N - 1)$. It was observed by Snir [1986] that (*s*, *d*)-optimal parallel prefix circuits with depth in the range

$$\lceil \log N \rceil \le d(N) \le \max(\lceil \log N \rceil, (2 \lceil \log N \rceil - 3)). \tag{*}$$

may not exist. Recently, Lakshmivarahan, Yang and Dhall [1987] gave a design of (*s*, *d*)-optimal parallel prefix circuits with the depth in the range given in (*). This design provides (*s*, *d*)-optimal circuits with a smaller depth than hitherto known in the literature. Furthermore, in many cases (at least for small values of N), their design provides *d*-optimal and (*s*, *d*)-optimal circuits. However, this design, like Snir's has unbounded fan-out.

The design of the overall circuit is essentially modular in nature. There are two major components in this design. The first is a well known circuit called $CR(m)$, defined in Section 6.2. The second is a *new* class of N-input, (*s*, *d*)-optimal parallel prefix circuits, called $Q(N)$, with depth = width = d, size = d^2 and $2N - 2 = d^2 + d$.

For the purpose of reference, we state the properties of the circuit $CR(m)$ in the following:

Lemma 1. For any integer $m \geq 2$, there exists a parallel prefix circuit $CR(m)$, such that

$$d(CR(m)) = \begin{cases} \lceil \log m \rceil & \text{if } m \leq 5 \\ 2r - 3 & \text{if } 3 \times 2^{r-2} < m < 2^r, r > 2 \\ 2r - 4 & \text{if } 2^{r-1} \leq m \leq 3 \times 2^{r-2}, r > 2 \end{cases}$$

and

$$s(CR(m)) = 2m - \lceil \log m \rceil - 2.$$

This Lemma follows from Property 3 in Section 6.2. Clearly, $CR(m)$ is *not* (s,d)-optimal, but is a restricted parallel prefix circuit.

6.4.1 A New (s, d)-Optimal Circuit Q(m)

We now introduce a new class of (s, d)-optimal circuits, called $Q(m)$. Let m be such that

$$2m - 2 = t^2 + t, \tag{1}$$

for some $t > 0$. Typical (m, t) pairs satisfying this relation are given below:

t:	1	2	3	4	5	6	7	8	9	10
m:	2	4	7	11	16	22	29	37	46	56

The circuit $Q(m)$ is defined by the connections at each level. Let g_i refer to the set of all product nodes at level i, and $g_{i,j}$ denote the jth product node at level i. Typically, $g_{i,j}$ is an ordered pair (a, b), where $a = l(g_{ij})$ and $b = r(g_{ij})$, refer to the left and right inputs of the product node $g_{i,j}$, respectively. The input is assumed to be at level 0.

(1) At level 1, $g_{1,1} = (1,2)$, $g_{1,2} = (3,4)$, and

$$g_{1,j} = (l(g_{1,j-1}) + (j-1),\ r(g_{1,j-1}) + (j-1)),\ \text{for } j = 3, 4,\ \cdots\ t.$$

(2) For levels $i = 2$ to t

$$g_{i,1} = (r(g_{i-1,1}), r(g_{i-1,2})),$$

and

$$g_{i,j} = (r(g_{i-1,j+1}),\ r(g_{i-1,j+1}) + 1), \quad \text{for } j = 2, 3, \cdots, t + 1 - i.$$

(3) The nodes at level $(t + 1)$ are given by

$$g_{t+1} = \left\{ r(g_{i,1}),\ r(g_{i,1}) + j) \,|\, i = 1, 2, \cdots, t-1, j = 1, 2, \cdots i \right\}$$

The circuits $Q(11)$ and $Q(29)$ are given in Figures 1 and 2, respectively. Informally, $Q(m)$ consists of blocks of serial prefix circuits with block sizes increasing in an arithmetic sequence. The results of these serial blocks are then combined to compute the required prefixes.

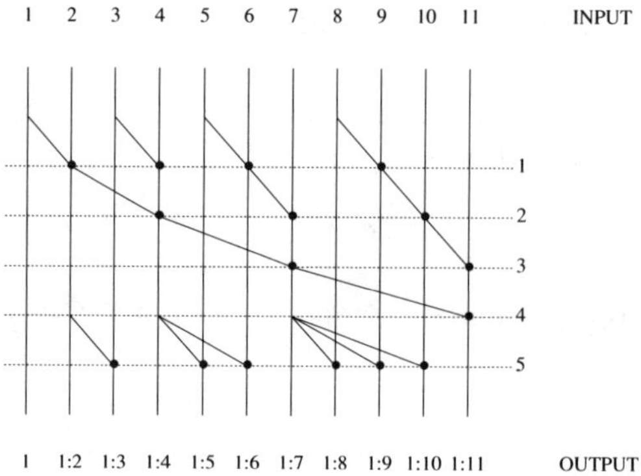

Figure 1. Prefix circuit $Q(11)$.

The following Lemma summarizes the properties of this class of circuits.

Lemma 1. The parallel prefix circuit $Q(m)$, with m inputs is (s, d)-optimal with

$$d(Q(m)) = t = O(m^{1/2}). \tag{2}$$

Proof: It follows that, for $i = 1$ to t, level i has $(t + 1 - i)$ product nodes. The first t levels have a total of

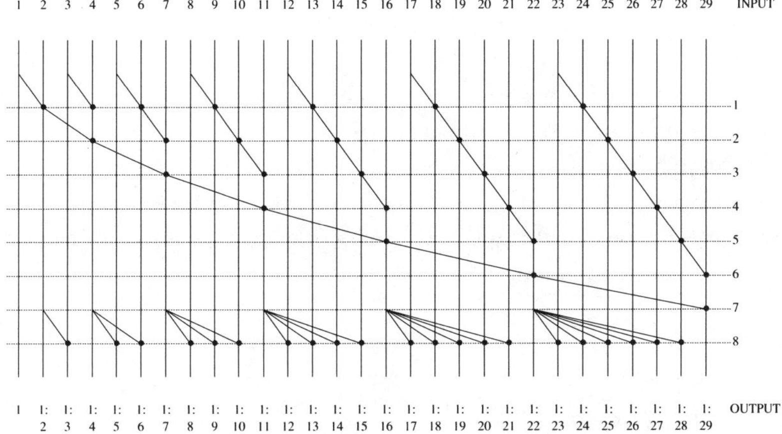

Figure 2. Prefix circuit $Q(29)$.

$$\sum_{i=1}^{t} i = \frac{t(t+1)}{2}$$

product nodes. The last level $(t+1)$ has

$$\sum_{i=1}^{t-1} i = \frac{t(t-1)}{2}$$

product nodes. Thus,

$$s(Q(m)) = t^2. \tag{3}$$

Furthermore, the depth of the overall circuit $Q(m)$ can be reduced to t, by overlapping all the computations at level $(t+1)$ with those at lower levels. Hence,

$$d(Q(m)) = t. \tag{4}$$

Clearly, in view of (1), $Q(m)$ is (s, d)-optimal, and

$$t = (2m - \frac{7}{4})^{1/2} - \frac{1}{2} \approx \left\lfloor (2m)^{1/2} \right\rfloor = O(m^{1/2}),$$

and the Lemma follows.

Since

$$\left\lfloor (2m)^{1/2} \right\rfloor < 2\lceil \log m \rceil - 2,$$

for $m < 32$, it follows that $Q(m)$, while being (s, d)-optimal, has also lower depth compared to Snir's circuit, for $2 \leq m < 32$.

Define the *width, w*, of a parallel prefix circuit to be the *maximum* of the number of product nodes at a given level. In Theorems 9 and 10, Snir [1986] gave a design for m-input *near-(s, d)-optimal* circuits with width w and depth d where

$$m > w^2 \text{ and } d \geq \frac{2m}{w + 1} \geq 2w.$$

In contrast, $Q(m)$ has

$$depth = width = O(m^{1/2}),$$

while maintaining (s, d)-optimality. As an example, consider $t = 50$. Then $t^2 + t = 2550 = 2m - 2$, and hence, $m = 1276$. The circuit $Q(1276)$ has *width* = *depth* = 50 and *size* = 2500. Although, according to Theorem 10 in Snir [1986], Snir's circuit, with 1276 inputs, and (maximum) width $w = 35$ (since $m > w^2$), has a depth ≥ 70.

6.4.2 LYD Circuits

The general schematic of the class of parallel prefix circuits introduced in this Section is illustrated in Figure 1. It consists of four parts, with Part i having n_i inputs, where

$$N = n_1 + n_2 + n_3 + n_4, \tag{1}$$

and $n_1, n_2, n_4 > 0$ and $n_3 \geq 0$.

As in Snir's circuit, Part 1 corresponds to the circuit $CR(n_1)$, described in Section 6.2. Part 2 is essentially derived from the new circuit $Q(n_2)$, described in Section 6.4.1. Parts 3 and 4 are serial circuits. The relation between the various parts may be described as follows:

Let $d(N)$ and $s(N)$ be the depth and size of the overall circuit.

(1) Part 1 is such that

$$s(CR(n_1)) = 2n_1 - \left\lceil \log n_1 \right\rceil - 2, \tag{2}$$

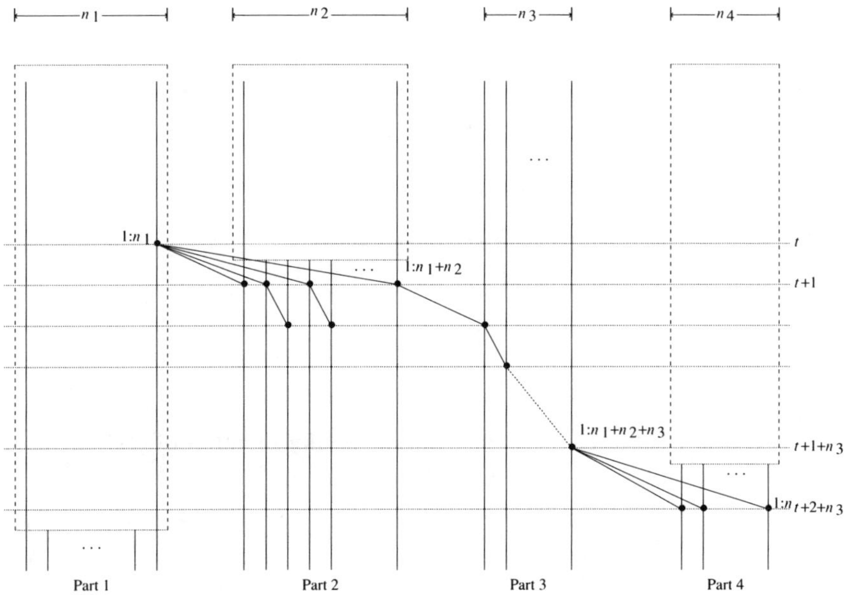

Figure 1. The structure of LYD(N), a class of (s, d)-optimal parallel prefix circuits.

$$d(CR(n_1)) \le d(N), \tag{3}$$

and the last output, $1\!:\!n_1$, is available at depth

$$t = \left\lceil \log n_1 \right\rceil \le d(N) - 2. \tag{4}$$

(2) Part 2 consists of n_2 nodes, given by the equation

$$n_2 = \frac{1}{2}(t^2 + t) + 1, \tag{5}$$

where $t > 0$ is defined in (4) above.

(3) Parts 1 and 2 are linked as follows. First, move all the product nodes of $Q(n_2)$ at the level $(t+1)$ vertically to level $(t+2)$. An example is shown in Figure 2 corresponding to Figure 1 of Section 6.4.1. This is equivalent to

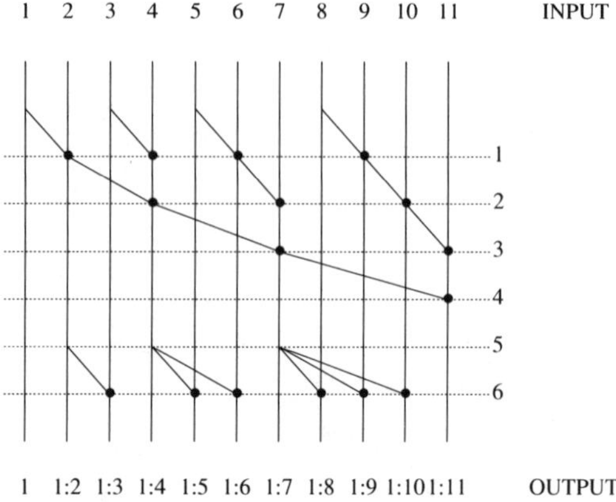

Figure 2.   An illustration of modification of $Q(11)$,
ready for use in Part 2.

$$g_{t+2} \leftarrow g_{t+1}$$

and

$$g_{t+1} \leftarrow \varnothing, \text{ the empty set.}$$

Now, create $(t+1)$ new product nodes at level $(t+1)$ of Part 2 by feeding the last output, $1{:}n_1$, from Part 1, as the left input to the lines at positions 1, 2, 4, 7, 11, 16, 22, $\cdots$ $\dfrac{t(t+1)}{2} + 1 = n_2$ in Part 2. Refer to Figures 3 and 4 for illustration.

The connection between Parts 1 and 2 guarantees that, (a) $1 : (n_1 + n_2)$ is available at level $t+1$, and (b) the resulting depth of Part 2, in view of (5), is less than, or equal to, $d(N)$ and

$$s(\text{Part } 2) = 2n_2 - 1. \tag{6}$$

(4) Part 4 is a serial circuit with n_4 inputs, where

$$n_4 \leq d(N), \tag{7}$$

$$d(Part4) \leq d(N) - 1, \tag{8}$$

and

$$s(Part4) = n_4 - 1. \tag{9}$$

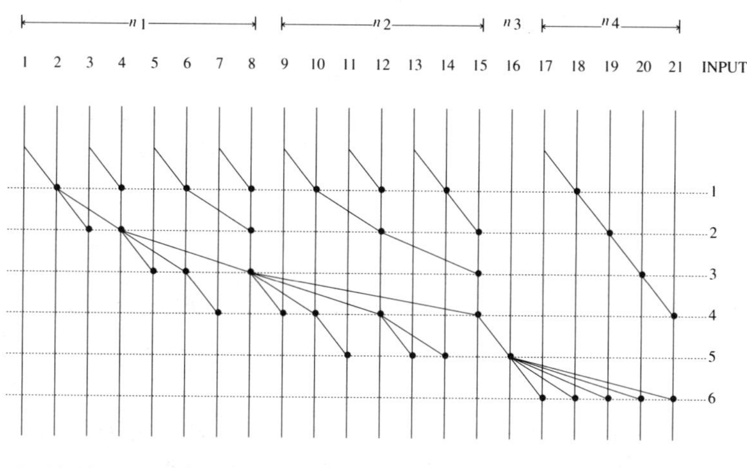

Figure 3. An example of an LYD circuit. $N = 21$, size = 34, *depth* = 6, *deficiency* = 0, $n_1 = 8$, $n_2 = 7$, $n_3 = 1$, $n_4 = 5$. (s, d)-optimal, not restricted prefix circuit.

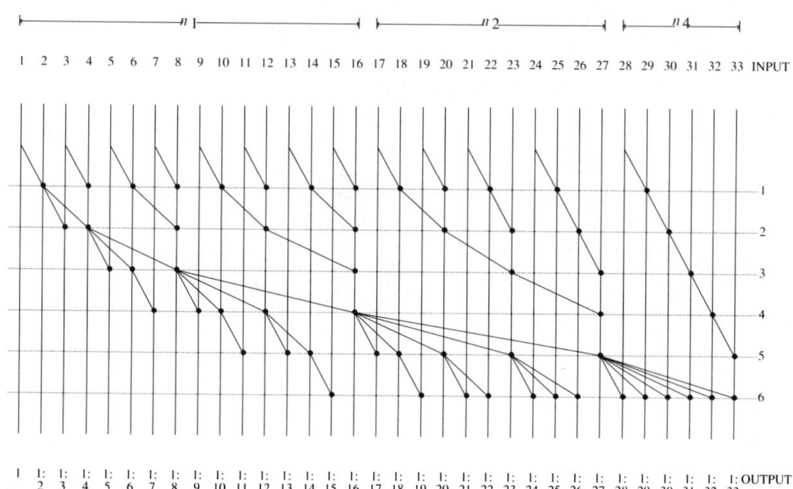

Figure 4. An example of an LYD circuit. $N = 33$, size = 58, *depth* = 6, *deficiency* = 0, $n_1 = 16$, $n_2 = 11$, $n_3 = 0$, $n_4 = 6$. (s, d)-optimal, restricted prefix circuit.

(5) Part 3 exists only if $n_3 > 0$. If it exists, it is sandwiched between Parts 2 and 4. The first product node of Part 3 has the first input of Part 3 as its right input, and the last output namely, $1 : (n_1 + n_2)$ of Part 2 as its left input. The last output of Part 3 computes $1 : (n_1 + n_2 + n_3)$, and feeds all the nodes just below Part 4 as their left input. Part 3 is a serial circuit. Thus,

$$s(Part\ 3) = n_3. \tag{10}$$

(6) Denoting Part 4 and the nodes below it as Part 4′, it follows, that

$$s(Part\ 4') = 2n_4 - 1. \tag{11}$$

(7) Note, the output $1 : (n_1 + n_2 + n_3)$ is available at level $(t + 1 + n_3)$ and the last output $1 : N$, is available at level $(t + 2 + n_3)$. The following Theorem summarizes the overall properties of this circuit.

Theorem 1. The structure of the parallel prefix circuit, $LYD\,(N)$, given in Figure 1 is $(s,\ d)$-optimal, if

$$d(N) = \left\lceil \log n_1 \right\rceil + 2 + n_3. \tag{12}$$

Proof: Combining (2) through (11), it follows that

$$s(N) = s\,(Part\ 1) + s(Part\ 2) + s(Part\ 3) + s(Part\ 4')$$

$$= (2N - 2) - (\left\lceil \log n_1 \right\rceil + 2 + n_3)$$

$$= (2N - 2) - d\,(N)$$

and the Theorem follows.

Now, given an $N > 0$, following is an algorithm for computing $d(N)$ and n_i, $i = 1, 2, 3, 4$, satisfying (1) and (12). Let $N \geq 2$. Consider two cases.

Case I. N is such that, for some $k \geq 7$, $2^{k-1} < N \leq 2^k$.

Algorithm for Case I.

Define a set of depth defining thresholds B_1, B_2, and B_3, as follows:

$$B_1 = 3 \times 2^{k-2} + (3k - 10) + \frac{k\,(k + 1)}{2}. \tag{13}$$

$$B_2 = 2^{k-1} + (3k - 11) + \frac{k(k-1)}{2}. \tag{14}$$

$$B_3 = 3 \times 2^{k-3} + (3k - 13) + \frac{k(k-1)}{2}. \tag{15}$$

Clearly,

$$B_3 < B_2 < B_1.$$

Typical values of B_1, B_2, and B_3 are given in Table 1.

Table 1. Table giving the range of B-values.

k	2^k	B_1	B_2	B_3
7	128	135	95	77
8	256	242	169	135
9	512	446	308	242
10	1024	843	576	446
11	2048	1625	1101	843
12	4096	3176	2139	1625
13	8192	6264	4202	3176
14	16384	12425	8314	6264
15	32768	24731	16523	12425
16	65536	49326	32925	24731

Step 1: Define the depth $d(N)$ as follows:

    Case A1. If $B_1 < N \le 2^k$, then $d(N) = 2k - 3$.
    Case A2. If $B_2 < N \le B_1$, then $2k - 4 \le d(N) \le 2k - 3$.
    Case A3. If $B_3 < N \le B_2$, then $2k - 5 \le d(N) \le 2k - 3$.
    Case A4. If $2^{k-1} < N \le B_3$, then $2k - 6 \le d(N) \le 2k - 3$.

Note that in all cases $d(N)$ satisfies (*) given at the beginning of Section 6.4.

Using the depth defined above, we now proceed to specify the sizes of various parts of the circuit. To this end, define a new set of size defining thresholds as follows:

$$b_1 = 2^{k-1} + 2d(N) + \frac{k(k-1)}{2} - 1. \tag{16}$$

$$b_2 = 2^{k-1} + 2d(N) + \frac{k(k-3)}{2}. \tag{17}$$

$$b_3 = 2^{k-2} + 2d(N) + \frac{k(k-3)}{2}. \tag{18}$$

The following Lemma is immediate.

Lemma 2. If $N > B_2$, then $B_2 < b_2 < b_1 < B_1$.

Proof: Since $d(N) \le 2k - 3$, it follows, that

$$B_1 - b_1 = 2^{k-2} + (4k - 8) - 2d(N) - 1$$

$$\ge 2^{k-2} - 3 > 0, \text{ for } k \ge 7.$$

Since $N > B_2$, $d(N) \ge 2k - 4$, and $b_2 - B_2 = 2d(N) - 4k + 11 > 0$. The other inequality is easily proved, and the proof is complete.

Step 2: To calculate the sizes, we consider four sub-cases and verify the conditions of Theorem 1 in each case.

Case 1. For $b_1 < N \le \min(B_1, 2^k)$,

$$\left. \begin{array}{rcl} n_4 &=& d(N) \\ n_3 &=& d(N) - (k + 2) \\ n_2 &=& k(k + 1)/2 + 1 \\ n_1 &=& N - (n_2 + n_3 + n_4) \end{array} \right\} \tag{19}$$

Claim 1.1. $n_3 \in \{k - 6, k - 5\}$

Proof: In view of Lemma 2 and Case A2, it follows that

$$2k - 4 \le d(N) \le 2k - 3,$$

and the claim follows from the definition of n_3.

Note that, for $B_1 < N \le 2^k$, there is only one design with depth $2k - 3$ (and $n_3 = k - 5$). But, for $b_1 < N \le B_1$, there are two designs: one with depth $2k - 3$, ($n_3 = k - 5$), and the other with depth $2k - 4$ ($n_3 = k - 6$). Also, note that, $B_1 > 2^k$ only if $k = 7$, and $B_1 < 2^k$, for all $k \ge 8$.

Claim 1.2. $n_1 > 2^{k-1}$ and $t = \lceil \log n_1 \rceil = k$.

Proof: Since $N \geq b_1 + 1$, it follows from simple substitution that

$$n_1 \geq (b_1 + 1) - (n_2 + n_3 + n_4) > 2^{k-1},$$

and the claim is proved.

Claim 1.3. This design is (s, d)-optimal.

Proof: Case 1. If $b_1 < N \leq B_1$, then

$$n_1 \leq B_1 - (n_2 + n_3 + n_4) < 3 \times 2^{k-2},$$

since $d(N) \geq 2k - 4$.

Now, by Lemma 1

$$d(CR(n_1)) = 2k - 4 \leq d(N).$$

Again, if $B_1 < N \leq 2^k$, by Lemma 1 and Case A1,

$$depth(CR(n_1)) = 2k - 3 = d(N).$$

Clearly, $\lceil \log n_1 \rceil + 2 + n_3 = d(N)$, and the design is (s, d)-optimal.

Example. For $N = 186$, there are two designs:

Design	n_1	n_2	n_3	n_4	t	$d(N)$
1	135	37	2	12	8	12
2	133	37	3	13	8	13

For $N = 245$, there is only one design:

$$n_1 = 192, n_2 = 37, n_3 = 3, n_4 = 13, t = 8, d(N) = 13.$$

Case 2. For $b_2 < N \leq b_1$, define

$$\left. \begin{array}{rcl} n_4 &=& N - (n_1 + n_2 + n_3) \\ n_3 &=& d(N) - (k + 2) \\ n_2 &=& k(k + 1)/2 + 1 \\ n_1 &=& 2^{k-1} + 1 \end{array} \right\} \tag{20}$$

Since $\lceil \log n_1 \rceil = k$, it readily follows that this design is (s, d)-optimal, provided $n_3 > 0$, and $n_4 > 0$.

Claim 2.1. $n_3 > 0$ and $n_4 > 0$.

Proof: In view of Lemma 2 and Case A2, since

$$2k - 4 \le d(N) \le 2k - 3,$$

it follows, that $n_3 \in \{k - 5, k - 6\}$ and $n_3 > 0$. Now,

$$n_4 \ge (b_2 + 1) - (n_1 + n_2 + n_3) = d(N) - k + 1 > 0$$

and the claim follows.

Example. For $N = 101$, there are two designs:

(1) $n_1 = 65$, $n_2 = 29$, $n_3 = 1$, $n_4 = 6$, $d(N) = 10$, $t = 7$.
(2) $n_1 = 65$, $n_2 = 29$, $n_3 = 1$, $n_4 = 5$, $d(N) = 11$, $t = 7$.

Case 3. For $b_3 < N \le b_2$, define

$$\left. \begin{aligned}
n_4 &= d(N) \\
n_3 &= d(N) - (k+1) \\
n_2 &= k(k-1)/2 + 1 \\
n_1 &= N - (n_2 + n_3 + n_4)
\end{aligned} \right\} \tag{21}$$

Note that this is very similar to Case 1.

Claim 3.1. For $k \ge 7$, $b_3 < B_3 < B_2 < b_2$.

Proof: Only the left-most inequality is to be proved. It can be shown by direct substitution that

$$B_3 - b_3 \ge 2^{k-3} - 7 > 0.$$

Claim 3.2.
a) $n_3 \in \{k - 7, k - 6, k - 5, k - 4\}$, if $b_3 < N < B_3$.
b) $n_3 \in \{k - 6, k - 5, k - 4\}$, if $B_3 \le N \le B_2$, and
c) $n_3 \in \{k - 5, k - 4\}$, if $B_2 < N \le b_2$

Proof: In view of Claim 3.1 and Case A4, since $2k - 6 \le d(N) \le 2k - 3$, (a) follows.

Likewise, from Case A3, since $2k - 5 \le d(N) \le 2k - 3$, (b) follows.

From Case A2, and Claim 3.1, since $2k - 4 \le d(N) \le 2k - 3$, (c) follows.

Claim 3.3. The design is (s, d)-optimal.

Proof: Since $N < b_2$, we obtain that

$$n_1 \le (b_2 + 1) - (n_2 + n_3 + n_4) \le 2^{k-1}.$$

Also,

$$n_1 \ge (b_3 + 1) - (n_2 + n_3 + n_4) \ge 2^{k-2} + 1.$$

Thus $\lceil \log n_1 \rceil = k - 1$ and the design is optimal.

Examples. For $N = 76$, there are four designs as shown below:

Design	n_1	n_2	n_3	n_4	t	$d(N)$
1	46	22	0	8	6	8
2	44	22	1	9	6	9
3	42	22	2	10	6	10
4	40	22	3	11	6	11

For $N = 147$, there are three designs:

Design	n_1	n_2	n_3	n_4	t	$d(N)$
1	105	29	2	11	7	11
2	103	29	3	12	7	12
3	101	29	4	13	7	13

For $N = 172$, there are two designs:

Design	n_1	n_2	n_3	n_4	t	$d(N)$
1	128	29	3	12	7	12
2	126	29	4	13	7	13

Case 4. The range of N to be considered is

$$2^{k-1} < N \le b_3. \tag{22}$$

Since, $d(N)$ is of the form $(2k - i)$, for $i \in \{3, 4, 5, 6\}$, from (18), it follows that

$$b_3 = 2^{k-2} + \frac{k(k+5)}{2} - 2i. \tag{23}$$

It can be seen, that

$$\frac{k(k+5)}{2} - 2i > 2^{k-2}, \tag{24}$$

only if, $k = 7$ and $i = 3$ *or* 4. Hence, this case applies only for $k = 7$, and there are only two circuits with depth $2k - 3$ and $2k - 4$. The design is

$$\left. \begin{array}{rcl} n_4 &=& N - (n_1 + n_2 + n_3) \\ n_3 &=& d(N) - (k+1) \\ n_2 &=& k(k-1)/2 + 1 \\ n_1 &=& 2^{k-2} + 1 \end{array} \right\} \tag{25}$$

It is readily seen that this design is (s, d)-optimal if the following holds.

Claim 4.1.
(a) $n_3 \in \{k-4, k-5\}$
(b) $n_4 > 0$.

Proof: (a) follows from the above discussions. Also, by direct substitution, it follows, that

$$n_4 \geq (2^{k-1} + 11) - (n_1 + n_2 + n_3) > 0.$$

Example. For $N = 65$, there are two designs:

Design	n_1	n_2	n_3	n_4	t	$d(N)$
1	33	22	3	7	6	11
2	33	22	2	8	6	10

From (24), it is clear that $b_3 < 2^{k-1}$, for all $k \geq 8$. (Also, refer to Table 1) Hence, Case 3 may be restated as follows:

Case 3′. If

$$\max [\, b_3, 2^{k-1} \,] < N \leq b_2 \tag{26}$$

then, define $n_i\text{'s}$ according to (21).

Example. When $N = 65$, and $d(N) = 2k - 5$ or $2k - 6$, Case 3′ applies and we obtain two more designs as follows:

Design	n_1	n_2	n_3	n_4	t	$d(N)$
1	33	22	1	9	6	9
2	35	22	0	8	6	8

Case II. Now, we complete the Algorithm by giving a design for N, in the range, $9 \leq n \leq 64$.

Case 1. Let $32 < N \leq 64$. Define $d(N)$ as follows:

For $32 < N \leq 33$, let $d(N) = 6$. For $33 < N \leq 54$, let $d(N) = 7$, and for $54 < N \leq 64$, let $d(N) = 8$.

(1) For $32 < N \leq 35$, define $n_1 = 16$, $n_2 = 11$, $n_3 = d(N) - 6$, and $n_4 = N - (d(N) + 21)$.

(2) For $35 < N \leq 39$, define $n_1 = 17$, $n_2 = 16$, $n_3 = 0$, and $n_4 = N - 33$.

(3) For $39 < N \leq 57$, define $n_1 = N - (2d(N) + 9)$, $n_2 = 16$, $n_3 = d(N) - 7$, and $n_4 = d(N)$.

(4) For $57 < N \leq 62$, define $n_1 = 33$, $n_2 = 22$, $n_3 = 0$, and $n_4 = N - 55$.

(5) For $62 < N \leq 64$, define $n_1 = N - 30$, $n_2 = 22$, $n_3 = 0$, and $n_4 = 8$.

Case 2. Let $16 < N \leq 32$. Define $d(N)$ as follows:
For $16 < N \leq 20$, let $d(N) = 5$ and, for $21 < N \leq 32$, let $d(N) = 6$.

(1) For $16 < N \leq 22$, define $n_1 = 8$, $n_2 = 7$, $n_3 = d(N) - 5$, and $n_4 = N - (d(N) + 10)$.

(2) For $22 < N \leq 25$, define $n_1 = 9$, $n_2 = 11$, $n_3 = 0$, and $n_4 = N - (d(N) + 14)$.

(3) For $25 < N \leq 32$, define $n_1 = N - (d(N) + 11)$, $n_2 = 11$, $n_3 = 0$, and $n_4 = d(N)$.

Case 3. Let $8 < N \leq 16$. Define $d(N)$ as follows:

For $8 < N \leq 12$, let $d(N) = 4$ and for $12 < N \leq 16$, let $d(N) = 5$.

(1) For $8 < N \leq 14$, define $n_1 = 4$, $n_2 = 4$, $n_3 = d(N) - 4$, and $n_4 = N - (d(N) + 4)$.

(2) For $14 < N \leq 16$, define $n_1 = 5$, $n_2 = 7$, $n_3 = d(N) - 5$, and $n_4 = N - (d(N) + 7)$.

For $N = 8$, there exists a depth 4, (s, d)-optimal circuit and likewise, for all $2 \leq N \leq 7$, (s, d)-optimal circuits can be readily obtained. Table 2 gives the (s, d)-optimal circuits for various values of N. From Table 2, it follows that the LYD circuits, for $N = 9$ to 12, $N = 17$ to 20, and $N = 33$ are not only (s, d)-optimal, but d-optimal as well. An intriguing open question is: does there exist a design of parallel prefix circuits that are simultaneously (s, d)-optimal and d-optimal?

Table 2. (s, d)-Optimal Design

N	n_1	n_2	n_3	n_4	$d(N)$	N	n_1	n_2	n_3	n_4	$d(N)$
9	4	4	0	1	4	37	17	16	0	4	7
10	4	4	0	2	4	38	17	16	0	5	7
11	4	4	0	3	4	39	17	16	0	6	7
12	4	4	0	4	4	40	17	16	0	7	7
13	4	4	1	4	5	41	18	16	0	7	7
14	4	4	1	5	5	42	19	16	0	7	7
15	5	7	0	3	5	43	20	16	0	7	7
16	5	7	0	4	5	44	21	16	0	7	7
17	8	7	0	2	5	45	22	16	0	7	7
18	8	7	0	3	5	46	23	16	0	7	7
19	8	7	0	4	5	47	24	16	0	7	7
20	8	7	0	4	5	48	25	16	0	7	7
21	8	7	1	5	6	49	26	16	0	7	7
22	8	7	1	6	6	50	27	16	0	7	7
23	9	11	0	3	6	51	28	16	0	7	7
24	9	11	0	4	6	52	29	16	0	7	7
25	9	11	0	5	6	53	30	16	0	7	7
26	9	11	0	6	6	54	31	16	0	7	7
27	10	11	0	6	6	55	30	16	1	8	8
28	11	11	0	6	6	56	31	16	1	8	8
29	12	11	0	6	6	57	32	16	1	8	8
30	13	11	0	6	6	58	33	22	0	3	8
31	14	11	0	6	6	59	33	22	0	4	8
32	15	11	0	6	6	60	33	22	0	5	8
33	16	11	0	6	6	61	33	22	0	6	8
34	16	11	1	6	7	62	33	22	0	7	8
35	16	11	1	7	7	63	33	22	0	8	8
36	17	16	0	3	7	64	34	22	0	8	8

6.5 Exercises

6.1   (Snir [1986]) Let $\theta_1, \theta_2, \cdots, \theta_t$ be a set of non-trivial binary (associative) operators. Define

$$f_1 = x_1$$

and

$$f_i = f_{i-1}\, \theta_{j_i}\, x_i, \quad i = 2, \cdots, N.$$

Show that, $\{\, f_1, f_2, \cdots, f_N \,\}$ constitutes a self-reducible family, if each operator θ_i admits a (right) unit element e_i.

6.2   (Snir [1986]) Let $D = \{\, 0, 1 \,\}$ and A be the set of non-trivial binary Boolean operators on D, (that is, A consists of all but the projections and the constants). Let

$$f_1 = x_1$$

and

$$f_i = f_{i-1}\, \theta_i\, x_i, \quad \theta_i \, \varepsilon \, A \text{ for } i = 2, 3, \cdots, N.$$

Show that, $\{\, f_i, \cdots, f_N \,\}$ is a self-reducible family, if, for each θ_i, there exists an element e_i (not necessarily the right unit) such that the mapping

$$x \rightarrow x\, \theta_i\, e_i$$

is one-to-one. As an example of the latter condition, let $\theta_i = +$, the modulo-2 addition. Clearly,

$$x \rightarrow x + 0 \text{ } is \text{ } one-to-one.$$

and

$$x \rightarrow x + 1 \text{ } is \text{ } also \text{ } one-to-one.$$

6.3   Let R be the set of all real numbers. Let $f_i(x_i, x_2, \cdots, x_i)$, $i = 1, 2, \cdots, N$, be a set of rational functions over R, such that, f_i depends on all of its i variables. Show that, $\{f_1, f_2, \cdots, f_N \}$ constitutes a self-reducible family of functions. (An example of such a family is

$$f_i(x_1, x_2, \cdots, x_i) = x_1^2 + x_2^2 + \cdots + x_i^2, \qquad \text{for } i = 1 \text{ to } N.$$

6.4   (Snir [1986]) Let

$$y_i = f_i(y_{i-1}, \; x_i), \quad i = 1, 2, \; \cdots \; , N$$

where f_i is an arbitrary rational function, including linear recurrence, continued fractions, etc. Show that, y_i, $i = 1, 2, ..., N$, constitutes a self-reducible family.

Hint: $y_1 = f_1(y_0, x_1)$, $y_2 = f_2(y_1, x_2)$, $y_3 = f_3(y_2, x_3) \; \cdots$

Clearly,

$$y_1 = f_1(y_0, x_1) = g_1(x_1)$$

$$y_2 = f_2(f_1(y_0, x_1), x_2) = g_2(x_1, x_2)$$

$$y_3 = f_3(f_2(f_1(y_0, x_1), x_2), x_3) = g_3(x_1, x_2, x_3)$$

and so on.

6.5   (Snir [1986]) Combining Theorem 1 of Section 6.1 and Exercise 6.3, show that the carry look-ahead circuit G with $2N + 1$ inputs (N generate signals $g_1, g_2, \; \cdots \; , g_N$, N propagate signals $p_1, p_2, \; \cdots \; , p_N$, and c_0, the initial carry bit), is such that

$$s(G) + d(G) \geq 4N$$

6.6   (Snir [1986]) Let R be the set of all real numbers. Let $f_0, f_1, \; \cdots \; , f_N$ be the linear recurrences defined by

$$f_0 = a_0$$

$$f_i = a_i f_{i-1} + b_i \quad i = 1, 2, \; \cdots \; , N$$

If G is a circuit that computes $f_0, f_1, \; \cdots \; , f_N$, then, show that

$$s(G) + d(G) \geq 4N.$$

6.7   Show that, the computation of the circuit $CR(N)$ given in Section 6.2 is a generalization of the computations resulting from the odd-even reduction described in Chapter 3. Also, compare this circuit with the Brent-Kung, $BK(N)$, circuit given in Figure 2, Section 5.2.

6.8   Prove the Property 1 in Section 6.2.

6.9   Prove the Property 2 in Section 6.2.

6.10   Prove the Property 3 in Section 6.2.

6.11   (Snir [1986]) Thus far, all the circuits we have considered for computing the prefixes in the text are *layered,* where, at each level there is a maximum of $\dfrac{N}{2}$ nodes. Number each node in a given level from 1 through $\dfrac{N}{2}$, such that

(a) the inputs are at level zero and the input x_i labels the (input) node with number i,

(b) the last node with number i computes $x_1 \circ x_2 \circ \cdots \circ x_i$, and

(c) if a node p at level r has a number j, then the left and right parents of p are, respectively, the last node with number i, for some $i < j$, and the last node with number j.

Circuits satisfying these conditions are called *conservative* circuits. Do there exist *non-conservative* parallel prefix circuits?

6.6 Notes And References

Section 6.1–6.3: These sections are derived from Snir [1986].

Section 6.4: The family of $Q(m)$ circuits (in Section 6.4.1) developed by Lakshmivarahan, Yang and Dhall [1987], while being (s, d)-optimal also have an interesting property of depth = width = $O(m^{1/2})$. Among all the *known* (s, d)-optimal designs, while LYD(N) have the least depth, this class of circuits also promotes the possibility of designs that are simultaneously d-optimal and (s, d)-optimal. As observed toward the end of Section 6.4 that, for $N = 9$ to 12, $N = 17$ to 20 and $N = 33$ (refer to Table 2 in Section 6.4.2), LYD(N) design is both (s, d)-optimal and d-optimal. Finding alternate designs that simultaneously satisfy different optimality conditions constitutes an important problem area that awaits attention. Also, refer to Yang [1987] for details.

Part Four

Analysis of Fan-In And Fan-Out In Circuits

Chapter 7

Bounding Fan-Out In Parallel Prefix Circuits

The depth-optimal and (size + depth)-optimal circuits described in Chapters 5 and 6 have the property that they have a constant or fixed fan-in but unbounded fan-out. From practical considerations, it is desirable to construct circuits with bounded fan-out as well. In this Chapter, we first describe general methods for bounding fan-out in circuits, and then demonstrate an application of these techniques to obtain parallel prefix circuits with fixed fan-in and fixed fan-out. However, bounding fan-out increases the size and depth. The principal result of this Chapter is to derive bounds on the increase in the size and depth resulting from fixing the fan-out.

7.1 Methods For Bounding Fan-Out

A glance at the structure of the d-optimal and (s, d)-optimal circuits defined in Chapters 5 and 6 reveals that these circuits have *unbounded* fan-out (that is, fan-out is a function of N, the number of inputs). However, in practice, such as, in VLSI implementation, for practical reasons stemming from *power, noise,* and *reliability* considerations, the fan-out has to be limited to a small, fixed number, for instance, k (such as 2 or 3). We first describe an *optimal* method for bounding fan-out and then apply it to prefix circuits.

7.1.1 An Optimal Method for Building k-ary trees

To understand the effect of limiting the fan-out, consider an example of a node a in Figure 1, with fan-out 9. This can be thought of as a 9-ary tree with a as its root, and b_i, $1 \le i \le 9$ as the leaves. Suppose that we have to limit the fan-out to 3. That is, we have to replace the 9-ary tree in Figure 1 by a 3-ary tree with a as its root and b_i, $1 \le i \le 9$, as the leaves with the constraint that the values of the leaves remain unchanged. One such tree is given in Figure 2. Clearly, restricting the fan-out simultaneously *increases* the depth and the size of the circuit. In this example, the size is increased by 3 and the depth by 1. The internal nodes (denoted by $\square$) of this equivalent tree, other than the root, are essentially repeater, relay or broadcast nodes. Our first task is to quantify the increase in the size and depth resulting from bounding fan-out of a single node. Applying this technique to every node in the prefix circuit with fan-out larger than k, we then compute the increase in size and depth for the entire circuit.

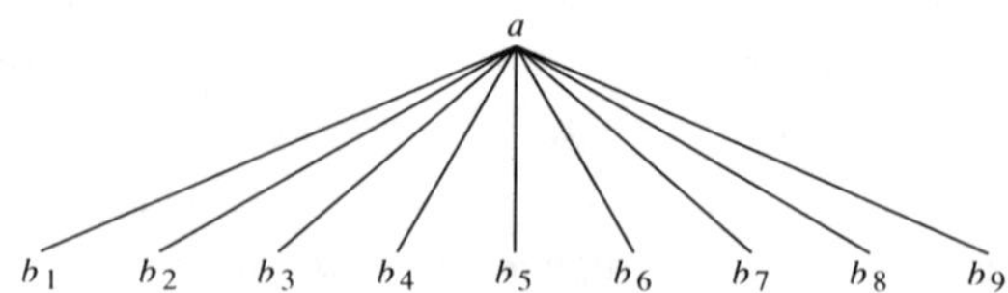

Figure 1. An example of a node with fan-out 9.

We begin by characterizing the size and depth of a k-ary tree with n leaves.

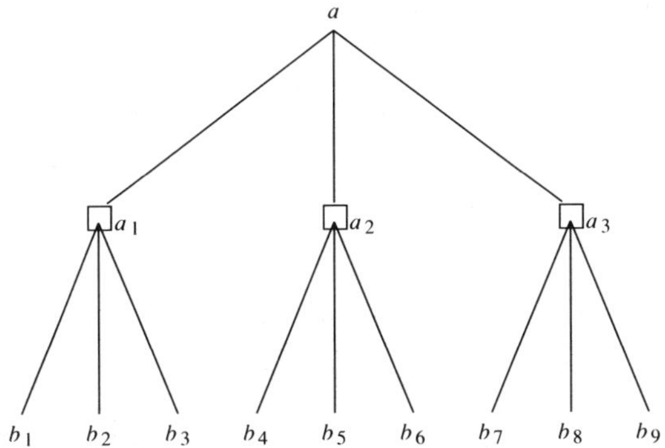

Figure 2. An equivalent tree obtained by limiting the fan-out to 3.

Lemma 1. A k-ary tree with n leaves has *at least* $\left\lceil \dfrac{n-1}{k-1} \right\rceil$ internal nodes and depth $\left\lceil \log_k n \right\rceil$.

Proof: Since a k-ary tree with p internal nodes can have a maximum of $pk - (p-1)$ leaves, we must have

$$p = \left\lceil \frac{n-1}{k-1} \right\rceil. \tag{1}$$

It can be verified that the depth of the tree is minimized by requiring that the leaves be, *at most,* at two adjacent levels. Combining this with the fact that the number of nodes at level i, is k^i (assuming that the root of the tree is at level 0), the lower bound on the depth is obtained.

Refer to Figure 3 for an illustration of Lemma 1. Returning to the example in Figures 1 and 2, it follows from Lemma 1 that the equivalent 3-ary tree in Figure 2 is an optimal replacement for the 9-ary tree in Figure 1.

A *rooted tree T*, is a *triple T* $= \ <M, r, h>$, where

    (i) M denotes the set of *all nodes* in the tree T,

    (ii) $r \in M$ is the *distinguished* node called the *root, and*

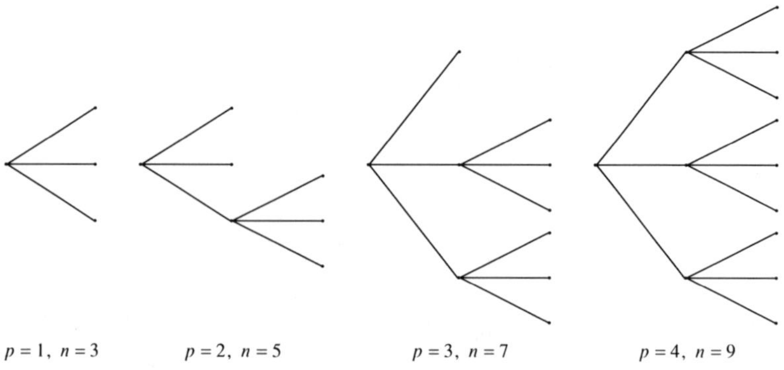

Figure 3. An example of lemma 1, with $k = 3$.

(iii) $h: M \setminus \{r\} \to M$ is called the *successor function, such that*

$$h^{(i)}(x) \neq x, \qquad \text{for all } i > 0 \text{ and } x \in M \setminus \{ r \},$$

where

$$h^{(i)}(x) = h(h^{(i-1)}(x))$$

is the i-fold iterate of h.

As an example, let $M = \{a, a_1, a_2, a_3, b_1, b_2, \cdots, b_9\}$. Let a be the distinguished root node and h be defined as in Table 1. The resulting tree is shown in Figure 2.

Table 1

x	$h(x)$	x	$h(x)$
b_1	a_1	b_7	a_3
b_2	a_1	b_8	a_3
b_3	a_1	b_9	a_3
b_4	a_2	a_1	a
b_5	a_2	a_2	a
b_6	a_2	a_3	a

Given a tree, $T = <M, r, h>$, if, for all $x \in M \setminus \{ r \}$, $| h^{-1}(x) | \leq k$, then T is called a k–ary tree. To further understand the structure of the

k-ary trees, consider an algorithm for assigning weights to the nodes of a tree as follows. Let $\omega(x)$ be the weight of node x.

Algorithm W.

(a) Leaves are assigned *arbitrary* integer weights.

(b) An internal node z is assigned weight

$$\omega(z) = 1 + \max \{\, \omega(y) \mid y \in h^{-1}(z) \,\}. \tag{2}$$

A k-ary tree T, with weights assigned as described above is often called a *weighted k-ary tree*. An example of a 3-ary weighted tree is given in Figure 4. Since the weights can be chosen to denote the levels of a node in a tree, the restriction to integer weights is essentially a convenience rather than a necessity. Verification of the following property is Exercise 7.1.

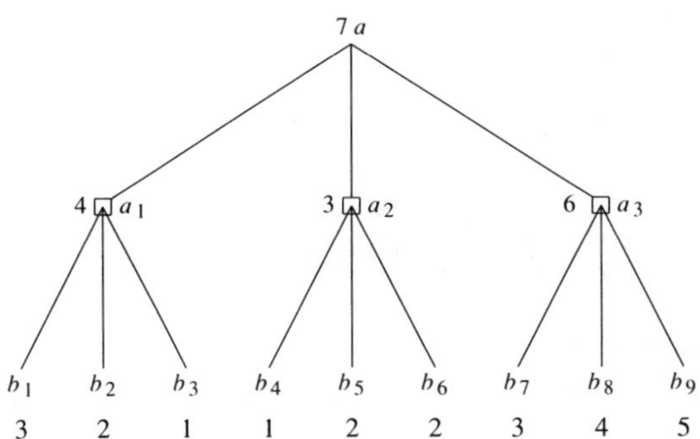

Figure 4. An example of assignment of weights.

Lemma 2. (a) The sequence of weights along a path from a leaf to the root is strictly increasing.

(b) There exists one or more paths along which the weights of the nodes increase by one at successive nodes from the leaf to the root.

The next Lemma relates to a lower bound on the weight assigned to the root of a weighted k-ary tree.

Lemma 3. Let T be a weighted k-ary tree with r as its root, and L as its leaves. Then

$$\sum_{x_i \in L} k^{\omega(x_i)} \le k^{\omega(r)}. \tag{3}$$

Proof: This is proved by induction on the level of the k-ary tree. Referring to Figure 5a, the inequality (3) can be easily verified for the two-level tree which constitutes the basis.

Let T_i be a k-ary tree with r_i as the root and A_i as its leaves, for $1 \le i \le t$, for some $2 \le t \le k$. Refer to Figure 5b. By induction hypothesis

$$\sum_{x_j \in A_i} k^{\omega(x_j)} \le k^{\omega(r_i)}, \qquad 1 \le i \le t.$$

Define

$$m = \max_{1 \le i \le t} \{ \omega(r_i) \}.$$

Let r be the root of a new k-ary tree obtained by combining the roots r_1, r_2, $\cdots$, r_t, as shown in Figure 5b. Clearly, $\omega(r) = 1 + m$. Let $A = \bigcup_{i=1}^{t} A_i$. Then

$$\sum_{x_j \in A} k^{\omega(x_j)} \le \sum_{i=1}^{t} k^{\omega(r_i)} \quad \text{(by induction hypothesis)}.$$

$$\le k^{m+1} = k^{\omega(r)},$$

and the Lemma follows.

The inequality (3) is known as the *Kraft's* inequality. Since $\omega(r)$ is integer-valued, on rewriting (3), we have

$$\omega(r) \ge \left\lceil \log_k \sum_{x_i \in L} k^{\omega(x_i)} \right\rceil. \tag{4}$$

Given a set L of leaf nodes with preassigned weights, the problem is to construct a k-ary tree T, such that

(a) the size $s(T)$ (number of internal or non-leaf nodes), of the tree is minimum, and

(b) the weight $\omega(r)$ of its root is minimum.

We now describe an algorithm from Golumbic [1976] that simultaneously minimizes the size and weight of the root T.

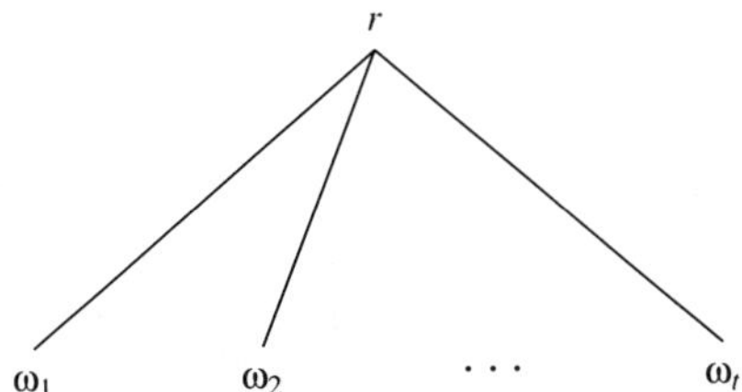

(a) Basis for induction. $2 \le t \le k$.

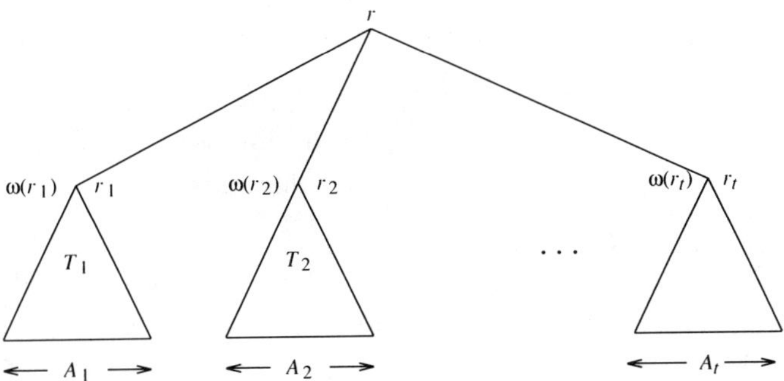

(b) Inductive step. T is obtained by combining $T_1, T_2, \cdots, T_t$.

Figure 5. Illustration of the proof of Lemma 3.

Algorithm G1.

Let P denote the set of nodes for which the successor function h is yet to be defined. Initially $P = L$, and the algorithm terminates when $|P| = 1$.

For $S \subseteq P$, define an operation **combine (S)** that creates a set Q of $\left\lceil \dfrac{|S|}{k} \right\rceil$ nodes, such that

$$Q = \{ \, y \mid x \in S, \, h(x) = y \text{ and } |h^{-1}(y)| \le k \, \},$$

where the weights of nodes in Q are assigned using the rule in (2).

Redefine,

$$P \leftarrow (P \setminus S) \cup Q,$$

that is, delete the elements of S from P and add those of Q to P, and the algorithm continues until $|P| = 1$.

The algorithm is complete by specifying how the set S is picked at each step. To this end, express

$$|L| = r(k - 1) + q, \tag{5}$$

where $2 \leq q \leq k$ (see Exercise 7.2).

At any step, S contains t elements of P with *smallest* weights, where

$$t = \begin{cases} q & \text{in the first step} \\ k & \text{in other steps.} \end{cases}$$

Illustrations of this algorithm are given in Figure 6. Two variations of this algorithm are pursued in Exercises 7.7 and 7.8.

The following two Lemmas characterize the size, $s(T)$, and weight $\omega(r)$ of the root of the tree T, with the set L as it leaves resulting from Algorithm G1.

Lemma 4.

$$(a) \qquad s(T) = \left\lceil \frac{|L| - 1}{k - 1} \right\rceil. \tag{7}$$

$$(b) \qquad \omega(r) = \left\lceil \log_k \sum_{x_i \in L} k^{\omega(x_i)} \right\rceil. \tag{8}$$

Proof: From (5), since $2 \leq q \leq k$, it follows that the number of internal nodes in the tree T is given by

$$s(T) = \frac{|L| - q}{k - 1} + 1 = \frac{|L| - 1}{k - 1},$$

and claim (a) follows.

The claim (b) is proved by induction. Clearly, (b) is true when $|L| = 1$. Let S be the set of q nodes in L with the minimum weight.

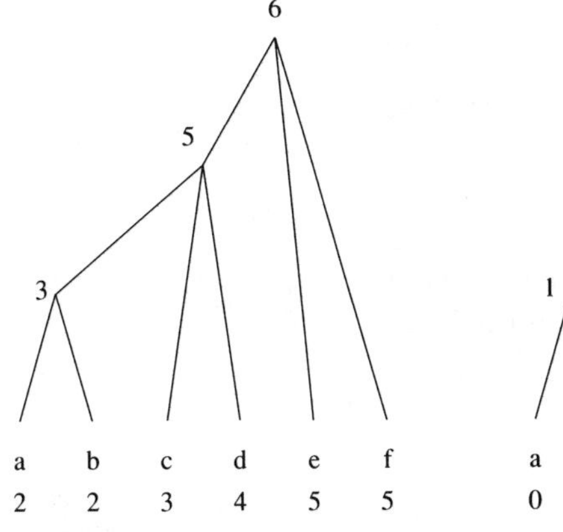

$$S = \{a, b\}, \quad \sum_{x_i \in S} 3^{\omega(x_i)} = 18$$

$$m = 2$$

$$\alpha = 2 \times 3^5 + 1 \times 3^4 + 1 \times 3^3 = 351$$
$$= 211000 \ (base \ 3)$$

$$n = 5$$

(a) Case 1

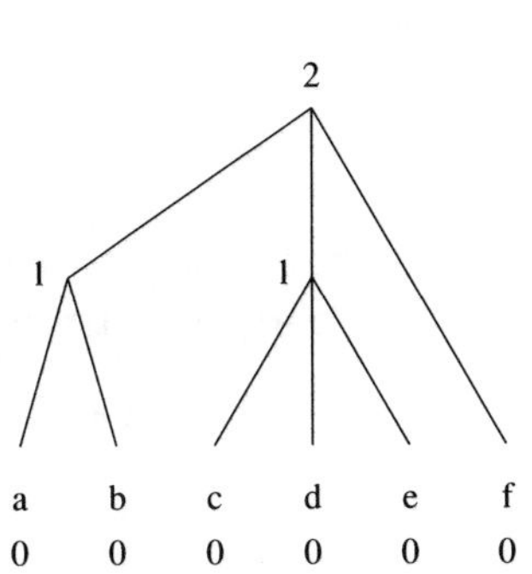

$$S = \{a, b\}, \quad \sum_{x_i \in S} 3^{\omega(x_i)} = 2$$

$$m = 0$$

$$\alpha = 4 \times 3^0 = 4 = 11 \ (base \ 3)$$

$$n = 1$$

(b) Case 1

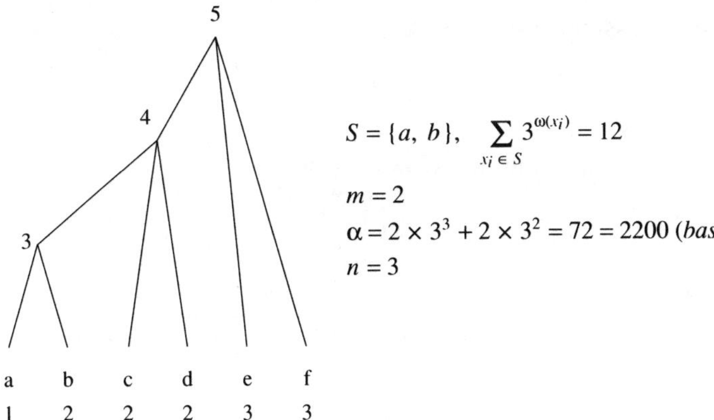

$$S = \{a, b\}, \quad \sum_{x_i \in S} 3^{\omega(x_i)} = 12$$

$$m = 2$$

$$\alpha = 2 \times 3^3 + 2 \times 3^2 = 72 = 2200 \ (base \ 3)$$

$$n = 3$$

(c) Case 2

Figure 6. Illustration of Golumbic's Algorithm G1.

Define

$$R = L \setminus S,$$

where, from (3), $|R| = r(k-1)$. Define

$$m = \max_{x_i \in S} \{\omega(x_i)\}.$$

Let y be the new node of weight $\omega(y) = 1 + m$, created by combining the nodes in S. Clearly, (see Exercise 7.5)

$$1 + k^m \le \sum_{x_i \in S} k^{\omega(x_i)} \le k^{m+1}. \tag{9}$$

Define

$$\alpha = \sum_{x_i \in R} k^{\omega(x_i)}. \tag{10}$$

Clearly,

$$\sum_{x_i \in L} k^{\omega(x_i)} = \sum_{x_i \in S} k^{\omega(x_i)} + \sum_{x_i \in R} k^{\omega(x_i)} \le \alpha + k^{m+1}. \tag{11}$$

Let

$$L' = R \cup \{\, y \,\}, \tag{12}$$

where $|L'| = 1 + r(k-1)$. The Algorithm G1, when applied to L', inductively assigns a weight

$$\left\lceil \log_k (\alpha + k^{m+1}) \right\rceil$$

to the root. Combining this with (11), we get

$$\left\lceil \log_k \sum_{x_i \in L} k^{\omega(x_i)} \right\rceil \le \left\lceil \log_k (\alpha + k^{m+1}) \right\rceil. \tag{13}$$

The proof is completed by showing (13) holds with equality. To this end, express α (in base k) as

$$\alpha = a_n\, a_{n-1}\, \cdots\, a_m\, 0\, 0\, \cdots\, 0$$

$$= a_n k^n + a_{n-1} k^{n-1} + \cdots + a_m k^m$$

where $n > m$ and $a_m \ge 0$, since $\omega(x) \ge m$, for all $m \in R$. Furthermore, since $(k-1)$ divides $|R|$, it follows that $(k-1)$ divides $\sum_{i=m}^{n} a_i$ (refer to Exercises 7.3 and 7.4). Two cases arise.

Case 1: $\alpha + k^{m+1} \le k^{n+1}$. From

$$k^n < \alpha + \sum_{x \in S} k^{\omega(x)} < \alpha + k^{m+1} \le k^{n+1},$$

it follows that equality holds in (13), and both sides are equal to $(n + 1)$.
　　Examples of Case 1 are given in Figures 6a and 6b.

Case 2: $\alpha + k^{m+1} > k^{n+1}$. From

$$\alpha + k^{m+1} = a_n k^n + \cdots + (a_{m+1} + 1)k^n + a_m k^n > k^{n+1}, \tag{14}$$

it follows that (see Exercise 7.6)

$$a_{m+1} = a_{m+2} = \cdots = a_n = (k - 1).$$

Combining this with the strict inequality in (14), and the fact that $(k - 1)$ divides $\sum_{i=m}^{n} a_i$, we get

$$a_m = k - 1.$$

Thus,

$$\alpha + \sum_{x_i \in S} k^{\omega(x_i)} = (k - 1) \sum_{i=m}^{n} k^i + \sum_{x_i \in S} k^{\omega(x_i)} > k^{n+1}. \quad \text{(from definition of } m) \tag{15}$$

Hence,

$$k^{n+1} < \alpha + \sum_{x_i \in S} k^{\omega(x_i)} \qquad \text{(from (15))}$$

$$\le \alpha + k^{m+1} \qquad \text{(from (5) and (6))}$$

$$= a_m k^m + k^{n+1} \qquad \text{(from } a_i = k - 1, \text{ for } m \le i \le n)$$

$$< k^{n+2}.$$

Clearly, equality holds in (13), and both sides are equal to $(n + 2)$.
　　The following Corollary to claim (b) in Lemma 4 is immediate.

Corollary 5. $$k^{\omega(r)} \le k \sum_{x_i \in L} k^{\omega(x_i)}.$$

　　An example of Case 2 is given in Figure 6c. Methods for deriving other upper bounds on $\omega(r)$ are contained in Exercise 7.7.

We now state a principal result of this Section.

Theorem 6. Algorithm G1 defines a weighted k-ary tree T with root r, such that, $s(T)$ and $\omega(r)$ are optimal.

Proof: That $s(T)$ is optimum follows by combining Lemma 1 with (7). Optimality of $\omega(r)$ follows from combining (4) with (8).

Refer to Exercise 7.10 for an alternate derivation from Hoover, Klawe, and Pippenger [1984].

7.1.2 Effect of Bounding Fan-out on Size and Depth

We now apply the above technique to bounding fan-out in circuits. For this purpose, a circuit may be modeled as a directed acyclic graph $G = (V, E)$ with N inputs and M outputs, where the direction of the edges is from the input to the output. For any node x, let $d_i(x)$ and $d_o(x)$ denote the in-degree and out-degree of x. (Clearly, in-degree of input nodes and the out-degree of output nodes are both zero.) In the following, we consider graphs with *fixed* in-degree, that is $d_i(x) = d^*$ for all x. It is useful to express G as the union of disjoint levels. For this purpose, the *output nodes are defined to be at level 0*. Level j nodes, denoted by L_j, consist of those nodes in G whose longest path from an output node is of length j. Refer to Figure 1 for an example. Let D be the depth of the graph G, which is the length of the longest path from an output node to an input node. Thus, the graph G is the union of disjoint levels L_j, $j = 0, 1, 2, \cdots, D$, and the edges connecting them.

The algorithm for bounding fan-out defines a sequence $G^{(i)}$ of graphs with $G^{(0)} = G$. Given $G^{(j)}$, $0 \le j < i$, the graph $G^{(i)}$ is obtained from $G^{(i-1)}$ by replacing all nodes at level L_i of out-degree greater than k, with a k-ary tree described in Section 7.1.1. Let $x \in L_i$ be, such that, $d_o(x) > k$. Define

$$V(x) = \{ \, y \mid (x, y) \text{ is a directed edge from } x \text{ to } y \, \},$$

that is, $V(x)$ is the set of *immediate descendants* of x in G and $|V(x)| > k$. For each y in $V(x)$ assign a weight $\omega(y)$ to be the length of the longest path from y to an output in $G^{(i-1)}$. $G^{(i)}$ is obtained from $G^{(i-1)}$, by replacing each node x and the edges to its immediate descendants by a k-ary tree using Algorithm G1.

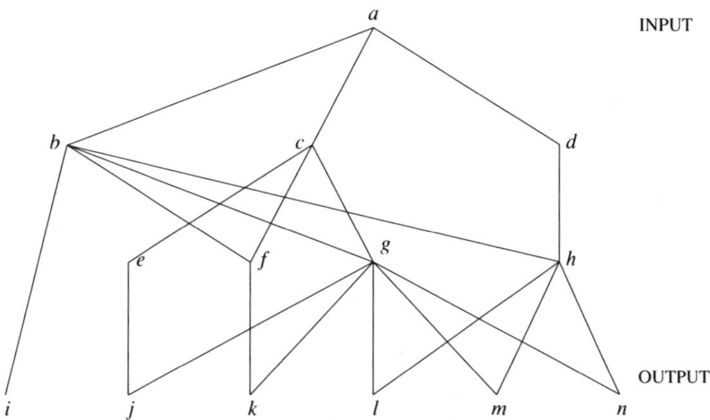

$$L_0 = \{i, j, k, l, m, n\}, \quad L_1 = \{e, f, g, h\}, \quad L_2 = \{b,c,d\}, \quad L_3 = \{a\}, \quad D = 3.$$

Figure 1. An example of a directed (top down) acyclic graph G, $\text{size}(G) = 14$, $\text{depth}(G) = 3$. (For simplicity, the arrows are not shown.)

The graph resulting from applying the above algorithm to that in Figure 1, with $k = 2$, is given in Figures 2(a) through 2(c). Note that the size of the resulting graph has increased by 8 and the depth by 3. Also note that, for $x \in L_i$, if the length of the longest path $\omega(x)$ from x to an output in $G^{(D)}$, then $\omega(x)$ is also the length of the longest path from x to an output in $G^{(i)}$. As a first step towards deriving bounds on the increase in size and depth, we state the following property whose proof is left as an Exercise 7.9.

Lemma 1. (a)
$$\sum_{x: d_0(x) > 0} d_o(x) \le d^* \text{size}(G).$$

(b)
$$\sum_{x: d_o(x) > 0} 1 = \text{size}(G) - M.$$

(c) Let a and b be two positive integers with $a > b$. Then

$$\left(\frac{a}{b} + 1\right) - \left\lceil \frac{a}{b} \right\rceil \ge \frac{1}{b}.$$

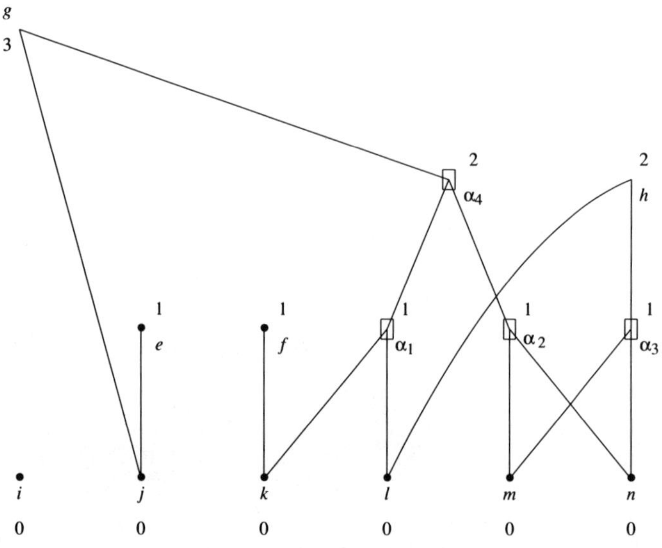

Figure 2a. Part of the graph $G^{(1)}$ contained between L_0 and L_1.

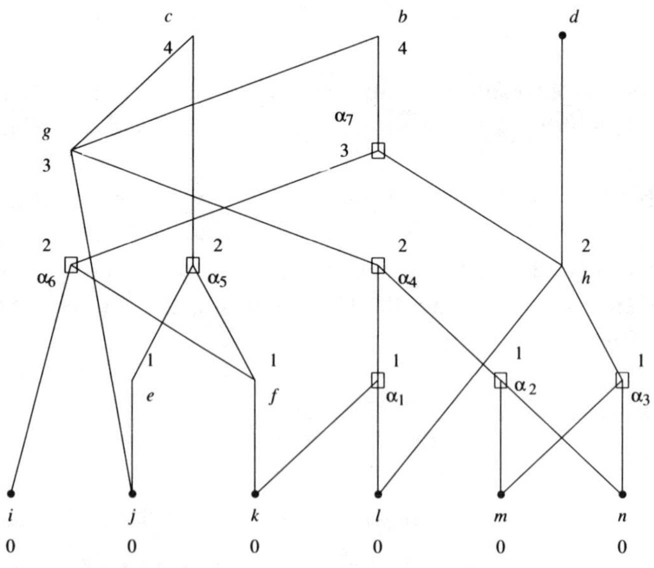

Figure 2b. Part of the graph $G^{(2)}$ contained between L_0 and L_2.

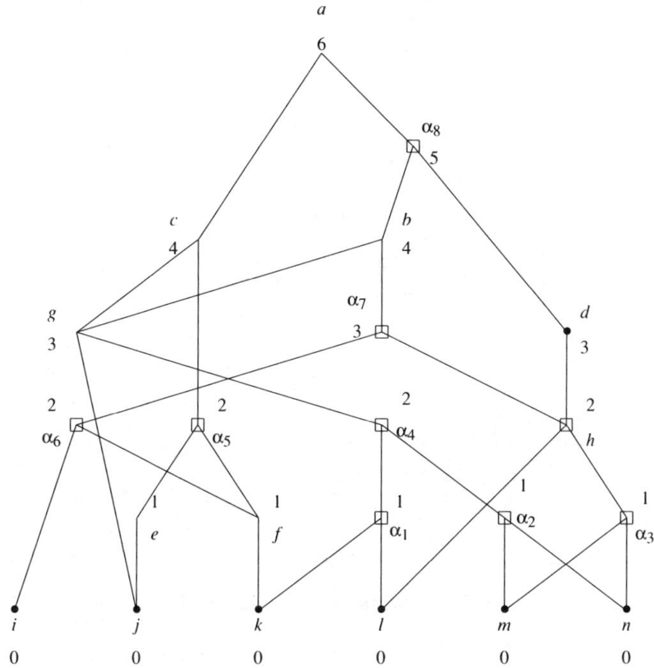

Figure 2c. The graph $G^{(3)}$ obtained from G in Figure 1. Size(G) = 22, depth(G) = 6.

The next two Lemmas contain one of the principal results of this Section, namely, that by bounding fan-out, the size and the depth increase, at most, by a constant factor.

Lemma 2. If G is a directed, acyclic graph of constant in-degree d^* with N inputs and M outputs, then

$$\text{size}(G^{(D)}) \le (1 + \frac{d^* - 1}{k - 1})\, \text{size}\,(G) + \frac{M - 1}{k - 1}. \tag{1}$$

Proof: If $d_o(x) \le k$, for all nodes x in G, then inequality (1) is true. Otherwise, there is at least one node x with $d_o(x) > k$. Let $V_k \subseteq V$ denote the set of nodes in G of out-degree greater than k. In replacing these nodes and the edges to their immediate descendants by a k-ary tree, the size of G, by Lemma 1 of Section 7.1.1, increases by

$$\sum_{x \in V_k} \left\{ \left\lceil \frac{d_o(x) - 1}{k - 1} \right\rceil - 1 \right\} \le \sum_{x \in V_k} \left\{ \left\lceil \frac{d_o(x) - 1}{k - 1} \right\rceil - \frac{1}{k - 1} \right\}$$

$$\le \sum_{x \in V_k} \left\{ \frac{d_o(x) - 1}{k - 1} \right\} - \frac{1}{k - 1} \quad \text{(by Lemma 1).} \qquad (2)$$

But

$$\sum_{x \in V_k} (d_o(x) - 1) \le \sum_{x : d_o(x) > 0} (d_o(x) - 1)$$

$$\le (d^* - 1) \ \text{size} \ (G) + M, \qquad \text{(by Lemma 1).}$$

Combining this with (2), we obtain

$$\text{size} \ (G^{(D)}) \le \left\lceil 1 + \frac{d^* - 1}{k - 1} \right\rceil \text{size}(G) + \frac{M - 1}{k - 1}.$$

To quantify the increase in depth, define, for $0 \le i \le D - 1$,

$$A_i = \{ \ x \in L_j \ | \ j \le i \ \text{and} \ x \ \text{is an immediate descendant}$$

$$\text{of some node} \ y \ \in \ L_r, \ \text{for} \ r > i \ \}.$$

Referring to Figure 1, it can be verified that

$$A_0 = \{ \ i, \ j, \ k, \ l, \ m, \ n \ \} = L_0$$

$$A_1 = \{ \ i, \ e, \ f, \ g, \ h \ \}, \quad A_0 \cap A_1 = \{ i \}$$

$$A_2 = \{ \ b, \ c, \ d \ \}, \quad A_1 \ \cap \ A_2 = \varnothing.$$

Another example is given in Figure 3. To further understand the relation between the sequence of sets A_i's and L_i's, consider an $x \in A_i$. Since A_i's are constructed sequentially, for $i = 0, 1, 2, \cdots, D - 1$, it follows that either $x \in L_i$ or $x \in L_{i-1}$. Since x is an immediate descendant of a node y in L_r, for $r > i$, it follows that in the latter case x also is in A_{i-1}. Thus, we obtain

$$A_i \subseteq (A_i \cap A_{i-1}) \cup L_i. \qquad (3)$$

Also, it follows from the definition that, (i) if $x \in L_i$, then all of its immediate descendants are in A_{i-1}, and (ii) if $x \in (A_i \cap A_{i-1})$, then x is an immediate descendant of at most $(d^* - 1)$ nodes in L_i. Refer to Figure 3 for an illustration.

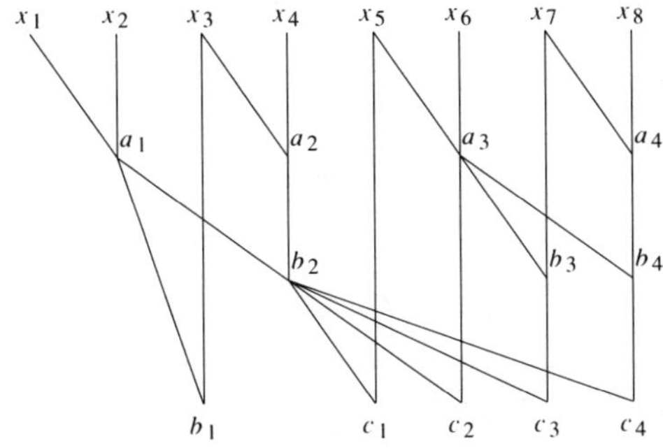

$$A_0 = \{b_1, c_1, c_2, c_3, c_4\}$$
$$A_1 = \{b_1, b_2, b_3, b_4, c_1, c_2\}, \qquad A_1 \cap A_0 = \{b_1, c_1, c_2\}$$
$$A_2 = \{a_1, a_2, a_3, a_4, b_1, c_1\}, \qquad A_2 \cap A_1 = \{b_1, c_1\}$$

Figure 3. Another example of a directed graph.

With these preliminaries, we now derive an important bound.

Lemma 3.
$$\sum_{x \in A_i} k^{\omega(x)} \le (kd^*)^i M.$$

Proof: The proof is by induction. Since $A_0 \le L_0$, the set of all output nodes, the claim is true, for $i = 0$. Now, assume that it is true, for $i - 1$. To prove it for A_i, observe from (3) that

$$\sum_{x \in A_i} k^{\omega(x)} \le \sum_{x \in A_i \cap A_{i-1}} k^{\omega(x)} + \sum_{x \in L_i} k^{\omega(x)}. \tag{4}$$

Before proceeding with the rest of the proof, we now digress to evaluate the right-hand-side of inequality (4) using an example. Referring to Figure 3, consider $A_1 \cap A_0$ and L_1. Clearly,

$$\sum_{x \in A_1 \cap A_0} k^{\omega(x)} = k^{\omega(b_1)} + k^{\omega(c_1)} + k^{\omega(c_2)}. \tag{5}$$

and

$$\sum_{x \in L_1} k^{\omega(x)} = k^{\omega(b_2)} + k^{\omega(b_3)} + k^{\omega(b_4)}. \tag{6}$$

From Corollary 5 of Section 7.1.1, it follows that

$$k^{\omega(b_2)} \le k \, [k^{\omega(c_1)} + k^{\omega(c_2)} + k^{\omega(c_3)} + k^{\omega(c_4)}]. \tag{7}$$

$$k^{\omega(b_3)} \le k \, [k^{\omega(c_3)}] \tag{8}$$

and

$$k^{\omega(b_4)} \le k \, [k^{\omega(c_4)}]. \tag{9}$$

Combining (6) – (9), we obtain

$$\sum_{x \in L_1} k^{\omega(x)} \le k \, [k^{\omega(c_1)} + k^{\omega(c_2)} + 2k^{\omega(c_3)} + 2k^{\omega(c_4)}]. \tag{10}$$

From (5) and (10)

$$\sum_{x \in A_1 \cap A_0} k^{\omega(x)} + \sum_{x \in L_1} k^{\omega(x)} \le 2k \sum_{x \in A_0} k^{\omega(x)},$$

where 2 is the fan-in for each node.

In continuing with the proof of Lemma 3, first recall that each node in $A_i \cap A_{i-1}$ is the immediate descendant of, at most, $(d^* - 1)$ nodes in L_i. Also, all the descendants of each node in L_i are in A_{i-1}. Thus, each node in A_{i-1} affects the weight of, at most, d^* nodes in L_i. Combining these observations with Corollary 5 of Section 7.1.1, we obtain

$$\sum_{x \in A_i} k^{\omega(x)} \le \sum_{x \in A_i \cap A_{i-1}} k^{\omega(x)} + \sum_{x \in L_i} k^{\omega(x)}$$

$$\le d^* k \sum_{x \in A_{i-1}} k^{\omega(x)}$$

$$\le (d^* k)^i \, M, \quad \text{by inductive hypothesis,}$$

and the Lemma follows.

The depth bound is the content of the following result.

Lemma 4. $\mathrm{depth}(G^{(D)}) \le (1 + \log_k d^*) \, \mathrm{depth}(G) + \log_k M. \tag{11}$

Proof: Let x be a node in G that receives the maximum weight $\omega(x)$. Let $x \in L_i$. Since all the immediate descendants of x are in A_{i-1}, from Lemma 3 it follows that

$$k^{\omega(x)} < (d^* k)(d^* k)^{i-1} \, M \le (d^* k)^D \, M. \tag{12}$$

Thus, since $D = \text{depth}(G)$, taking logarithm on both sides of (12), the Lemma follows.

Consequently, it follows from Lemmas 2 and 4 that the effect of bounding the fan-out is to effectively increase the size and depth of the resulting circuit, at most, by a constant factor that depends on the fixed fan-in d^* and fan-out k.

7.2 Prefix Circuits with Bounded Fan-out.

In this section we illustrate the method of Section 7.1.2 by applying it to parallel prefix circuits. For definiteness, let $d^* = 2$ and $k = 2$. For N elements, the bounds on the size and depth now become

$$\text{size}(G^D) \le 2\text{size}(G) + (N - 1) \tag{1}$$

and

$$\text{depth}(G^D) \le 2\text{depth}(G) + \log_2 N. \tag{2}$$

In a parallel prefix circuit, since not all internal nodes are of fan-out larger than two, it turns our that the circuit G^D obtained by applying the methods of Section 7.1.2 is of size and depth much smaller than the bounds given above.

Consider Snir's circuit as an example. (Refer to Section 6.3.) Recall that it consists of two components $CR(N_1)$ and $S(N_2)$. From the fan-out point of view $S(N_2)$ poses no problem. As for $CR(N_1)$, it consists of two parts — g_t for $1 \le t \le m = \lceil \log N_1 \rceil$ and g_{m+t} for $1 \le t \le m - 1$. In the "compressed" version of $CR(N_1)$, each operation is scheduled as early as possible by overlapping operations from successive levels. It is this compression process that is responsible for increased fan-out. Thus, if we leave the circuit "uncompressed", the circuit will have fan-out equal to two. Refer to Figure 1 for an example of the Snir's circuit in this uncompressed form. At the cost of only 14 extra repeater nodes with no increase in depth, we have a circuit with fan-in and fan-out both equal to two. Thus, the resulting size and depth are much smaller than the bounds in (1) and (2) indicate. We invite the reader to verify that the prefix circuit resulting from the application of the algorithm of Section 7.1.2 to compressed version of Snir's circuit is the same Snir's circuit with the $CR(N_1)$ kept in the "uncompressed" form. (Exercises 7.11 to 7.14.)

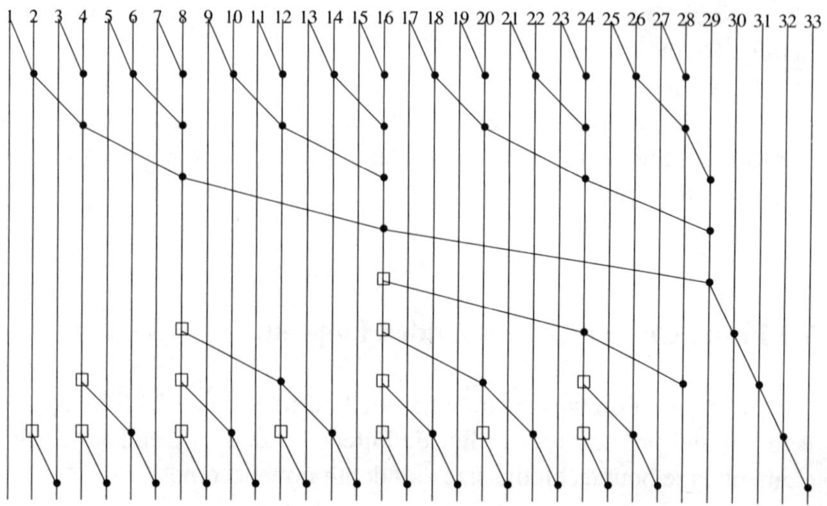

Figure 1. An uncompressed version of Snir's circuit. • denotes semigroup operation, and □ denotes the repeater node.

7.3 Exercises

7.1   Prove Lemma 2 in Section 7.1.1.

7.2   Given $|L|$ and k, prove that $|L|$ can be expressed as

$$|L| = q + r(k - 1),$$

where $2 \leq q \leq k$.

Hint: Recall, given any two integers m and n, $m > n$, we can express $m = an + b$, where $0 \leq b \leq n - 1$.

7.3   Let n be an integer with a decimal expansion $n = a_k a_{k-1} \cdots a_2 a_1$. Show that 9 divides $\sum_{i=1}^{k} a_i$, if and only if 9 divides n.

Hint: Recall $10^i (\bmod\ 9) \equiv 1$.

7.4   Show that $\sum_{i=1}^{p} 10^{m_i}$ is divisible by 9 if an only if p is divisible by 9.

7.5   Prove that inequality in (9) in Section 7.1.1.

Hint: In the first step $t = q$, and $2 \leq q = |S| \leq k$.

7.6   From the relation (14) in Section 7.1.1, show that

$$a_{m+1} = a_{m+2} = \cdots = a_{n-1} = a_n = k - 1.$$

7.7   (Golumbic [1976]) A variation of the Algorithm G1 is pursued in this Exercise.

As the first variation, combine min $\{k, |P|\}$ nodes from P with the smallest weight in P. An example of this algorithm with $k = 3$ is given below.

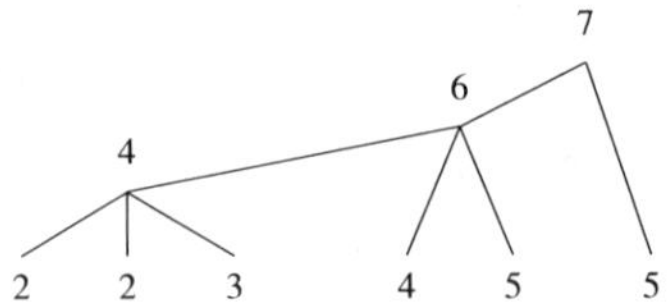

Compare this with Figure 6a. Show that this procedure builds a k-ary tree with $\left\lceil \dfrac{|L| - 1}{k - 1} \right\rceil$ internal nodes and assigns a weight $\omega'(r)$ to the root r, where

$$\omega'(r) = 1 + \omega(r),$$

and $\omega(r)$ is given by equation (13) in Lemma 4 in Section 7.1.1.

Remark: This procedure clearly leads to a k-ary tree of *optimal* size, but depth at most one more than the optimum value.

7.8   (Golumbic [1976]) As a second variation, define

$$S = \{\, x \in P \mid \omega(x) = \min_{y \in P} \omega(y) \,\},$$

and **combine**(S). An example of this algorithm with $k = 3$ is illustrated below.

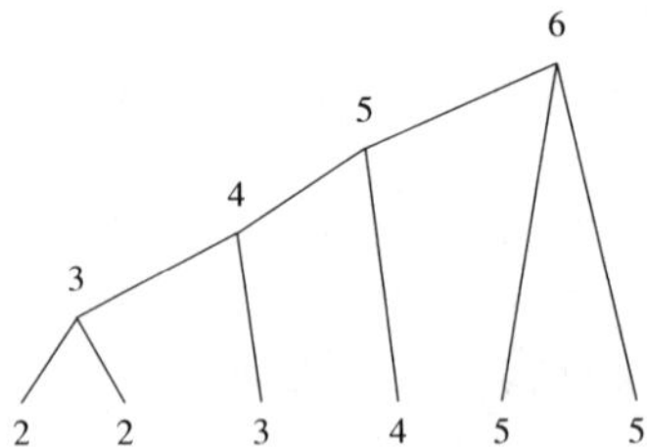

Compare this with Figure 6a and the example in Exercise 7.7. Show that this procedure builds a k-ary tree with optimal depth (that is, the weight assigned to the root is that given by Lemma 4 in Section 7.1.1).

7.9   Prove Lemma 1 in Section 7.1.2.

7.10 (Hoover, Klawe and Pippenger [1984]). Given L, a set of weight leaves, let L^* be a set, where $|L^*| \equiv 1 (\mod k - 1))$, obtained by adding at most $k - 2$ dummy leaves with weight $-\infty$. A weighted k-ary tree $T(k, L^*)$ can be defined as follows: If $|L^*| = 1$, the tree is trivial. For $|L^*| > 1$, let $x_1, x_2, \cdots, x_k$ be the k nodes with the *smallest* weight. Let $L' = L \setminus \{ x_1, x_2, \cdots, x_k \} \cup \{ y \}$ where y is the new node, obtained by combining $x_1, x_2, \cdots, x_k$, with weight

$$\omega(y) = 1 + \max \{ \omega(x_i) \mid 1 \leq i \leq k \}.$$

It can be verified that $|L'| \equiv 1 (\mod (k - 1))$. Then $T(k, L^*)$ is obtained from $T(k, L')$ by joining y to $x_1, x_2, \cdots,$ and x_k. Finally $T(k, L)$ is obtained from $T(k, L^*)$ by removing the dummy nodes.

Let $\alpha = \dfrac{(|L^*| - 1)}{(k - 1)}$ and define a sequence of trees $T^{(i)}$ for $0 \leq i \leq d$ with $T^{(0)} = T(k, L^*)$ and $T^{(i+1)}$ obtained from $T^{(i)}$ by removing the k leaves in $T^{(i)}$ with the smallest weight. Clearly $T^{(d)}$ is a trivial tree with a single node, say, r. Let $x(i, 1), x(i, 2), \cdots, x(i, k)$ be the k nodes with the smallest weight in $T^{(i)}$ and let $\omega(x(i, 1)) \leq \omega(x(i, 2)) \leq \cdots \leq \omega(x(i, k))$. As an example

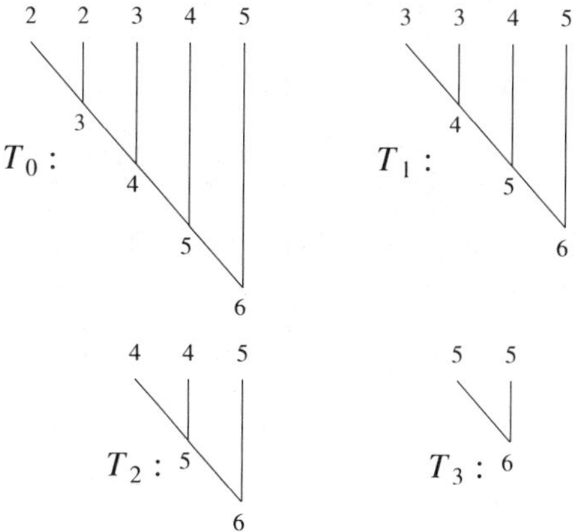

Since $x(i, j)$, $1 \leq j \leq k$ are the immediate descendants of a node y (say) in $T^{(i)}$ of weight $\omega(y) = \omega(x(i, k)) + 1$, therefore,

$$\sum \left\{ k^{\omega(x)} \mid x \ \text{is a leaf of} \ T^{(i+1)} \right\}$$

$$= k^{\omega(y)} - \sum_{j=1}^{k} k^{\omega(x(i,\ j))} + \sum \left\{ k^{\omega(x)} \mid x \ \text{is a leaf of} \ T^{(i)} \right\}$$

$$= (k-1)k^{\omega(x(i,\ k))} - \sum_{j=1}^{k-1} k^{\omega(x(i,\ j))} + \sum \left\{ k^{\omega(x)} \mid x \ \text{is a leaf of} \ T^{(i)} \right\}$$

(a) Applying this repeatedly and using the inequality

$$(k-1)k^{\omega(x(i,\ k))} \le k^{\omega(x(i+1,\ 1))} + \ \cdots \ + k^{\omega(x(i+1,\ k-1))}$$

verify that

$$k^{\omega(r)} < (k-1)k^{\omega(x(d-1,\ k))} + \sum_{x \in L^*} k^{\omega(x)}.$$

(b) Using the fact $\omega(r) = 1 + \omega(x(d-1,\ k))$, verify that

$$k^{\omega(r)} < k \sum_{x \in L^*} k^{\omega(x)}.$$

7.11   Consider the "compressed" version of the Snir's circuit for $N = 33$. By identifying all the nodes with fan-out greater than two, apply the algorithm of Section 7.1.2 to these nodes and derive a circuit of fan-out two. Compute the increase in size and depth and compare this with the bounds given by (1) and (2) of Section 7.2.

7.12   (Chi-Ming Yang [1987]) Show that the sum of the net increase in size and depth resulting from the application of algorithm in Section 7.1.2 to Snir's circuit is bounded by $\dfrac{N}{2}$.

7.13   Repeat Exercise 7.11 for LYD circuit with $N = 33$.

7.14   Compute the net increase in the size and depth resulting from the application of the algorithm in Section 7.1.2 to LYD circuits.

7.4 Notes And References

Section 7.1 - 7.2: The developments in this Section closely follow Golumbic [1976] and Hoover, Klawe, and Pippenger [1984]. The Algorithm G1 in Section 7.1.1 due to Golumbic is essentially the now classical Huffman'a Algorithm for design of *optimal prefix coding* (Huffman [1952]). The second variation of the Golumbic's algorithm given in Exercise 7.8 is very similar to that used by Hicks and Bernstein [1964] for minimizing the number of stages in realizing a switching function using gates with limited fan-in.

For a discussion of *Kraft inequality* (refer to Lemma 3 in Section 7.1.1) and its applications to coding theory, refer to Abramson [1963] and Jelinek [1968].

Earlier attempts to bound fan-out in switching circuits resulted in an increase in size very similar to that in Lemma 2, Section 7.1.2. But the depth of the resulting "equivalent" circuit also increased by a factor as large as the logarithm of the number of inputs. A discussion of these techniques is contained in Savage [1976]. It is only recently that Hoover, Klawe and Pippenger [1984] showed that the increase in the size and depth resulting from bounding fan-out can be simultaneously bounded by a constant that depends only on fan-in d^* and fan-out k.

Hoover, Klawe, and Pippenger [1981] analyzes the effect of bounding fan-out on the *size, depth* and *width*. Chi-Ming Yang [1987] provides a comparison of the size and depth of parallel prefix circuits obtained from Snir's and LYD circuits by restricting fan-out to two. Very little is known about the structure of optimal (in the sense of depth, size, (size + depth), (size + depth + width), etc.) circuits with bounded fan-in and bounded fan-out.

Chapter 8

Constant Depth Prefix Circuits With Unbounded Fan-In

It is well known that among the three classes of the PRAM models, namely, CRCW, CREW, and EREW, the CRCW models are the *weakest,* in the sense that, they permit concurrent read/write by processors. Accordingly, algorithms on the CRCW model mainly concentrate on the core computations without much ado about data access. Consequently, this model, at least in principle, allows for the design of the *fastest* algorithm for a problem. It is intriguing to ask how fast prefixes can be computed on the CRCW models. Since CRCW models are *equivalent* to the *unbounded fan-in* circuits (refer to Chapter 2), the task of developing the fastest algorithms for the prefix problems is pursued in the context of the unbounded fan-in circuits.

Recall from Chapter 2, that while the standard measures, such as, size and depth are still used to quantify the goodness of unbounded fan-in circuits, the *size* of the circuit is measured by the *total number of edges* incident on all of its operation nodes, instead of by the number of operations nodes. It turns out that the size and depth of unbounded fan-in circuits for computing prefixes, depends critically on the structure of the underlying semigroup from which the input elements are drawn. The principal result of this concluding Chapter may be stated as follows: There exists unbounded fan-in parallel prefix circuits of *constant depth* and *polynomial size* if, and only if, the underlying semigroup is group free. The proof of this result involves a very clever synthesis of a number of ideas drawn from different directions — structure of *group free semigroups,* their relations to a special class of regular sets, called *non-counting regular sets,* the relation of this latter class of regular sets to yet another class of regular sets defined by *star-free regular expressions,* and the design of a special class of finite state deterministic automata called *RS machines* that accept star-free regular expressions. In this context, it is convenient to define the notion of *small circuits* as the class of circuits with constant depth and polynomial size. A fundamental (negative) result from the complexity theory of Boolean functions states that, there exists no small circuit for computing the parity function (which is the mod 2 sum of a set of n bits). To render this exposition self-contained, Appendices A, B and C provide the necessary background information in all of these areas. The reader is encouraged to read through these Appendices before proceeding with this chapter.

8.1 The Need For Group-Free Semigroups

Let $S = \{0, 1\}$ and $\oplus$ denote the mod 2 sum or the exclusive-OR operation. Given $x \in \{0, 1\}^N$, where $x = x_n x_{n-1} \cdots x_2 x_1$, define the parity function

$$PARITY : \{0, 1\}^N \rightarrow \{0, 1\}$$

as

$$PARITY(x) = (\sum_{i=1}^{N} x_i) \,(\mathrm{mod}\ 2) \tag{1}$$

where $\sum$ denotes the integer sum. The system $< S, \oplus >$ is often called the *parity semigroup.*

The parity semigroup is an extreme, or the smallest instance of a more general semigroup $< Z_n, +_n >$, where $Z_n = \{0, 1, \cdots, n-1\}$ and $+_n$ denotes the sum (mod n) function $+_n : Z_n \times Z_n \to Z_n$, where

$$i +_n j \equiv (i + j) \,(\mathrm{mod}\, n). \tag{2}$$

It can be verified that $< Z_n, +_n >$ is a *group* with 0 as the identity.

For reasons that will become apparent, we now present some preparatory results. Let $a \in Z_n$. If h is the *smallest positive integer*, such that, $a^h \equiv 1(\mathrm{mod}\, n)$, then h is called the order of $a(\mathrm{mod}\, n)$ and is denoted by $h = ord_n^a$. It can be verified that

$$a, a^2, a^3, \cdots, a^h \equiv 1 \tag{3}$$

are all *distinct* (mod n). Consequently, if $a^k \equiv 1$ (mod n), then clearly h *divides k.* Thus, for any s

$$a^s \equiv a^r (\mathrm{mod}\, n), \tag{4}$$

where

$$s = qh + r, \qquad 0 \le r < h. \tag{5}$$

In other words, the exponent or the index of the powers of a under (mod n) are to be computed under (mod h).

Lemma 1. Let S be a semigroup containing a nontrivial subgroup G, and let $C(N)$ be a circuit of size $s(N)$, and depth $d(N)$ for computing the product of N elements taken from S. Let $|G| = n$. Then, there exists a circuit $C'(N)$ for computing the $+_n$ (the sum mod n) where

$$s'(N) = s(N) + O(N)$$

$$d'(N) = d(N) + \text{constant}.$$

Proof: Let e be the identity of G, and let $e \ne a \in G$. Let h be the order of a, that is, $a^h = e$. The circuit $C(N)$ in Figure 1, that computes the product of $y_1, y_2, \cdots, y_N$, where $y_i \in S$, for $1 \le i \le N$, is given.

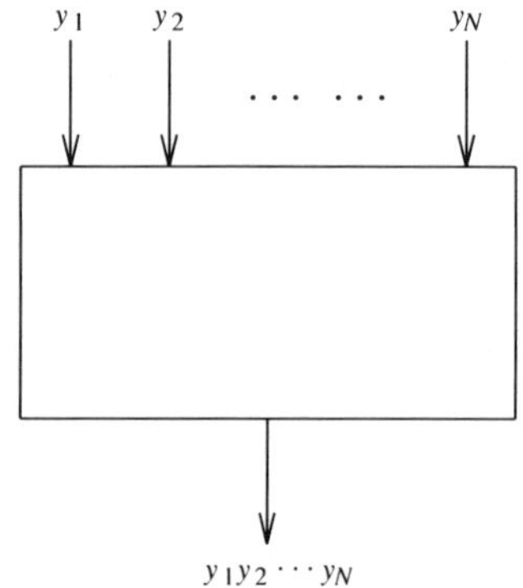

Figure 1. A circuit $C(N)$ for computing the product.

Let $x_i \in Z_n$, for $1 \le i \le N$. As a first step towards the design of the circuit $C'(N)$ for computing

$$(\sum_{i=1}^{N} x_i) \bmod n$$

we introduce two auxiliary circuits.

Let A_i be a circuit that takes a and x_i as inputs and computes

$$y_i = a^{x_i}.$$

From Exercise 8.1, it follows that the depth of each A_i that computes a^{x_i} is $O(\log n)$ (which is constant since n is fixed), and the total size of all A_i's is $N\, O(\log n) = O(N)$.

Let B be a circuit that computes r as the output, given $b = a^r$ as the input. Since there are only h distinct powers of a, namely, $a, a^2, a^3, \cdots, a^h = 1$, B can be realized as a simple table-look-up as follows. Compare b in parallel with $a, a^2, \cdots, a^h$ using h comparators in parallel. Since b is equal to only one of these powers, only the one with $b = a^r$ outputs r. Clearly, the size of B is $O(n)$, and depth of B is constant.

The circuit $C'(N)$ is built around $C(N)$ with the input connected to the outputs of A_i and its output to the input of B, as shown in Figure 2.

From (4) and (5), it follows that the output of $C(N)$ is given by

$$a^{(\sum_{i=1}^{N} x_i) \bmod n}$$

and the output of the entire circuit is the required sum. Clearly,

$$s'(N) = s(N) + O(N) + O(n) = s(N) + O(N),$$

$$d'(N) = d(N) + \text{constant}.$$

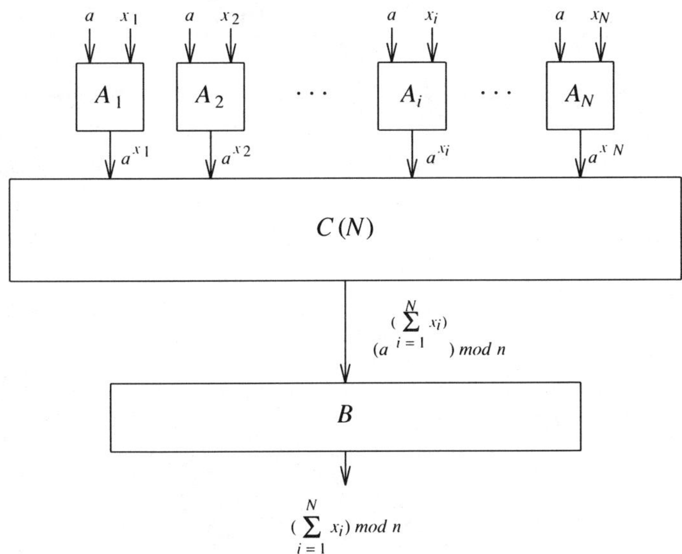

Figure 2. A circuit $C'(N)$ for computing sum mod n.

The next result is very basic and is proved in Appendix C.

Lemma 2. There exists no small circuit (polynomial size and constant depth) for computing the parity function.

As a consequence there exists no small circuit for computing the sum (mod n) function. Combining these we get the following necessary condition.

Theorem 3. There exists a small circuit for computing the products of N elements taken from a semigroup S, only if, S is group-free.

It turns out that this necessary condition is also *sufficient,* and the construction of such circuits is given in the following Section.

8.2 Small Prefix Circuits With Unbounded Fan-In

Let $N = 2^n$. Consider a complete binary tree with N leaves corresponding to the input numbered 1 to N from left to right as shown in the example in Figure 1. We define the notion of a *principal interval* as the segment of the input that are leaves of a subtree rooted at an internal (non-leaf) node. Thus, the interval [5, 8] is a principal interval, but

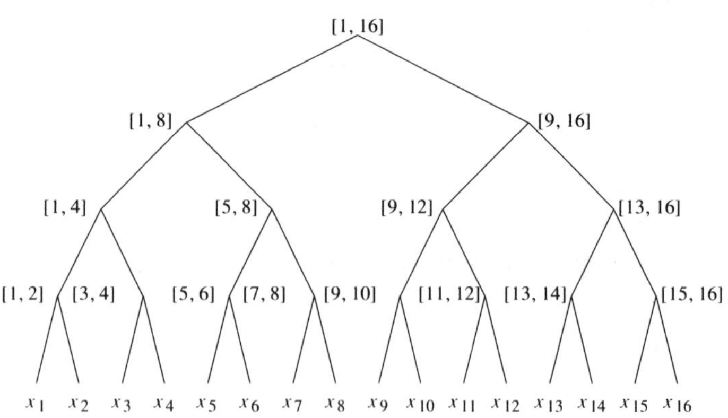

Figure 1. An illustration of the principal intervals.

[5, 11] is not a principal interval. The *length* of a principal interval is equal to the number of indices in it. Thus, the length of the interval [5, 8] is four. Clearly, there are $\dfrac{N}{2^i}$ principal intervals, each of length 2^i, for $1 \le i \le n$. Thus, if I_{ij} denotes the jth principal interval at level i, then

$$I_{ij} = \{k \mid (j-1)2^{n-i} + 1 \le k \le j2^{n-i}\}, \quad 1 \le j \le 2^{n-i}, \quad 0 \le i \le n.$$

It can be verified that, for any $1 \le j \le N$, the interval [1, j] can be expressed as the sum of at most $\log N$ principal intervals (see Exercise 8.2).

Based on this property of principal intervals, we now describe a class of unbounded fan-in parallel prefix circuits as follows:

Step 1: For each principal interval, say, [i, j], compute $x_i \wedge x_{i+1} \wedge x_{i+2} \wedge \cdots \wedge x_j$ (denoted by $i:j$) in parallel using an *AND* gate with unbounded fan-in (refer to Figure 2).

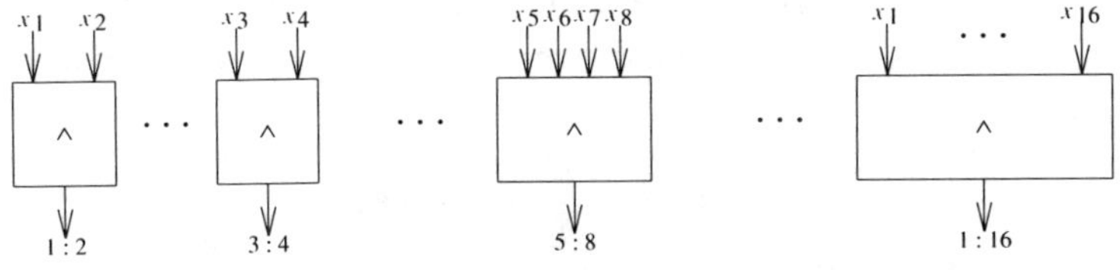

Figure 2. Computation of AND of variables in principal intervals.

Since there are $\dfrac{N}{2^i}$ principal intervals, each of length 2^i, for $1 \le i \le n$, it follows that this step requires depth = 1, and size given by

$$size = \sum_{i=1}^{n} \left(\dfrac{N}{2^i}\right)2^i = N \log N.$$

Step 2: For $1 \le j \le N$, since [1, j] is the sum (or concatenation) of, at most, $\log N$ principal intervals, all the prefixes can be computed in parallel by combining, at most, $\log N$ results of Step 1. Refer to Figure 3 for an example.

Clearly, this step requires depth = 1 and size, at most, $N \log N$.

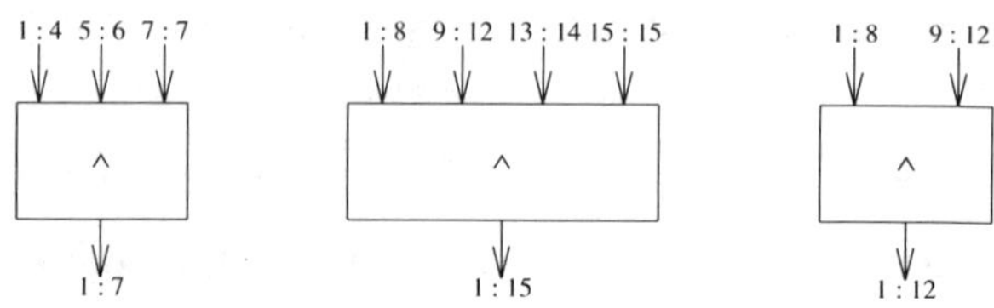

Figure 3. Computing the prefixes using the principal intervals.

Combining these, we obtain the following.

Lemma 1. There exist unbounded fan-in parallel prefix circuits of depth 2 and size, at most, $2N \log N$.

While the circuit defined above is indeed a small circuit with unbounded fan-in, using this construction as a building block, we now define a strategy to further reduce the size. We begin by introducing two related functions - the *repeated exponentiation* and *iterated logarithm*. Let $f(0) = 1$, and

$$f(k) = 2^{f(k-1)}, \qquad \text{for } k \geq 1.$$

From Table 1, it follows that the repeated exponentiation function $f(k)$ grows astronomically large even for small values of k.

Table 1. Values of $f(k)$.

k	0	1	2	3	4	5
$f(k)$	1	2	$2^2 = 4$	$2^{2^2} = 16$	$2^{2^{2^2}} = 65,536$	$2^{2^{2^{2^2}}} = 2^{65,536}$

The notion of iterated logarithm is defined as follows:

$$\log^{(k)} n = \log(\log^{(k-1)} n),$$

where $\log^{(1)} n = \log n$. Given n, define

$$\log^* n = \min\{\, k \geq 1 \mid \log^{(k)} n \leq 1 \,\}.$$

As Table 2 indicates, this function is a very slowly increasing function.

Table 2. Iterated logarithm.

n	2	4	16	65,536	2^{65536}
$\log^* n$	1	2	3	4	5

Since $2^{65536} \approx 10^{19727}$, which is astronomically large,[1] for practical purposes $\log^* n$ is bounded above by 5. (See Exercise 8.3.)

Given N, we now extend the idea of principal intervals by defining a tree of nested intervals as follows.

At the root which is at level 0, there is $n_0 = 1$ interval of length $t_0 = N$. In going from level $(i - 1)$ to level i, each of the subintervals of length t_{i-1} is further divided into

$$n_i := \frac{t_{i-1}}{t_i}$$

intervals each of length $t_i = \log t_{i-1} = \log^{(i)} N$. Thus, there are

$$n_1 \, n_2 \, \cdots \, n_i = \frac{N}{t_i} = \frac{N}{\log^{(i)} N}$$

intervals of length t_i, at level $i = 1, 2, \cdots, \log^* N$.

Refer to Figure 4 for an illustration. At level 0, there is one interval of length $t_0 = N = 2^{16}$. At level 1, there are $n_1 = 2^{12}$ intervals, $I_1, I_2, \cdots, I_{n_1}$, each of length $t_1 = 2^4$. At level 2, the interval I_1 is

---

[1] The number $f(5) = 10^{19727}$ is significantly larger than the number of atoms in the observable universe, which is roughly 10^{80}.

subdivided into $n_2 = 4$ subintervals, I_{11}, I_{12}, I_{13}, and I_{1n_2}, each of length $t_2 = 2^2$. This process is repeated to acquire the entire sequence of nested intervals.

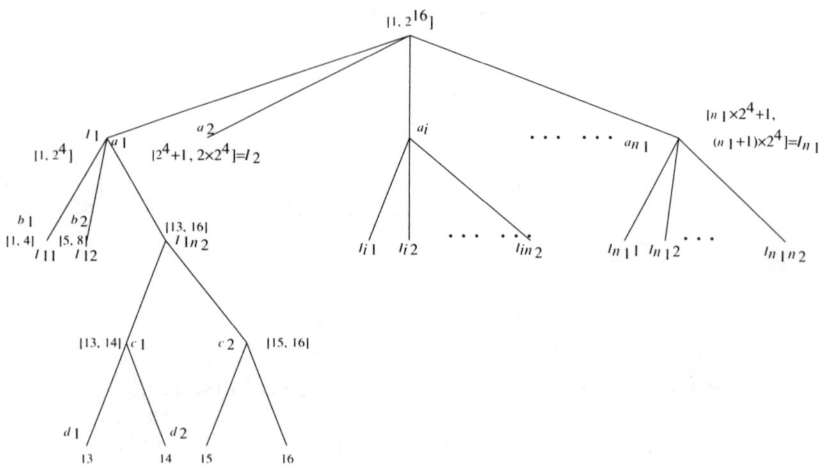

Figure 4. Tree of nested intervals. $t_0 = 2^{16}$, $t_1 = 2^4$, $t_2 = 2^2$, and $t_3 = 2$.

We now give an algorithm for the design of small circuits which is clearly an extension of the one that leads to Lemma 1.

Step 1: Compute, in parallel, the *AND* of the input variables in each of the intervals of length t_i, for all $1 \le i \le k$, using a single *AND* gate for each interval.

Referring to Figure 5, let a_i be the *AND* of input variables in interval I_i, $1 \le i \le n_1 = 16$, at level 1. Similarly, let b_i be the *AND* of the input variables in the subinterval I_{1i}, $1 \le i \le n_2 = 4$, $i = 1, 2, 3, 4$, and so on.

At level i, since the size of the circuit that computes the *AND* of each subinterval is t_i, and there are $\dfrac{N}{t_i}$ such subintervals. The total size for computing the *AND* of all intervals at this level is N. There are a total of $\log^* N$ levels and the overall size for Step 1 is $N \log^* N$. It is evident that the depth for Step 1 is one.

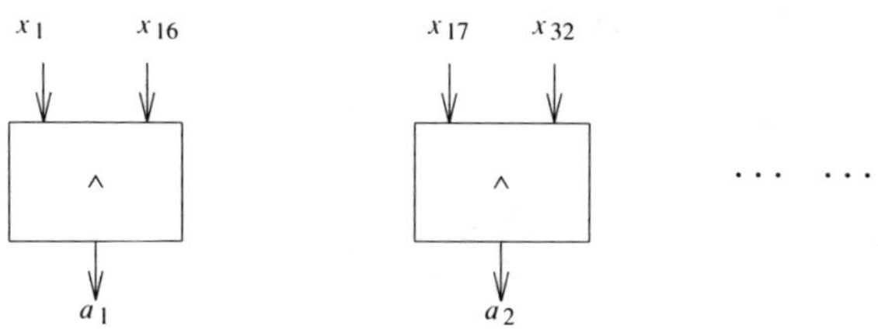

Figure 5. Sample computations.

Step 2: Let $z_1, z_2, \cdots, z_{n_i}$ be the *AND* (computed in Step 1) of the $n_i = \dfrac{t_{i-1}}{t_i}$ subintervals of length t_i arising from the division of an interval, say, Z, of length t_{i-1}. For this interval Z, compute the subinterval prefixes

$$z_1, \quad z_1 z_2, \quad z_1 z_2 z_3, \quad \cdots \quad, \quad z_1 z_2 z_3 \cdots z_{n_i}$$

using the algorithm that leads to Lemma 1. This subinterval prefix computation is performed in parallel for all intervals.

As an illustration, referring to Figure 4, subinterval prefixes for the interval of length t_0 are

$$a_1, \quad a_1 a_2, \quad a_1 a_2 a_3, \cdots, \quad a_1 a_2 a_3 \cdots a_{n_1}.$$

The subinterval prefixes for the interval I_1 are

$$b_1, \quad b_1 b_2, \quad b_1 b_2 b_3, \text{ and } b_1 b_2 b_3 b_4.$$

This process is repeated for all intervals.

From Lemma 1, for computing the subinterval prefixes for interval of length t_0, we need a size of (since $n_1 = \dfrac{N}{\log N}$)

$$2n_1 \log n_1 \le 2N.$$

For intervals of length t_1, there are n_1 circuits, each of size $2n_2 \log n_2$.

Thus, the total size for these subinterval prefixes is given by

$$2n_1 n_2 \log n_2 \le 2N,$$

since $n_1 n_2 = \dfrac{N}{\log \log N}$ and $n_2 = \dfrac{\log N}{\log \log N}$.

Continuing in this way, it can be seen that the total size required to compute the subinterval prefixes of all sizes is $2N \log^* N$. From Lemma 1, it follows that Step 2 requires a depth of two.

Comparing the tree of nested intervals in Figures 1 and 4, observe that in the former tree an interval is always divided into two subintervals, but in the latter, an interval is divided into two or more subintervals. Consequently, the subinterval prefix computation is *not* required for the algorithm leading to Lemma 1.

Step 3: Since any prefix can be expressed as the *AND* of, at most, $\log^* N$ subinterval prefixes (Exercise 8.4), compute in parallel all the prefixes of the input using the results of Step 2. Clearly, this step requires $N \log^* N$ size and depth one.

Combining all the arguments, we obtain Lemma 2.

Lemma 2. There exist small circuits with unbounded fan-in of depth *four* and size $4N \log^* N$ for computing prefixes.

Note that in both Lemmas 1 and 2, the constant of proportionality in the size bound is linear in the depth of the circuit. This fact will be later exploited in Section 8.3 (Theorems 3 and 4) in deriving linear size circuits for binary addition.

The above results demonstrate the existence of depth-size trade-off for the unbounded fan-in prefix circuits. A drastic reduction in size from $O(N \log N)$ to $O(N \log^* N)$ is made possible by increasing the depth from two to four. In the following, we further extend this trade-off by generalizing the constructions that lead to Lemmas 1 and 2. The extension depends critically on the properties of a class of functions called Ackermann's function, $A_m(n)$ defined for integers m, $n \ge 1$, as follows:

$$A_1(n) = 2^n, \qquad\qquad \text{for } n \geq 1$$

$$A_m(1) = A_{m-1}(2), \qquad\qquad \text{for } m \geq 2$$

$$A_m(n) = A_{m-1}(A_m(n-1)), \qquad \text{for } m, n \geq 2.$$

It can be verified that

$$A_{m+1}(n) = A_m^{(n)}(2), \tag{1}$$

where $A_m^{(n)}(x)$ is the nth iterate of $A_m(x)$, and

$$A_{m+1}(n) \geq A_m(n) \geq 2^n.$$

$A_n(n)$ is often denoted by $A_\omega(n)$.

This class of functions exhibits explosive growth even for small values of m and n as shown in Table 3. Note that the elements of the $(i+1)^{th}$ row make a sparse subset of the ith row, for $i \geq 1$. Note that $A_2(n)$ is the repeated exponentiation introduced in Table 1. In fact, this function $A_m(n)$ and its inverse play a role quite akin to exponentiation and logarithm in Lemma 1 and repeated exponentiation and iterated logarithm in Lemma 2.

Table 3. Some sample values of Ackermann's function.

			n		
m		1	2	3	4
1		2	2^2	2^3	2^4
2		2^2	2^{2^2}	$2^{2^{2^2}}$	$2^{2^{2^{2^2}}}$
3		$2^{2^{2^2}} = 2^{16}$	$\left.2^{2^{2^{\cdot^{\cdot^2}}}}\right\}16$	$\left.2^{2^{2^{\cdot^{\cdot^2}}}}\right\}\left.2^{2^{\cdot^{\cdot^2}}}\right\}16$	$\left.2^{2^{2^{\cdot^{\cdot^2}}}}\right\}\left.2^{2^{\cdot^{\cdot^2}}}\right\}\left.2^{2^{\cdot^{\cdot^2}}}\right\}16$

Given N, we now further extend the notion of principal intervals by defining a tree of nested intervals as follows. Let $t_0 = N$ and define

$$t_i = A_m^{-1}(t_{i-1}) \qquad \text{for } i > 0.$$

Let k be an integer, such that $t_k = 2$. Then, from

$$2 = t_k = A_m^{-1}(t_{k-1})$$

$$= A_m^{-1}(A_m^{-1}(t_{k-2}))$$

$$= A_m^{-1}(A_m^{-1}(\cdots A_m^{-1}(N)\cdots)) = k\text{-}fold\ iterate\ of\ A_m^{-1}(N),$$

and (1), we obtain

$$N = A_m^{(k)}(2) = A_{m+1}^{(k)},$$

that is,

$$k = A_{m+1}^{-1}(N). \tag{2}$$

Now, given m, N and k, define a tree of nested intervals as follows. At the root, which is at level 0, there is $n_0 = 1$ interval of length $t_0 = n$. In going from level $(i-1)$ to i, divide each subinterval of length t_{i-1} into

$$n_i = \frac{t_{i-1}}{t_i}$$

intervals, each of length t_i. Thus, at level i there are

$$n_1\ n_2\ \cdots\ n_i = \frac{N}{t_i} = \frac{N}{A_m^{(-i)}(N)}$$

subintervals, where $A_m^{(-i)}(x)$ denotes the ith iterate of $A_m^{-1}(x)$. Note that except for the length and the number of subintervals, this process of subdivision is exactly the same as the one described in Figure 4. With this background, we are now ready to prove one of the principal results of this Section.

Theorem 3. For each m, the prefix of *AND* of N inputs can be computed using unbounded fan-in circuit of size $O(N\ A_m^{-1}(N))$ and depth $2m$.

Proof: The proof is by induction on m, with $m = 1$, as the basis. Since $A_1^{-1}(N) = \log N$, Lemma 1 establishes the existence of depth two circuits of size $O(N \log N)$ for computing prefix *AND*.

Now, assume that for each N, circuits of size $O(N\, A_m^{-1}(N))$ and depth $2m$ exist to compute prefix AND. The circuit of depth $2(m+1)$ is constructed as follows.

Step 1: Compute, in parallel, the AND of the input variables in each of the intervals of length t_i, for all $1 \le i \le k$, using a single AND gate for each interval.

The size of an AND gate for interval of length t_i is also t_i. There are $\dfrac{N}{t_i}$ such gates giving a total size of N for intervals of size t_i. Since there are $k = A_{m+1}^{-1}(N)$ different interval lengths, this step requires a total size of $NA_{m+1}^{-1}(N)$ and depth one.

Step 2: An interval, say, Z, of length t_{i-1}, $1 \le i \le k$, is divided into $n_i = \dfrac{t_{i-1}}{t_i}$ subintervals, each of length t_i. Let $z_1, z_2, \cdots, z_{n_i}$ be the AND of the input variables in each of these n_i subintervals computed in Step 1. For each interval of length t_{i-1}, $1 \le i \le k$, inductively compute in parallel the subinterval prefixes

$$z_1, \quad z_1 z_2, \quad z_1 z_2 z_3, \quad \cdots \quad , \quad z_1 z_2 \cdots z_{n_i}$$

using prefix circuits of depth $2m$ and size $O(n_i\, A_m^{-1}(n_i))$. Recall that the constant of proportionality in this asymptotic size bound is linear in the depth $2m$.

For the $n_0 = 1$ interval of length $t_0 = N$, the size of the subinterval prefix circuit is

$$O(n_1\, A_m^{-1}(n_1)) = O\left(\frac{N}{t_1} A_m^{-1}\left(\frac{N}{t_1}\right)\right)$$

$$\le O\left(\frac{N}{A_m^{-1}(N)}\, A_m^{-1}(N)\right) \quad \text{(from the definition of } t_i)$$

$$= O(N).$$

The subinterval prefix circuit for an interval of length t_{i-1}, for $1 \le i \le k-1$ is of size

$$O\left(\frac{t_{i-1}}{t_i} A_m^{-1}\left(\frac{t_{i-1}}{t_i}\right)\right) \le O\left(\frac{t_{i-1}}{A_m^{-1}(t_{i-1})} \cdot A_m^{-1}(t_{i-1})\right) = O(t_{i-1}).$$

Summing this over $n_1, n_2, \cdots, n_{t_{i-1}} = \dfrac{N}{t_{i-1}}$ intervals, we get a size of

$O(N)$ for this type of intervals. Since there are $k = A_{m+1}^{-1}(N)$ interval lengths, this step requires a size of $O(NA_{m+1}^{-1}(N))$ and depth $2m$.

Step 3: Compute each of the prefixes as the *AND* of, at most, $A_{m+1}^{-1}(N)$ subinterval prefixes.

Clearly, this step requires a depth of one and a total size of $O(NA_{m+1}^{-1}(N))$.

The circuit resulting from this construction has a depth $(2m + 2)$ and overall size of $O(NA_{m+1}^{-1}(N))$, where the constant of proportionality is linear in $2(m + 1)$, and the theorem is proved.

While the above construction is cast using the *AND* operation, it applies to *OR* and other similar associative binary operations.

Thus far, our analysis has centered around depth-size trade-off in unbounded fan-in circuits of constant depth. It turns out that by letting the depth to grow very slowly we can obtain linear size circuits. To this end, given N find the minimum m such that

$$A_m(m) \geq N \tag{6}$$

that is, $A_m^{-1}(N) = m = A_\omega^{-1}(N)$. Let $k = m^2$. We now describe a method for the design of linear size circuits.

Divide the N inputs into $n = \dfrac{N}{k}$ consecutive intervals of length k.

Step 1: Compute z_i, the *AND* of the k input variables in the ith interval, for $1 \leq i \leq n$, using one *AND* gate of size k. This requires a total size of N. Then compute the subinterval prefixes

$$z_1, \; z_1 z_2, \; z_1 z_2 z_3, \; \cdots \; , z_1 z_2 \cdots z_n$$

using the prefix circuit of depth $2m$ and size $c\,m\,n\,A_m^{-1}(n)$ (refer to Theorem 3). Since $n = \dfrac{N}{m^2}$, combining it with (6) we get

$$c\,m\,n\,A_m^{-1}(N) \leq cN.$$

Combining these, it follows that this step requires a depth of $(2m + 1)$ and size $O(N)$.

Step 2: Now, compute the prefix of the input in each of the intervals of size using the prefix circuits of size $O(k) = O(m^2)$ and depth $O(\log k) = O(\log m)$ described in Chapter 6 (such as Ladner-Fischer or Snir or LYD circuits).

Step 3: Compute each of the required prefixes as the *AND* of a subinterval prefix in Step 1 and a prefix from an interval in Step 2. Clearly, this computation requires a size $O(N)$ and constant depth of one.

Summing all the sizes, the overall circuit is of size $O(N)$. Total depth is given by

$$2m + 1 + O(\log m) + 1 = O(m) = O(A_\omega^{-1}(N)).$$

We conclude this Section by summarizing the above result.

Theorem 4. There are circuits of size $O(N)$ and depth $O(A_\omega^{-1}(N))$ for computing the prefix of *AND* of N inputs.

8.3 Small Circuits For Binary Addition

In this Section, we extend the above construction of small circuits to semigroup products of interest in binary addition. Let, $a = a_N\, a_{N-1}\, \cdots\, a_2\, a_1$ and $b = b_N\, b_{N-1}\, \cdots\, b_2\, b_1$ be two binary N-bit integers to be added. As shown in Section 1.2.2 and in Example 7 of Appendix A, the computation of carry can be reduced to that of prefixes in a properly chosen semigroup. To this end, define

$$x_i = \begin{cases} s & \text{if } a_i = b_i = 1 \\ p & \text{if } a_i \neq b_i \\ r & \text{if } a_i = b_i = 0, \end{cases} \tag{1}$$

for $1 \leq i \leq N$. The *carry semigroup* (S, α), with $S = \{s, p, r\}$ and $\alpha(y, z) = yz$ is defined by

$$ys = s; \qquad yr = r \qquad yp = y$$

for all $y \in S$. It can be verified that there is a carry bit into the $(k + 1)^{th}$ position exactly when the prefix (product)

$$x_1\, x_2\, \cdots\, x_k = s. \tag{2}$$

In this Section, we describe an algorithm for the design of small circuits with unbounded fan-in for computing the prefixes $x_1\, x_2\, \cdots\, x_k$, for $1 \leq k \leq N$.

From (1), it follows that p is the *right* identity and s and r are the *right zeros*. (Refer to Appendix A for the definitions of right/left zero and identity.) Thus, the value of the product $x_1\, x_2\, \cdots\, x_k$ is either the last s or the r to appear or p if there is no occurrence of s and r. Let

$< i : j > = \{i, i+1, \cdots, j\}$, for $i \leq j$. From this, we obtain that, for $1 \leq k \leq N$

$$x_1 \, x_2 \, \cdots \, x_k = s$$

exactly when

$$C(< 1 : k >, s) = \bigvee_{i \in < 1 : k >} [(x_i = s) \wedge \{ \bigwedge_{j \in < i+1 : k >} (x_j = p)\}] \tag{3}$$

is true. The following result can be easily verified (Exercise 8.5).

Lemma 1. $C(< 1 : k >, s)$ can be computed using depth two circuits of size $O(k^2)$.

For $i \leq k$, let

$$C(< i : k >, p) = \bigwedge_{j \in < i : k >} (x_j = p). \tag{4}$$

Using (4), the expression on the right hand side of (3) can be rewritten as

$$C(< 1 : k >, s) = \bigvee_{i \in < 1 : k >} [(x_i = s) \wedge C(< i+1 : k >, p)]. \tag{5}$$

In fact, $C(< i+1 : k >, p)$ are suffixes and can be computed using the obvious modification of small circuits for computing prefixes described in Section 8.2. In the following, we develop small circuits for computing $C(< 1 : k >, s)$. The following Lemma is readily verified (Exercise 8.5), and constitutes the basis for much of the discussion below.

Lemma 2. For $i < k$, let $< i : k >$ be expressed as the concatenation of q subintervals, that is, $< i : j > = J_1 \cup J_2 \cup \cdots \cup J_q$. Then,

$$C(< i : k >, s) = \bigvee_{j=1}^{q} [C(J_j, s) \wedge \{ \bigwedge_{h=j+1}^{q} C(J_h, p)\}].$$

Let $N = 2^n$ and consider a system of principal intervals leading to Lemma 1 of Section 8.2. Let I_{ij} be the jth principal interval at level i. Then, for $0 \leq i \leq n$,

$$I_{ij} = \; < (j-1)2^{n-i} + 1 \; ; \; j2^{n-i} > , \quad 1 \leq j \leq 2^i.$$

Step 1: Compute $C(I_{ij}, p)$, for $1 \leq j \leq 2^i$, and $1 \leq i \leq n$ in parallel using (unbounded fan-in) circuit of size $O(N \log N)$ and depth one. (This is the same as Step 1 leading to Lemma 1 of Section 8.2.)

Step 2: Compute $C(I_{ij}, s)$, for all $1 \leq j \leq 2^i$ and $0 \leq i \leq n-1$ in parallel, where

$$C(I_{ij}, s) = \bigvee_{t \in I_{ij}} [(x_t = s) \wedge \{C(<t+1 : j2^{n-i}>, p)\}]. \tag{6}$$

Since $|<t+1 : j2^{n-i}>| \leq 2^{n-i}$, for each t, from Exercise 8.2, this interval can be expressed as the concatenation of at most $(n-i)$ principal intervals. Let

$$<t+1 : j2^{n-i}> = J_1 \bigcup J_2 \bigcup J_3 \bigcup \cdots \bigcup J_{m_t}, \quad m_t < n-i.$$

Then

$$C(<t+1 : j2^{n-i}>, p) = \bigwedge_{r=1}^{m_t} C(J_r, p), \tag{7}$$

where $C(J_r, p)$ is computed in Step 1. Clearly, the computation of

$$[(x_t = s) \wedge \{\bigwedge_{r=1}^{m_t} C(J_r, p)\}]$$

for each t requires a depth one and size $(1 + m_t)$. The *OR* of this quantity, for $t \in I_{ij}$, requires an extra depth one and size 2^{n-i}. Thus, the expression (6) requires depth two and size

$$2^{n-i} + 2^{n-i}(1 + m_t) \leq 2^{n-i}(n-i+2).$$

Summing this over all of the principal intervals, we obtain

$$\text{size} \leq \sum_{i=0}^{n-1} 2^i \times 2^{n-i}(n-i+2)$$

$$= N \sum_{i=0}^{n-1} (n-i+2)$$

$$= O(N(\log N)^2).$$

The primary reason for this increased size is that the right-hand-side of (6) requires all of the suffixes of each of the principal intervals. In the usual prefix/suffix computation, we normally do not compute all the prefixes/suffixes of each subinterval as required here.

Step 3: Compute $C(<1:k>, s)$, for $1 \le k \le N$. Recall that $<1:k>$ is the union of, at most, $\log N$ principal intervals. Let

$$<1:k> = J_1 \cup J_2 \cup J_3 \cup \cdots \cup J_{m_k}, \quad m_k \le \log N.$$

Then (from Lemma 2)

$$C(<1:k>, s) = \bigvee_{t=1}^{m_k} [C(J_t, s) \wedge \{ \bigwedge_{r=t+1}^{m_k} C(J_r, p)\}]. \tag{8}$$

This computation requires a depth of two and size of $(1 + 2m_k) \le (1 + 2\log N)$. Summing this over all k, $1 \le k \le N$, it follows that this step requires depth two and size $O((\log N)^2)$.

Combining these, we obtain

Lemma 3. $C(<1:k>, s)$, for $1 \le k \le N$ can be computed using unbounded fan-in circuits of depth five and size $O(N(\log N)^2)$.

It must be kept in mind that the computation of $C(<1:k>, s))$ in Steps 2 and 3 together requires a depth four. This fact will be used in the inductive proof of Theorem 4 below.

Note that the algorithm leading to this Lemma is quite similar to the one leading to Lemma 1 of Section 8.2. Thus, following the developments in Section 8.2, we now generalize this algorithm. To this end, define a tree of nested intervals as follows. Let $t_0 = N$, and define

$$t_i = [A_m^{-1}(t_{i-1})]^2, \quad \text{for } i > 0$$

Let r be an integer, such that, $t_r = 2$. While it is obvious that $t_{i+1} \ge A_m^{-1}(t_i)$, it can be shown that (see Exercise 8.6)

$$t_{i+1} \ge A_m^{-1}(t_i) \ge t_{i+2}. \tag{9}$$

Iterating the second inequality, we obtain

$$2 = t_r \le A_m^{-1}(t_{r-2})$$

$$\le A_m^{-1}(A_m^{-1}(t_{r-4}))$$

$$\le A_m^{-1}(A_m^{-1} \cdots (A_m^{-1}(t_0) \cdots) = A_m^{(-r/2)}(t_0).$$

That is,

$$A_m^{(r/2)}(2) = A_{m+1}(\frac{r}{2}) \leq N$$

and

$$r \leq 2A_{m+1}^{-1}(N). \tag{10}$$

Now, given m, N and r, define a tree of nested intervals as follows. At the root level, there is $n_0 = 1$ interval I_{01} of length $t_0 = N$. In going from level $(i - 1)$ to i, divide each subinterval of length t_{i-1} into $n_i = \dfrac{t_{i-1}}{t_i}$ intervals of length t_i. Thus, at level i, $0 \leq i \leq r$, there are I_{ij}, $1 \leq j \leq n_1 n_2 \cdots n_i = \dfrac{N}{t_i}$ intervals each of length t_i, where

$$I_{ij} = \; < (j - 1)t_i + 1 : jt_i > , \quad |I_{ij}| = t_i.$$

With these preliminaries, we now state one of the principal results of this Section.

Theorem 4. $C(< 1 : k >, s)$, for $1 \leq k \leq N$, can be computed using unbounded fan-in circuits of depth, at most, $6m$ and size $O(N(A_m^{-1}(N))^2)$, for $m \geq 1$.

Proof: The proof is by induction on m. For $m = 1$, Lemma 1 provides the basis. Assume that for each N, circuits of size $O(N(A_m^{-1}(N))^2)$ and depth $6m$ exist for computing $C(< 1 : k >, s)$, for $1 \leq k \leq N$. The required circuit is computed as follows.

Step 1: Compute $C(I_{ij}, p)$, for $1 \leq j \leq n_1 n_2 \cdots n_i = \dfrac{N}{t_i}$, and, for $1 \leq i \leq r$, in parallel. Each of the $C(I_{ij}, p)$ takes one *AND* gate (hence, depth one) of size t_i. Summing this over all j's and i's gives a total size of $O(NA_{m+1}^{-1}(N))$. Now, compute $C(< h + 1 : jt_i >, p)$, for $h \in I_{ij}$, in parallel. This corresponds to computation of all *suffixes* corresponding to indices in I_{ij}. These suffixes can be computed using an obvious modification of the circuits in Theorem 3 of Section 8.2. Computation of the suffixes in I_{ij} requires a size of $O(t_i A_{m+1}^{-1}(t_i))$ and depth $2m + 1$. Summing this over all the $\dfrac{N}{t_i}$ values of j, we get the size for a given i to be

$$\frac{N}{t_i} \, O(t_i A_{m+1}^{-1}(t_i)) = O(NA_{m+1}^{-1}(N)).$$

Summing this term over all i's gives a size of $O(N(A_{m+1}^{-1}(N))^2)$.

Thus, computation of $C(I_{ij}, p)$ and all the suffixes requires a total size of $O(N(A_{m+1}^{-1}(N))^2)$ and depth $(2m + 2)$. As observed in Step 2 leading to Lemma 3, this increased size results from the computation of all suffixes of all intervals.

Step 2: Compute $C(I_{ij}, s)$ using

$$C(I_{ij}, s) = \bigvee_{h \in I_{ij}} [(x_h = s) \wedge C(< h + 1 : jt_i > , p)].$$

Since $C(< h + 1 : jt_i > , p)$ is available from Step 1, this computation requires a depth of two and a size $O(t_i)$. Summing this over all j's and i's gives a total size of $O(NA_{m+1}^{-1}(N))$.

Step 3: Let Z be an interval of length t_{i-1} divided into subintervals $z_1, z_2, \cdots, z_{n_i}$, each of length t_i, where $n_i = \dfrac{t_{i-1}}{t_i}$, and, $1 \le i \le r$. Compute $C(Z, s)$ *inductively* using the values of $C(z_i, p)$ computed in Step 1, and $C(z_i, s)$ computed in Step 2. The size of this circuit for this interval Z is given by

$$O((\frac{t_{i-1}}{t_i})(A_m^{-1}(\frac{t_{i-1}}{t_i}))^2) \le O(\frac{t_{i-1}}{(A_m^{-1}(t_{i-1}))^2} (A_m^{-1}(t_{i-1}))^2) \quad \text{(definition of } t_i)$$

$$= O(t_{i-1}).$$

Summing this over all j's and i's gives a total size of $O(NA_{m+1}^{-1}(N))$. Inductively this part requires a depth of $4m$.

Step 4: Compute $C(< 1 : k >, s)$ for $1 \le k \le N$. Recall that $< 1 : k >$ is the concatenation of subintervals, say, $J_1, J_2, \cdots, J_q$, where $q \le 2A_{m+1}^{-1}(N)$. Then, compute (from Lemma 2)

$$C(< 1 : k >, s) = \bigvee_{i = 1}^{q_k} [C(J_i, s) \wedge \{ \bigwedge_{j = i+1}^{q_k} C(J_j, p)\}]$$

using a circuit of size $(A_{m+1}^{-1}(N))^2$ and *depth two* (see Lemma 1). Thus, for all $1 \le k \le n$, this requires a total size of $O(N(A_{m+1}^{-1}(N))^2)$.

The sum of all the sizes in all the Steps is $O(N(A_{m+1}^{-1}(N))^2)$. As for the overall depth, the computation of Step 1 requires a depth of $(2m + 2)$. Computations in Step 2, 3 and 4 require a depth of $4m + 4$. Since the Steps 2, 3, and 4 depend on results of Step 1, the overall depth is the sum given by $6(m + 1)$. Hence, the Theorem.

The following Corollary is immediate.

Corollary 5. For any m, there exist unbounded fan-in circuits of size $O(N(A_{m+1}^{-1}(N))^2)$, and depth $6m + 3$ for computing the sum of two N-bit binary integers.

Proof: Let $a = a_N a_{N-1} \cdots a_2 a_1$ and $b = b_N b_{N-1} \cdots b_2 b_1$ be two N-bit binary integers. Let $s = s_{N+1} s_N \cdots s_2 s_1$ be the sum. Then

$$s_i = a_i \oplus b_i \oplus c_{i-1},$$

where c_{i-1} is the carry bit into the ith position. Clearly, $c_{i-1} = 1$ if, and only if, $x_1 x_2 \cdots x_{i-1} = s$ and x_i's are defined in (1).

Computation of x_i's using (1) takes size $O(N)$ and depth one. $a_i \oplus b_i$, for $1 \le i \le N$ can be computed in size $O(N)$ while c_i's are being computed. Now once c_i's are available, $(a_i \oplus b_i) \oplus c_{i-1}$ can be computed using circuit of size $O(N)$ and an additional depth of two. Combining this with Theorem 4, the corollary follows.

Thus far, our analysis has centered around constant depth circuits. It turns out that by letting the depth vary very slowly, we can indeed obtain linear size circuits for computing $C(<1:r>, s)$ and $C(<1:r>, p)$, for $1 \le r \le N$. Given N, let m be the smallest integer, such that

$$A_m(m) \ge N \tag{11}$$

that is, $m = A_m^{-1}(N) = A_\omega^{-1}(N)$. Let $k = m^3$ and divide the N inputs into $n = \dfrac{N}{k}$ intervals, each of length k. Using these parameters, we obtain the following analogue of Theorem 4 of Section 8.2, whose proof is left as an Exercise.

Theorem 6. $C(<1:r>, p)$ and $C(<1:r>, s)$, for $1 \le r \le s$ can be computed using circuits of size $O(N)$ and depth $O(A_\omega^{-1}(N))$.

The following Corollary is immediate.

Corollary 7. There exist unbounded fan-in circuits of linear size and depth $O(A_\omega^{-1}(N))$ for binary addition.

Bounded fan-in circuits for binary addition require a depth of $\lceil \log_2 N \rceil + 0.5(\lceil 2 \log_2 N \rceil)^{1/2} + L$ and size $O(N \log N)$, for some small constant $L \leq 4$, using Brent's adder (Brent [1970]) or require a depth of $\lceil \log N \rceil + 7(\lceil 2 \log N \rceil)^{1/2} + 16$ and size of nearly $9N$ using the Krapchenko adder (Krapchenko [1970]).

We conclude this Section with a discussion of the optimality of these circuits. A circuit is said to be *synchronous* if all paths between input and output have the same length. The following theorem provides the lower bound on the size.

Theorem 8. (a) A circuit for computing $C(<1:k>, p)$ and $C(<1:k>, s)$, $1 \leq k \leq N$ of depth $2m$ has size at least $\Omega(NA_m^{-1}(N))$.

(b) Any synchronous circuit for computing the same quantities requires a size of at least $\Omega(NA_m^{-1}(N))$.

The proof of these results depends on the lower bound on the size of a class of graphs called weak superconcentrators and is beyond our scope. For details, refer to Chandra, Fortune, and Lipton [1983][1982], and Dolev, Dwork, Pippenger, and Wigderson [1983]. Also, refer to Pippenger [1990].

8.4 Small Circuits And Group-Free Semigroups

Let $\mathbf{S}$ be a group-free semigroup. For $a, b \in \mathbf{S}$, the associative binary operation (called product) on $\mathbf{S}$ is denoted by ab. Let $q \in \mathbf{S}$ and $x_1 x_2 \cdots x_N$ be a word of length N over $\mathbf{S}$, that is, $x_i \in \mathbf{S}$, for $1 \leq i \leq N$. Let

$$\mathbf{L}(q, \mathbf{S}) = \{x_1 x_2 \cdots x_N \mid x_1 x_2 \cdots x_N = q \quad \text{for} \quad N \geq 1\},$$

that is, $\mathbf{L}(q, \mathbf{S})$ is the set of all words over $\mathbf{S}$ each of whose product evaluates to q. By exploiting the strong interrelation between group-free semigroups, non-counting regular events, star-free regular expressions and a class of machines called **RS**-machines, it is shown in Appendix B that there exist unbounded fan-in constant depth circuits of size $O(N^3)$ for deciding whether a string $x_1 x_2 \cdots x_N$ belongs to $\mathbf{L}(q, \mathbf{S})$. (Refer to Theorem 4 in Appendix B.) Following the developments in Section 8.3, we now present an improved version of Theorem 4 in Appendix B.

Theorem 1. Let **M** be an **RS**-machine with k flip-flops. Then, for any m, there exist unbounded fan-in circuits of depth $k(6m+3)+3$ and size $O(N(A_{m-1}(N))^2)$ which decides whether a string $x_1 x_2 \cdots x_N$ belongs to **L(M)**.

Proof: From Theorem 4 of Appendix B, it is sufficient to compute $F_i^{(t)}$ using small circuits, for $1 \le i \le k$, (k fixed), and $1 \le t \le N$. Recall from Appendix B that

$$F_i^{(t)} = \bigvee_{j=0}^{t} [\alpha_j \wedge (\bigwedge_{p=j+1}^{t} \beta_p)]. \tag{1}$$

Structurally, this expression is the same as that for $C(<1:k>, s)$ given in equation (3) of Section 8.3. Hence, by Theorem 4 of Section 8.3, $F_i^{(t)}$, for each i, can be computed by unbounded fan-in circuits of depth $6m$ and size $O(N(A_{m-1}(N))^2)$. Since $F_i^{(t)}$ is computed serially, for $1 \le i \le k$ and k is fixed, computation of $F_i^{(t)}$, for $1 \le t \le N$ and $1 \le i \le k$ requires a depth of $6km$ and a size of $O(N(A_{m-1}(N))^2)$.

It can be verified that the computation of α_j, and β_j, for each $1 \le j \le k$ requires a circuit of depth 3 and size $O(N)$.

Finally, given the state $F_i^{(N)}$, for $1 \le i \le N$, to check if it is an accepting configuration requires a circuit of depth 3 and constant size. Combining these, the Theorem follows.

We conclude this Section by stating a result which is an analogue of Theorem 4 of Section 8.2, and Theorem 6 of Section 8.3, whose proof is left as an Exercise.

Theorem 2. For any **RS**-machine **M**, there exist circuits of size $O(N)$ and depth $O(A_\omega^{-1}(N))$ that recognize **L(M)**).

This is paramount to saying that any associative function can be computed using linear sized circuits of depth proportional to $A_\omega^{-1}(N)$.

8.5 Exercises

8.1   Show that z^k can be computed using 2 processors in $\lceil \log k \rceil$ steps.

        Hint: Let $k = b_r b_{r-1} \cdots b_2 b_1$ in binary. One of the two processors computes $z^2, z^4, z^8, \cdots, z^{2^r}$, while the other processor accumulates the product of appropriate powers of z corresponding to the 1 bit in the binary expansion of k. Thus, z^k can be computed by circuits of *size* $O(\log k)$ and *depth* $O(\log k)$.

8.2   Show that $[1, j]$, for any $1 \le j \le N$, can be expressed as the sum of at most $\log N$ principal intervals.

8.3   Show that any prefix $x_1 \wedge x_2 \wedge \cdots \wedge x_j$, can be obtained as the *AND* of at most $\log^* N$ subinterval prefixes, where $1 \le j \le N$.

8.4   If $g(n)$ is a monotonically increasing function, then define the *inverse $g^{-1}(N)$ as*

$$g^{-1}(N) = \min_{x}\{x \mid g(x) \ge n\}.$$

        Verify that $\log^* n$ is the inverse of the repeated exponentiation, that is, if $f(k) = N$ then $\log^* N = k$ for $N \ge 2$.

8.5   Verify Lemmas 1 and 2 of Section 8.3.

8.6   Let $f(x)$ be a strictly monotonically increasing function increasing faster than x^2. Define a sequence with $t_0 = N$, and

$$t_i = [f^{-1}(t_{i-1})]^2 \quad \text{for } i > 0.$$

        (a) For $N = e^{20}$, compute the sequence t_0, t_1, t_2, t_3, t_4, and t_5, when $f(x) = e^x$. Find the range of values of i, for which the inequality

$$t_{i+1} \ge f^{-1}(t_i) \ge t_{i+2} \tag{*}$$

        holds.

        Hint: If $f^{-1}(t_i) = x$, then $t_{i+1} = x^2$, and $t_{i+2} = 4(\log_e x)^2$.

        (b) Plot e^x, x^2 and x and graphically verify the results in (a).

        (c) Prove the inequality (*) when $f(n) = A_m(n)$, the Ackermann's function.

8.6 Notes And References

Sections 8.1–8.4: This Chapter is patterned after Chandra, Fortune, and Lipton [1983]. The relations between star-free regular expressions, group-free semigroups and *RS*-machines are developed in the monograph by McNaughton and Pappert [1971].

Lemma 2 of Section 8.1 on the non-existence of polynomial size circuits of constant depth for computing parity is now classic. A proof of this result is contained in Appendix C. Analysis and relation among the complexity of computing many functions, such as, parity and threshold, among others, using constant depth circuits are contained in Furst, Saxe, and Sipser [1984], Chandra, Stockmeyer, and Vishkin [1984], and Håstad [1987].

Appendices

Appendix A

Semigroups And Monoids

Since semigroup constitutes the proper mathematical system for the analysis of the prefix problem, to render our exposition self-contained, in this Appendix we provide a summary of the properties of two related systems of *binary algebra,* namely *semigroup* and *monoid.* However, the reader is advised that many of these properties are used only in Chapter 8. To save space, we merely state the properties without proof.

A1. Definitions and Properties

A *binary* operation α on a set $\mathbf{X}$ is a function

$$\alpha : \mathbf{X} \times \mathbf{X} \to \mathbf{X}$$

and $\alpha(x, y)$ is called the *result* or *value* in $\mathbf{X}$. In general, such an operation is *not commutative,* that is

$$\alpha(x, y) \neq \alpha(y, x),$$

nor *associative,* that is

$$\alpha(x,\ \alpha(y,\ z)) \neq \alpha(\alpha(x,\ y),\ z).$$

The operation α is normally called the *product,* and is denoted by $\alpha(x,\ y) \equiv xy$ when convenient.

Example 1. $X =$ set of all $n \times n$ matrices and α is matrix addition. Then, α is both commutative and associative.

Example 2. $X =$ set of all $n \times n$ matrices and α is matrix multiplication. Then, α is associative but not commutative.

Example 3. $X =$ set of all real numbers and α is subtraction. Then, α is neither associative nor commutative.

A set X along with a binary operation α on it constitutes a *binary algebra* and is denoted by $<X, \alpha>$. The structure and properties of a binary algebra are very much dependent on those of the binary operation. It turns out that associativity is the least restrictive of the properties one can require of this binary operation.

A binary algebra $<X, \alpha>$ with an added constraint that α be *associative* is called a *semigroup.* In addition, if the operation α is also commutative, then it is called a *commutative semigroup.* The number of elements, $|\,X\,|$, in X is called the *order* of the semigroup.

Example 4. $S = \{0,\ 1\}$ with logical *OR* (denoted by $\vee$) and defined by

$\vee$	0	1
0	0	1
1	1	1

is a commutative semigroup. The computation logical *OR* of n bits is based on this semigroup.

Example 5. Let $Z_n = \{0,\ 1,\ 2,\ \cdots,\ n - 1\}$, and $\times_n$ and $+_n$ denote the multiplication of integers mod n and the addition of integers mod n, respectively. It can be verified that $<Z_n,\ +_n>$ and $<Z_n,\ \times_n>$ are both commutative semigroups. As an example,

$<\mathbf{Z}_4, +_4>$ $<\mathbf{Z}_4, \times_4>$

$+_n$	0	1	2	3
0	0	1	2	3
1	1	2	3	0
2	2	3	0	1
3	3	0	1	2

$\times_n$	0	1	2	3
0	0	0	0	0
1	0	1	2	3
2	0	2	0	2
3	0	3	2	1

Clearly, $<\mathbf{Z}_2, +_2>$ is the well-known *exclusive OR* or *mod 2 sum* or *parity* semigroup.

Example 6. Let $S = \{0, 1, 2, \cdots, n\}$, and $\alpha : S \times S \to S$ is, such that

$$\alpha(i, j) = \min\{i + j, n\}.$$

$<S, \alpha>$ is called the *threshold-n addition* semigroup and α is commutative.

Example 7. Consider a three element set, $S = \{s, r, p\}$, with an associative binary operation, $\alpha(x, y), \equiv xy$ defined as follows:

x	y		
	s	r	p
s	s	r	s
r	s	r	r
p	s	r	p

It can be verified that $<S, \alpha>$ is a non-commutative semigroup.

The computation of the carry bits arising in the addition of two n-bit binary integers (refer to Section 1.2.2) can be reformulated as a semigroup product as follows. For each i,

$$x_i = \begin{cases} s & \text{if } a_i = b_i = 1 \\ p & \text{if } a_i \neq b_i \\ r & \text{if } a_i = b_i = 0. \end{cases}$$

Accordingly, s may be thought of as *set carry*, p as *propagate carry if it exists,* and r is *reset carry.* It can be verified that there is a carry into the $(i + 1)^{th}$ bit exactly when the semigroup product $x_1 x_2 \cdots x_i$ is equal to s.

As an example, let

$$a = a_5 a_4 a_3 a_2 a_1 = 1\,0\,1\,1\,1$$

and

$$b = b_5 b_4 b_3 b_2 b_1 = 1\,0\,1\,1\,0.$$

Then

$$x_1 = p \qquad x_2 = s \qquad x_3 = s \qquad x_4 = r \qquad x_5 = s.$$

Clearly, $c_0 = 0$, and it can be verified that

$$
\begin{aligned}
x_1 &= p, & c_1 &= 0 \\
x_1 x_2 &= s, & c_2 &= 1 \\
x_1 x_2 x_3 &= s, & c_3 &= 1 \\
x_1 x_2 x_3 x_4 &= r, & c_4 &= 0 \\
x_1 x_2 x_3 x_4 x_5 &= s, & c_5 &= 1
\end{aligned}
$$

This semigroup is called *set-reset semigroup* or *carry semigroup.*

Let $<\mathbf{S}, \alpha>$ be a semigroup. An element $e_l \in \mathbf{S}$, such that

$$\alpha(e_l, x) \equiv e_l x = x \quad \textit{for all } x \in \mathbf{S}$$

is called the *left identity.* Similarly, a *right identity* can be defined.

An element $e \in \mathbf{S}$, such that

$$\alpha(e, x) = \alpha(x, e) = x \ \forall \ x \in \mathbf{S}$$

is called a *two-sided identity* or simply *an identity* (which is both left and right identity).

A semigroup $<\mathbf{S}, \alpha>$, with an *identity* is called a *monoid.* If α is commutative, it is called *commutative monoid.*

The logical-*OR* semigroup in Example 4 is a monoid with identity 0. The $<\mathbf{Z}_n, +_4>$ semigroup in Example 5 is a monoid with identity 0, and the $<\mathbf{Z}_n, \times_4>$ is a monoid with 1 as an identity. The threshold-n addition semigroup in Example 6 is a monoid with identity 0. The semigroup in Example 7 is a monoid with the symbol p as the identity.

The following results can be readily established (Birkoff and Bartee [1970]).

Property 1. If a binary algebra $<\mathbf{X}, \alpha>$ is, such that, it has a left and a right identity, then each of these is unique and both of them are equal to the same identity.

It follows from this that a *monoid can have only one identity.*

Property 2. Any semigroup $<S, \alpha>$ can be extended to a monoid by adjoining an identity element.

Let $<X, \alpha>$ be a binary algebra. An element $\theta_l \in X$, such that

$$\alpha(\theta_l, x) = \theta_l, \quad \forall \ x \in X,$$

is called the *left zero.* The *right zero* θ_r can likewise be defined. An element $\theta \in X$, such that

$$\alpha(\theta, x) = \alpha(x, \theta) = \theta, \quad \forall \ x \in X,$$

is called the *zero* element. The following analogue of Property 1 holds.

Property 3. If a binary algebra $<X, \alpha>$ is, such that, it has a left and a right zero, then each of these is unique and both of them are equal to the same zero.

Referring to Example 5, it can be verified that, $<Z_n, +_n>$ has no zero element and 0 is the zero element for $<Z_n, \times_n>$. In the carry semigroup of Example 7, both s and r are the right zeros but there are no left zeros, and hence, no zero element.

We now list several of the other semigroups of interest.

Example 8. Let Σ be a finite alphabet and α denote the usual concatenation or juxtaposition operation. The set of all strings of finite length denoted by Σ^* along with the concatenation operation constitutes a *non-commutative monoid* with Λ, the *null-string* as the identity. Clearly, this monoid has no zero element. This is often called the *free monoid* generated by Σ.

Example 9. Let X be a set and X^X denote the set of all functions $f : X \rightarrow X$. (Recall that a function is a *unary* operation, much like the *sign change* or the *negation* operation). Define the operation of (left) composition as

$$f \circ g(x) = f(g(x)).$$

It can be verified that $(X^X, \circ)$ is a non-commutative monoid with the identity $e : X \rightarrow X$, such that, $e(x) = x$, for all x, as the identity element.

As an example, consider $X = \{0, 1\}$. Then X^X has four functions given by

Functions	0	1
e	0	1
f_1	1	0
f_2	0	0
f_3	1	1

The monoid (X^X, o) for this example may be described using the following table:

o	e	f_1	f_2	f_3
e	e	f_1	f_2	f_3
f_1	f_1	e	f_3	f_2
f_2	f_2	f_2	f_2	f_2
f_3	f_3	f_3	f_3	f_3

Clearly, f_2 and f_3 are the left zero's for the left composition.

We invite the reader to verify that (X^X, Δ), where Δ is the right composition defined as

$$f \Delta g(x) = g(f(x)),$$

is also a non-commutative monoid.

Example 10. Let **A** be a set, and $\mathcal{P}(\mathbf{A})$ denote the power set which is a set of all subsets of **A**. If $\cup$ and $\cap$ denote the usual set *union* and *intersection* operations, then $< \mathcal{P}(\mathbf{A}), \cup >$ is a commutative monoid with **A** as the zero, and $\varnothing$, the null set, as the identity. Likewise, $< \mathcal{P}(\mathbf{A}), \cap >$ is a commutative monoid with **A** as the identity and $\varnothing$ as the zero element.

Example 11. Given a set **X**, let $\mathcal{R}(\mathbf{X})$ denote the set of all *binary relations* on **X**. Define the product of two relations $a, b \in \mathcal{R}(\mathbf{X})$ as follows. For any $x, y \in \mathbf{X}$

$$x(ab)y, \quad \text{if and only if,} \quad xaz \text{ and } zby$$

for some $z \in \mathbf{X}$. It can be verified that $\mathcal{R}(\mathbf{X})$ under this product is a non-commutative monoid with the *identity* relation as the identity and the *null* relation as the zero element.

Example 12. Let **X** be a set of numbers and MIN and MAX denote the usual minimum and the maximum operations, respectively. It can be verified that <**X**, MIN> and <**X**, MAX> are semigroups. We invite the reader to identify the identity and the zero elements for this semigroup.

Let <**X**, α> be a monoid, with α denoting the *product* $\alpha(x, y) = xy$. Given $x \in$ **X**, define the powers of x as follows. For any integer n

$$x^{n+1} = x^n x,$$

where $x^0 = e$, the identity of the monoid, and $x^1 = x$. A monoid is called *cyclic* if all of its elements can be obtained as the powers of some one of its elements, say, a. Such a monoid is said to be *generated* by a. Since

$$x^k x^n = x^{k+n} = x^n x^k,$$

a cyclic monoid is commutative.

Example 13. The set **N** of all non-negative integers under the operation of integer addition is a cyclic monoid generated by 1, with the number 0 (zero) as the identity. It can be verified that this monoid has no zero element. But the same set **N**, of all non-negative integers under the multiplication operation is a non-cyclic monoid with 1 as an identity and 0 as zero.

If the powers x^k are all distinct, then it is an infinite cyclic monoid. Every infinite cyclic monoid is *isomorphic* to <**N**, +>. If the powers x^k are not all distinct, then there exists a least integer $t > 0$, such that, for some $0 \le m < t$, we have $x^t = x^m$. Such a t is called the *order* of the finite monoid <**M**$_{m,n}$, α>, where $n = t - m$,

$$\mathbf{M} = \{1, x, x^2, \cdots, x^{t-1}\}$$

$$\alpha(x^i, x^j) = x^{\phi(i, j)}$$

with

$$\phi(i, j) = i + j - kn$$

and

$$k = \left\lceil \frac{i + j - t}{n} \right\rceil.$$

This type of cyclic monoids can be graphically represented as in Figure 1.

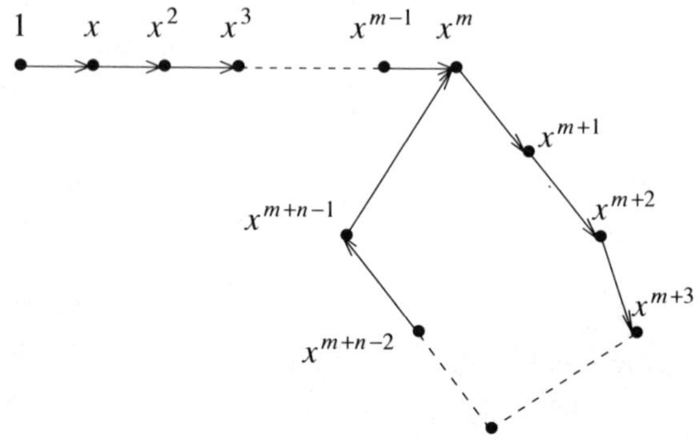

Figure 1. Graphical representation of a cyclic monoid.

It follows from the above argument that every finite cyclic monoid is isomorphic to $<\mathbf{M}_{m,n}, \alpha>$, for some m and n.

If x is an element of a semigroup $<\mathbf{X}, \alpha>$, such that, $\alpha(x, x) = x^2 = x$, then x is called an *idempotent*. Clearly, the identity is always an idempotent.

Property 4. In any finite cyclic monoid $<\mathbf{M}_{m,n}, \alpha>$, there are two idempotents, namely, the identity and x^n, if $m \neq 0$, and identity is the only idempotent if $m = 0$.

Property 5. In a finite cyclic monoid $<\mathbf{M}_{m,n}, \alpha>$, for each element x there exists an integer $k > 0$, such that, x^k is an idempotent.

Given a monoid $<\mathbf{X}, \alpha>$ with identity e, let $\mathbf{S} \subseteq \mathbf{X}$, such that

(a) $e \in \mathbf{S}$

(b) $\alpha(x, y) \in \mathbf{S}$, if $x, y \in \mathbf{S}$.

Then $<\mathbf{S}, \alpha>$ is called a *submonoid* of $<\mathbf{X}, \alpha>$. Clearly, the cyclic monoid generated by the powers of a given element is a submonoid called *cyclic submonoid*.

Let $<\mathbf{X}, \alpha>$ be a monoid with identity e. An element $a \in \mathbf{X}$ is said to be *left invertible* if there exists a $z \in \mathbf{X}$, such that, $za = e$, and z is called a left inverse of *a*. Similarly, we can define *right invertibility*. An element which is both left and right invertible, is called *invertible,* and the inverse acts both as the left and the right inverse. The inverse of x is denoted by x^{-1}.

Using Property 5, the following result can be readily established.

Property 6. Given a monoid, the set $\mathbf{X}_l$ of all left invertible elements of **X** forms a submonoid. Similarly, the set $\mathbf{X}_r$ of all right invertible elements of **X** forms a submonoid. Thus, $\mathbf{X}_l \cap \mathbf{X}_r$ is also a submonoid.

If *every element* of a monoid is invertible, then it is called a *group.* Thus, $<\mathbf{X}, \alpha>$ is a group if

G1. $\alpha(x, \alpha(y, z)) = \alpha(\alpha(x, y), z)$ (associative).
G2. $\alpha(x, e) = \alpha(e, x) = x$ (identity).
G3. $\alpha(x^{-1,} x) = \alpha(x, x^{-1}) = e$ (inverse).

From the definition of the submonoid, the following can be readily verified.

Property 7. In a commutative monoid, the subset of all idempotents forms a submonoid.

Let, $<\mathbf{X}, \alpha>$ be a semigroup with α denoting the *product.* Let a, x, $y \in \mathbf{X}$. If $ax = ay$ implies $x = y$, then the element a is *left-cancellative* and it is *right-cancellative* when $xa = ya$ implies $x = y$. The following conclusion is immediate.

Property 8. In a monoid, every right-invertible element is right-cancellative, and every left-invertible element is left-cancellative.

In addition, if the monoid is finite, even a stronger result holds.

Property 9. For $a \in \mathbf{X}$, the mapping $f_a : \mathbf{X} \to \mathbf{X}$, such that, $f_a(x) = ax$, for $x \in \mathbf{X}$ is one-to-one, if and only if, a has left inverse.

Based on this, the following conclusion results.

Property 10. In a *finite* monoid, an element $a \in \mathbf{X}$ has a left inverse, if and only if, it has a right inverse.

In other words, in a finite monoid, the right or the left inverse is unique and is indeed the (two-sided) inverse. Consequently, the right (left) invertible element is left (right) cancellative.

Example 14. Consider $(\mathbf{Z}_8, \times_8)$. It can be verified that $a = 1, 3, 5, 7$ are invertible, that is, there exists x, such that, $ax \equiv 1$ (mod 8). The inverses are given below.

a	1	3	5	7
x	1	3	5	7

A2. A Classification of Semigroups

We now present a graphical representation and a useful classification for the semigroups. Let, $\langle \mathbf{X}, \alpha \rangle$ be a finite semigroup of order t, with α denoting the product. Define a labeled directed graph $G = (V, E)$, where

$$V = \mathbf{X}$$

$$E = \{(x, xy)_y \mid (x, y) \in V \times V \text{ and } \alpha(x, y) = xy\}.$$

that is, the edge (x, xy) is labeled by y. This graph is called the *Cayley graph* of the semigroup. Clearly, the out-degree of each node is $|V| = t$. If $x, y, z \in V$, then from the definition of edges, it follows that

$$(x, xy)_y \in E \text{ and } (xy, xyz)_z \in E \implies (x, x(yz))_{yz} \in E,$$

that is, G is *transitively closed*. Furthermore, it can be verified that the labels of the self-loops constitute a sub-semigroup. Examples of the graph of the semigroup in Example 7 is given in Figure 1, and that of threshold-n addition semigroup, with $n = 4$, in Example 6 is given in Figure 2.

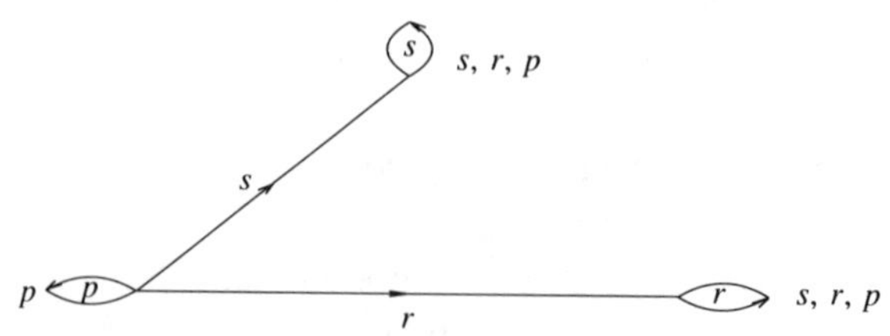

Figure 1. Graph of the semigroup in Example 7.

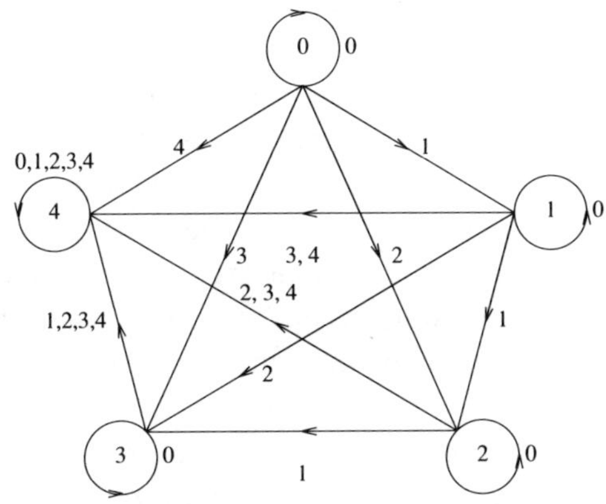

Figure 2. Graph of threshold-4 addition semigroup
of Example 6 with $n = 4$.

A semigroup is said to be *cycle-free* if the self loops are the only
cycles present in its Cayley graph. Otherwise, it is *non-cycle-free*. The
example in Figure 1 is non-cycle free, but, in Figure 2 is cycle-free.
Clearly, if $<X, \alpha>$ is a monoid, and if $x \neq e$ has the inverse, then the
edges (e, x), and $(x, xx^{-1} = e)$ constitute a cycle of length two.
Consequently, every group is non-cycle-free.

A semigroup, $<X, \alpha>$, with α denoting the product is said to be an
insertion semigroup if, for all x, y, w, and $z \in X$

$$xyz = xy \implies xwyz = xwy.$$

It can be be verified that every commutative cycle-free semigroup is an
insertion semigroup. Semigroups in Examples 6, 10 and 12 are all
insertion semigroups.

A semigroup is said to be *group-free* if it contains no non-trivial
subgroup as a subset. It can be verified that $<Z_n, +_n>$ is a semigroup
that is *not* group-free, for it constitutes a group. The threshold-k
semigroup in Example 6 is group-free.

A3. Notes And References

Most of the material in Section A1 is adopted from Birkoff and Bartee [1970] and the reader is referred to it for details of proof. Many of the examples in Section A1, and the developments in Section A2 are derived from Chandra, Fortune, and Lipton [1985], and Bilardi and Preparata [1987]. Cayley graphs are discussed in detail in Biggs [1974]. Cayley graphs of finite groups constitute the basis for the design of regular symmetric interconnection networks for parallel computers (Lakshmivarahan, Jwo, and Dhall [1991]).

Group-free semigroups play a vital role in the design of unbounded fan-in, constant depth and polynomial size prefix circuits. (See Chapter 8.) Likewise, the size of the circuit depends on whether or not the underlying semigroup is cycle-free. More specifically, the size of the circuits computing prefixes over a cycle-free semigroup is less than that for non-cycle free semigroup. See Chapter 8 for details.

Appendix B

Group-Free Semigroups, Star-Free Regular Expressions And Unbounded Fan-In Circuits

This appendix is rather technical in nature and describes the close relationship between the group-free semigroup, a class of regular languages, called *non-counting events,* described by star-free regular expressions. Based on this fundamental result, we then derive an unbounded fan-in circuit capable of performing computations over the group-free semigroups. This result is crucial for the developments in Chapter 8.

B1. Star-Free Regular Expressions

Let, Σ be a *finite* alphabet, set and $\circ$ denote the usual *concatenation* operation. Let Σ^n denote the set Σ^* of all strings of length n over Σ. Then

Σ^*, the set of all strings of finite length is define by

$$\Sigma^* = \bigcup_{n=0}^{\infty} \Sigma^n$$

where $\Sigma^0 = \{ \Lambda \}$, the set consisting of only the empty string. If x and y are strings, we write $x \circ y = xy$, for simplicity. Any $\mathbf{A} \subseteq \Sigma^*$ is called a language over Σ. First, we define a number of useful operations on languages. Let $\mathbf{A}, \mathbf{B} \subseteq \Sigma^*$.

1. *Union* of languages

$$\mathbf{A} \cup \mathbf{B} = \{x \mid x \in \mathbf{A} \ or \ x \in \mathbf{B}\}.$$

2. *Intersection* of languages

$$\mathbf{A} \cap \mathbf{B} = \{x \mid x \in \mathbf{A} \ and \ x \in \mathbf{B}\}.$$

3. *Product* of languages

$$\mathbf{AB} = \{z = xy \mid x \in \mathbf{A} \ and \ y \in \mathbf{B}\}.$$

4. *Complement* of a language

$$\neg \mathbf{A} = \{x \mid x \in \Sigma^* \ and \ x \notin \mathbf{A}\}.$$

Note that $\neg(\varnothing) = \Sigma^*$.

5. *Kleene Star* operation

$$\mathbf{A}^* = \bigcup_{n=0}^{\infty} \mathbf{A}^n$$

where

$$\mathbf{A}^{i+1} = \mathbf{A}^i\mathbf{A} \ \text{and} \ \mathbf{A}^0 = \{\Lambda\}.$$

Not every language is *finitely representable*. A special class of finitely representable languages called *regular sets* has received considerable attention in the literature. Regular sets are finitely represented using a class of expressions called *general regular expressions,* which are recursively defined over an alphabet set Σ as follows.

Any letter of the alphabet set Σ, the symbols Λ and $\varnothing$ denoting the *empty* string and the null set are generalized regular expressions. If α and β are generalized regular expressions, then so are

(a) $(\alpha) \cup (\beta)$ (union)

(b) $(\alpha) \cap (\beta)$ (intersection)

(c) $\neg (\alpha)$ (complement)

(d) $\alpha\beta$ (concatenation)

(e) α^* (Kleene-Star)

By further restricting the permissible operations, special classes of expressions are defined. For example, by disallowing the *intersection* and the *complement* operations we obtain the, so called, *restricted regular expressions*. Similarly, we define a *star-free* regular expression as a generalized regular expression without any occurrence of the Kleene-Star operation. As an example, $\neg (\varnothing) b$ is a star-free regular expression denoting the set of all strings that end in b. The expression $\neg (\varnothing) b \neg (\varnothing) b \neg (\varnothing)$, denoting the set of all strings with two or more b's is star-free. The expression $(b^* a b^* a)^* b^*$, denotes the set of all strings with an *even* number of a's is clearly *non-star-free*. The expression $\neg(\varnothing)(aaa)$, denoting the set of all strings that end in three or more a's is also star-free.

The set of languages corresponding to the regular expressions are the same as those accepted by finite state deterministic automata. There are well established algorithms for converting a regular expression into an automata and vice versa.

As an example, the set $A = (b^* a b^* a)^* b^*$, of all strings with even number of a's is acceptable by the finite state automaton in Figure 1. Similarly, the automaton in Figure 2 accepts $B = \neg (\varnothing)aaa$, which is the set of all strings that end in aaa.

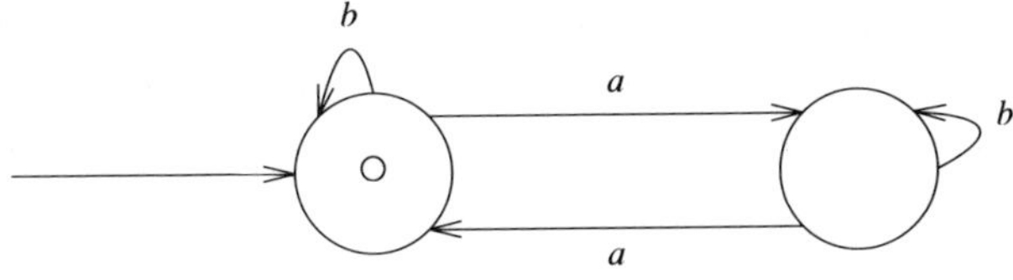

Figure 1. Automaton accepting $A = (b^* a b^* a)^* b^*$.

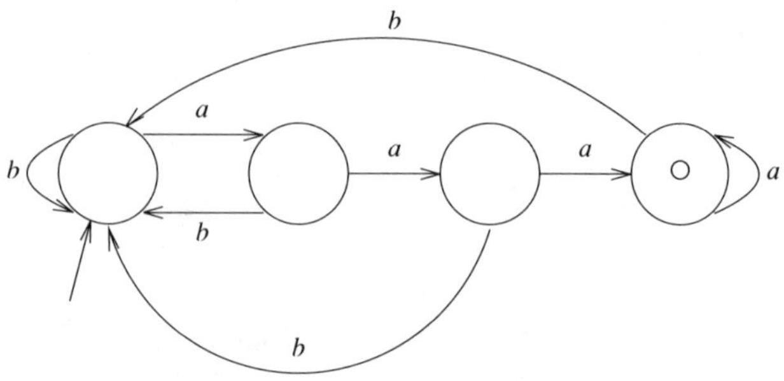

Figure 2. Automaton accepting $\mathbf{B} = \neg\,(\varnothing)aaa$.

Motivated by these examples, we now define two *distinct* notions of counting:

(a) counting modulo an integer $k \geq 2$, and

(b) *threshold* counting.

The example in Figure 1 illustrates the former and that in Figure 2, the latter. In a threshold counting, the automaton looks for a specific number (depending on the threshold) of repetitions of a given pattern of symbols. After the first occurrence of the desired pattern, the automaton ignores other occurrences of the pattern. On the other hand, counting mod k ($k \geq 2$), dictates the use of an explicit counter. In the literature the word counting is used to mean counting modulo $k(k \geq 2)$. Accordingly, the notion of *non-counting events* corresponds to languages defined by finite state deterministic automata that does *not* use any form of counting modulo k ($k \geq 2$). Thus, the sets $\neg(\varnothing)aaa$, and $\neg\,(\varnothing)\,b\,\neg\,(\varnothing)\,b\,\neg\,(\varnothing)\,b$ are non-counting. In other words, there is a close relation between star-free regular expressions and non-counting events.

Since star-free regular expressions, or non-counting events, are special classes of regular sets, we now define a restricted class of finite state automata called *RS-machine* that corresponds to them. A *RS*-machine consists of the following.

(a) An ordered set, $\mathbf{F} = \{F_1, F_2, \cdots, F_m\}$ of flip-flops, where each flip-flop is either in 1 (set) state or 0 (reset) state. Clearly, the set $\{0, 1\}^m$ of all m-bit binary strings constitutes the state space.

(b) Two sets of functions, $\mathbf{R} = \{R_1, R_2, \cdots, R_m\}$ and $\mathbf{S} = \{S_1, S_2, \cdots, S_m\}$, where R_j and S_j, for $j = 1$ to m, are two (or Boolean) valued functions whose values depend on the states of the flip-flops, $F_1, F_2, \cdots, F_{j-1}$, and the current input. However, it is restricted that R_j and S_j cannot both take on value 1 simultaneously.

(c) The *initial* state of the flip-flops in $\mathbf{F}$ is chosen in a pre-specified fashion.

(d) At time t, the tth input symbol of the input string is read and the states of the flip-flops are updated depending on the functions R_j and S_j. If $S_j = 1$, then the jth flip-flop F_j is forced to the 1 state; if $R_j = 1$, the F_j is forced to the 0 state; and if both R_j and S_j are 0, then the state of the flip-flop, F_j is unchanged. (Recall that $R_j = S_j = 1$ is prohibited).

(e) $\mathbf{A} \subseteq \{0, 1\}^m$ is the specified set of *final* or *accepting* states.

The *RS*-machine is said to accept an input string if that string leads to a state in the set $\mathbf{A}$. If M is an *RS*-machine, then the set of all strings accepted by M is denoted by $\mathbf{L(M)}$. From this description, it follows that every *RS*-machine accepts a regular set.

The steps involved in the computation of sequence of states leading to the acceptance or rejection of an input string is shown in Figure 3. Let $F_i^{(t)}$ be the state of the ith flip-flop at time t, where $1 \leq i \leq m$, and $0 \leq t \leq n$, where n is the length of the input string $x = x_1 x_2 \cdots x_n$. Recall that at time t, the values of R_i and S_i depend on the tth symbol, x_t of the input strings, and the states $F_j^{(t-1)}$, for $1 \leq j \leq i - 1$. Refer to Figure 4. Consequently, at any given time t, first compute R_i and S_i, for $1 \leq i \leq m$ (based on x_t and $F_j^{(t-1)}$, for $1 \leq j \leq m$) and then compute $F_i^{(t)}$ according to the state transition rule given in (d), above. Referring to Figure 3, in this way, the states of the flip-flops are calculated *row-wise*.

Alternatively, we can also compute the states *column-wise* as follows. From the definition, the (R_1, S_1) pair, at any time t, depends only on x_t. Consequently, values of R_1 and S_1 and, hence, $F_1^{(t)}$ can be computed, for all $1 \leq t \leq n$, once the input is given. Now, given $F_1^{(t)}$, for $0 \leq t \leq n$, since the pair (R_2, S_2) depends only on x_2 and $F_1^{(t)}$, for $1 \leq t \leq n$, we can readily compute $F_2^{(t)}$, for $1 \leq t \leq n$. Continuing in this way, at step k, compute $F_k^{(t)}$, for $1 \leq t \leq n$ based on

$m = 4$. Input string $x = x_1 x_2 x_3 x_4$. $n = |x| = 4$.

Initial State $t = 0$	$F_1^{(0)}$	$F_2^{(0)}$	$F_3^{(0)}$	$F_4^{(0)}$
Given x_1, compute **R** and **S**	R_1 S_1	R_2 S_2	R_3 S_3	R_4 S_4
Compute state at $t = 1$	$F_1^{(1)}$	$F_2^{(1)}$	$F_3^{(1)}$	$F_4^{(1)}$
Given x_2, compute **R** and **S**	R_1 S_1	R_2 S_2	R_3 S_3	R_4 S_4
Compute state at $t = 2$	$F_1^{(2)}$	$F_2^{(2)}$	$F_3^{(2)}$	$F_4^{(2)}$
Given x_3, compute **R** and **S**	R_1 S_1	R_2 S_2	R_3 S_3	R_4 S_4
Compute state at $t = 3$	$F_1^{(3)}$	$F_2^{(3)}$	$F_3^{(3)}$	$F_4^{(3)}$
Given x_4, compute **R** and **S**	R_1 S_1	R_2 S_2	R_3 S_3	R_4 S_4
Compute state at $t = 4$	$F_1^{(4)}$	$F_2^{(4)}$	$F_3^{(4)}$	$F_4^{(4)}$

Figure 3. Evolution of the states of an RS-machine.

$$\{F_j^{(t)} \mid 1 \leq j \leq k \text{ and } 0 \leq t \leq n\}.$$

Clearly, if the input *does not* change, the state of the jth flip-flop does not change after the jth step, that is, $F_j^{(t)} = F_j^{(j)}$, for all $t \geq j$, if the input is constant. An immediate consequence of this observation is that it is not always possible to design a RS-machine that will change the state of some flip-flop on every input. Hence, *not* every regular set is accepted by an RS-machine.

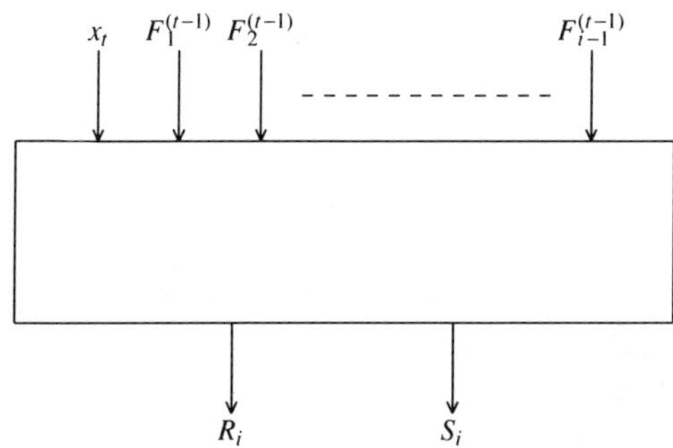

Figure 4: A circuit for the computation of R_i and S_i.

There is an intrinsic relation connecting the *RS*-machines, non-counting regular events and star-free regular expressions.

Theorem 1: If **L** is a regular set not containing the empty string, the following are equivalent:

> (a) **L** is accepted by an *RS*-machine.
>
> (b) **L** is a non-counting event.
>
> (c) **L** is star-free.

The proof of this fundamental Theorem is given in McNaughton and Papert [1971].

B2. Relating Star-Free Regular Expression to Group-Free Semigroup

Now, by way of linking the group-free semigroups and non-counting regular events, we establish the connection between regular sets and semigroups.

Let **S** be a semigroup. Define a deterministic finite state automaton as follows:

> (a) The state set, $\mathbf{Q} = \mathbf{S} \cup \{\ \varepsilon\ \}$.
>
> (b) The input alphabet set, $\Sigma = \{\bar{a} \mid a \in \mathbf{S}\}$.
>
> (c) The initial state is ε.
>
> (d) The state transition function

$$\delta : Q \times \Sigma \to \mathbf{Q}$$

where

$$\delta(s,\overline{a}) = sa.$$

It can be verified that the automaton is in state q on input $\overline{a}_1, \overline{a}_2, \cdots, \overline{a}_k$, if and only if,

$$a_1 a_2 \cdots a_k = q \in \mathbf{S}$$

Thus, given an element $q \in \mathbf{S}$, define

$$\mathbf{L}(q, \mathbf{S}) = \{x \mid x \in \Sigma^* \text{ such that, } x = x_1 x_2 \cdots x_t = q, \text{ for } t \geq 1\}.$$

Clearly, $\mathbf{L}(q, \mathbf{S})$ is regular.

Now, to connect the group-free semigroups with non-counting regular events, we need a technical definition of non-counting regular sets. A regular set $\mathbf{L}$, is said to be non-counting if there is an integer n, such that, for all strings x, y and z, and all $m \geq n$,

$$xy^m z \in \mathbf{L}, \text{ if and only if, } xy^{m+1}z \in \mathbf{L}.$$

In the light of this definition, the following result is crucial.

Theorem 2: Let $\mathbf{S}$ be a group-free semigroup. Then for any $q \in \mathbf{S}$, $\mathbf{L}(q, \mathbf{S})$ is non-counting.

Proof: Choose $n > |\mathbf{S}|$. First observe, that for any $b \in \mathbf{S}$ and, for $m > n$, we have $b^m = b^{m+1}$. Because, if $b^m \neq b^{m+1}$, then since $\mathbf{S}$ is finite, the sequence $b, b^2, b^3, \cdots$ must repeat with a period $k > 1$. Now, choose a least integer p, such that, $b^p = b^{p+k}$. Let i be an integer, such that, $0 \leq i < k$, and $(p + i) \equiv 0 \pmod{k}$. Then $\{b^p, b^{p+1}, \cdots, b^{p+k-1}\}$ is a group with b^{p+i} as the identity, which contradicts that $\mathbf{S}$ is group-free.

Now, construct the automaton that accepts $\mathbf{L}(q, \mathbf{S})$. If $x, y, z \in \Sigma^*$, then let a, b, c be the three semigroup elements that correspond to the product of the symbols in strings x, y, and z, respectively. Thus,

$$xy^m z \in \mathbf{L}(q, \mathbf{S}), \text{ if and only if, } ab^m c = q.$$

Since $b^m = b^{m+1}$, clearly, $xy^m z \in \mathbf{L}(q, \mathbf{S})$, if and only if, $ab^{m+1}c = q$, that is, if and only if, $xy^{m+1}z \in \mathbf{L}(q, \mathbf{S})$. Thus, $\mathbf{L}(q, \mathbf{S})$ is non-counting.

B3. Relating Group-Free Semigroups to Unbounded Fan-in Circuits

For reasons that will soon become apparent, we now describe a circuit that simulates the RS-machine.

Theorem 3: Let $\mathbf{M}$ be an RS-machine with m (fixed) flip-flops. Let $x = x_1 x_2 \cdots x_N$ be a string of length N. The behavior of $\mathbf{M}$ on the input string x can be simulated using an unbounded fan-in circuit $\mathbf{C}$, of constant depth and size $O(N^3)$.

Proof: This simulation exploits the *column-wise* computation of the states of the flip-flops described in the paragraph preceding Theorem 1.

The circuit is built by induction on the flip-flops in $\mathbf{M}$. Consider the stage where the states

$$\{F_j^{(t)} \mid 1 \le t \le N, \text{ for } j < i\}$$

of the first $(i - 1)$ flip-flops are given. A circuit for computing the states of the ith flip-flop F_i as a function of time namely $F_i^{(t)}$, for $1 \le t \le N$ may be described as follows. Define two Boolean quantities α_t and β_t, such that

$$\alpha_t = 1, \text{ if and only if, } F_i \text{ is forced to state 1 at time } t.$$

and

$$\beta_t = 1, \text{ if and only if, } F_i \text{ does not change at time } t,$$

where $\alpha_0 = 1$, if initially, the flip-flop F_i was in state 1.

Clearly, α_t and β_t depend only on the values of R_i and S_i at time t. Since the number m of flip-flops in the given RS-machine is fixed, referring to Figure 4, it follows that, for each t in the range, $1 \le t \le N$, the quantities R_i and S_i at time t and hence α_t and β_t can be computed using unbounded fan-in Boolean circuits of *constant* (depending only on m) depth and size.

We can now compute $F_i^{(t)}$, for $1 \le t \le N$ as follows:

$$F_i^{(t)} = [\alpha_0 \wedge (\beta_1 \wedge \beta_2 \wedge \cdots \wedge \beta_t)]$$

$$\vee \, [\alpha_1 \wedge (\beta_2 \wedge \beta_3 \wedge \cdots \wedge \beta_t)]$$

$$\vee \, [\alpha_2 \wedge (\beta_3 \wedge \beta_4 \wedge \cdots \wedge \beta_t)]$$

$$\vdots$$

$$\vee\, [\alpha_{t-1} \,\wedge\, (\beta_t)]$$

$$\vee\, [\alpha_t]$$

$$= \bigvee_{j=0}^{t} [\alpha_j \,\wedge\, (\bigwedge_{p=j+1}^{t} \beta_p)], \tag{1}$$

that is, $F_i^{(t)}$ is either α_0 (the initial state of F_i), and the state of F_i does not change in the rest of the steps, or α_1 and the state of F_i does not change in the rest of the steps, or $\cdots$ or α_t.

A schematic of the circuit for computing $F_i^{(t)}$ is given in Figure 5. This circuit is of depth two. As for the size,[1] the total number of lines incident on the $\wedge$ gates in the first row of Figure 5, is

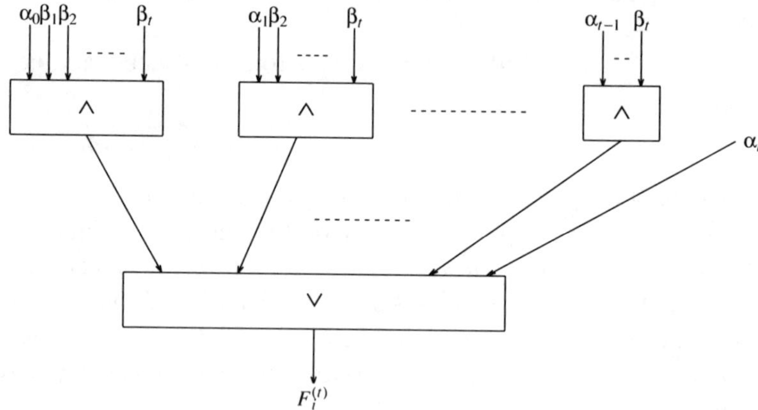

Figure 5: A circuit for computing $F_i^{(t)}$.

---

[1] Recall from Chapters 1 and 8 that in the case of unbounded fan-in circuits, size is measured by the total number of lines incident on all its gates.

$$s_1(t) = \sum_{i=2}^{t+1} i = \frac{(t+1)(t+2)}{2} - 1.$$

The number of lines incident on the $\vee$ gate in the second row, is

$$s_2(t) = t + 1.$$

Thus, the size of the circuit in Figure 5, is

$$s(t) = s_1(t) + s_2(t) = \frac{t^2 + 5t + 2}{2}.$$

Since, one such circuit is needed for each t, and each i, the total size of the circuit for computing $F_i^{(t)}$, for $1 \leq t \leq N$, and $1 \leq i \leq m$, is given by

$$\sum_{i=1}^{m} \sum_{t=1}^{N} s(t) < \sum_{i=1}^{m} \sum_{t=1}^{N} \left(\frac{t^2 + 5t + 2}{2} \right) = O(N^3).$$

(Recall that m is fixed).

We now conclude this Appendix with an important Theorem that combines all of the above results.

Theorem 4: Given a group-free semigroup, S and $q \in S$, there exists an unbounded fan-in circuit of constant depth and size $O(N^3)$, to decide if a string x (of length $|x| = N$) belongs to $L(q, S)$.

B4. Notes And References

This appendix derives much of its material from the classic monograph by McNaughton and Papert [1971] and the paper by Chandra, Fortune and Lipton [1985]. Hopcroft and Ullman [1979] is a standard reference on automata and formal language theory.

Appendix C

Boolean Circuits For Computing Parity

This Appendix analyzes the complexity of computing parity using unbounded fan-in Boolean circuits. It is shown that *unbounded fan-in, constant depth* circuits for computing parity must *necessarily* be of *exponential size*. Combining this with the fact that parity is a *group* (Example 5 in Appendix A), we readily obtain a proof of Theorem 3 in Section 8.1, namely, unbounded fan-in, constant depth and polynomial size circuits for computing the semigroup products exist only if the semigroup is group-free.

C1. Definition and Properties of Parity.

Let $\mathbf{X} = \{x_1, x_2, \cdots, x_N\}$ be a set of Boolean *variables*. The set $\{x_i, \bar{x}_i \mid 1 \leq i \leq N\}$ is called the set of *literals* over $\mathbf{X}$. Let B_N denote the set of all Boolean functions $f : \{0, 1\}^N \rightarrow \{0, 1\}$. A *monomial* (also called the *product*) is a *conjunction* of literals. The *size* of a monomial is measured by the number of literals it contains. A *polynomial p* is a

Boolean function which is a disjunction (also called the *sum)* of monomials. The size of a polynomial is the sum of the sizes of the monomials it contains. Given a function $f \in B_N$, a polynomial p is said to compute f, if

$$p(x) = f(x) \quad \text{for} \quad x \in \{0, 1\}^N.$$

p is called the *minimum* polynomial for f if among all polynomials computing f, $p(x)$ is of *minimum size*.

Let $\mathbf{a} = (a_1, a_2, \cdots, a_N) \in \{0, 1\}^N$. Define a *minterm* for $\mathbf{a}$, as

$$m_{\mathbf{a}}(x) = x_1^{a_1} \wedge x_2^{a_2} \wedge \cdots \wedge x_N^{a_N},$$

where $x_i^1 = x_i$ and $x_i^0 = \bar{x}_i$. Clearly,

$$m_{\mathbf{a}}(x) = 1, \text{ if and only if, } x = \mathbf{a}. \tag{1}$$

Given an $f \in B_N$, it can be expressed in an *OR* of *AND*s form,

$$f(x) = \bigvee_{\mathbf{a} \in f^{-1}(1)} m_{\mathbf{a}}(x). \tag{2}$$

This representation of $f(x)$ is often called the *disjunctive normal form (DNF)*, which is clearly, a polynomial. Simplifying the right-hand-side of (2) by applying the various laws and identities from Boolean algebra, we can arrive at the minimum polynomial for f.

Similarly, $\bar{f}(x)$ can also be expressed in the DNF,

$$\bar{f}(x) = \bigvee_{\mathbf{a} \in f^{-1}(0)} m_{\mathbf{a}}(x). \tag{3}$$

The dual of an *OR* of *AND*s is an *AND* of *OR*s. To obtain the dual, define the *maxterm* for $\mathbf{a}$ as

$$M_{\mathbf{a}}(x) = x_1^{\bar{a}_1} \vee x_2^{\bar{a}_2} \vee \cdots \vee x_N^{\bar{a}_N}.$$

It can be verified that

$$M_{\mathbf{a}}(x) = 0, \text{ if and only if, } \quad x = \mathbf{a}. \tag{4}$$

Now, given an $f \in B_N$, it can be expressed in an *AND* of *OR*s form,

$$f(x) = \bigwedge_{\mathbf{a} \in f^{-1}(0)} M_{\mathbf{a}}(x), \tag{5}$$

and

$$\bar{f}(x) = \bigwedge_{\mathbf{a} \in f^{-1}(1)} M_{\mathbf{a}}(x). \tag{6}$$

The expansion in (5) is often called the *conjunctive normal form* for f. It is obvious that (5) and (6) can be obtained from (3) and (2), respectively, by applying De Morgan's law.

We now illustrate these forms using a simple example. Let

$$g(x) = x_1 \oplus x_2 \oplus x_3 = (x_1 + x_2 + x_3) \bmod 2. \tag{7}$$

It can be verified that the *DNF (OR of ANDs)* for $g(x)$ and $\bar{g}(x)$ are given by

$$g(x) = (\bar{x}_1 \wedge \bar{x}_2 \wedge x_3) \vee (\bar{x}_1 \wedge x_2 \wedge \bar{x}_3) \vee (x_1 \wedge \bar{x}_2 \wedge \bar{x}_3) \vee (x_1 \wedge x_2 \wedge x_3)$$

and

$$\bar{g}(x) = (x_1 \wedge x_2 \wedge \bar{x}_3) \vee (x_1 \wedge \bar{x}_2 \wedge x_3) \vee (\bar{x}_1 \wedge x_2 \wedge x_3) \vee (\bar{x}_1 \wedge \bar{x}_2 \wedge \bar{x}_3).$$

Similarly, the *CNF (AND of ORs)*, for $g(x)$ and $\bar{g}(x)$ are given by

$$g(x) = (\bar{x}_1 \vee \bar{x}_2 \vee x_3) \wedge (\bar{x}_1 \vee x_2 \vee \bar{x}_3) \wedge (x_1 \vee \bar{x}_2 \vee \bar{x}_3) \wedge (x_1 \vee x_2 \vee x_3)$$

and

$$\bar{g}(x) = (x_1 \vee x_2 \vee \bar{x}_3) \wedge (x_1 \vee \bar{x}_2 \vee x_3) \wedge (\bar{x}_1 \vee x_2 \vee x_3) \wedge (\bar{x}_1 \vee \bar{x}_2 \vee \bar{x}_3)$$

The importance of, and the interest in, these forms primarily stems from the fact that the *OR* of *ANDs*, and the *AND* of *ORs*, can be implemented using Boolean circuits of depth-two. Refer to Figures 1 and 2 for such circuits.

In this appendix, we are particularly interested in analyzing the Boolean circuit implementation of the parity function

$$g(x) = x_1 \oplus x_2 \oplus \cdots \oplus x_N = \left(\sum_{i=1}^{N} x_i \right) \bmod 2. \tag{8}$$

We begin by listing a number of properties of $g(x)$.

P1. $g(x) = 0$, for exactly 2^{N-1} values of $x \in \{0, 1\}^N$ and $g(x) = 1$, for the rest of the values.

P2.   The value of $g(x)$ changes if the value of any *one* of its input changes.

P3.   Let $p(x)$ be a DNF (*OR* of *ANDs*) for $g(x)$. Let q be a monomial in

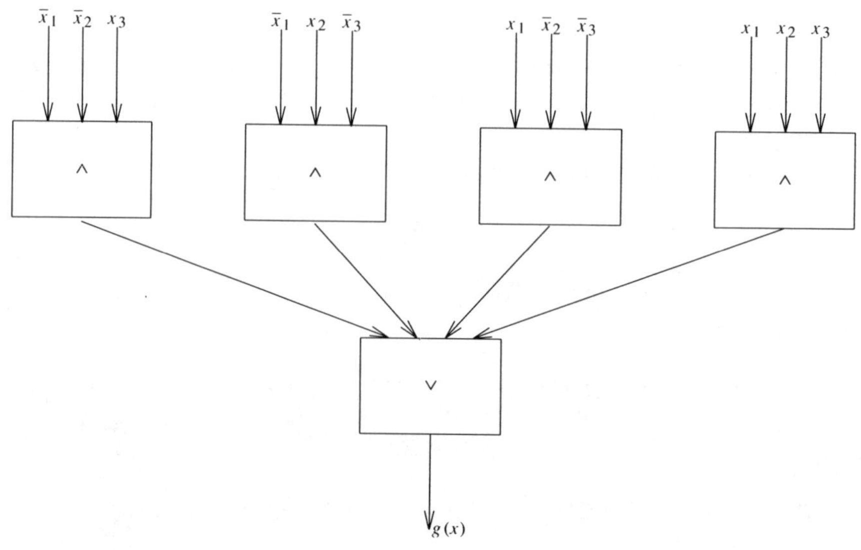

Figure 1. A depth-2 circuit for computing $g(x)$ using the *OR* of *AND*s form.

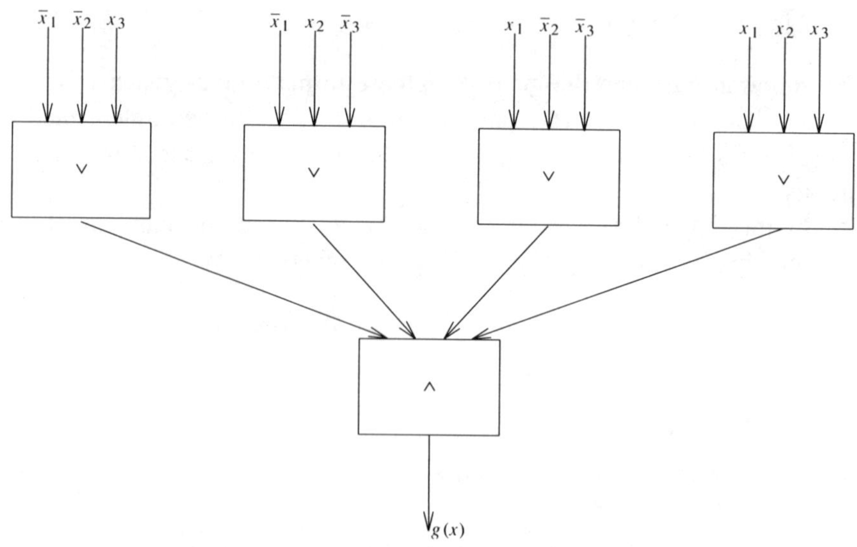

Figure 2. A depth-2 circuit for computing $g(x)$ using the *AND* of *OR*s form.

$p(x)$, such that a variable, say, x_k or its complement does not appear in q. Then there exist two instances of inputs, say, y and z, both from $\{0, 1\}^N$ differing in x_k, and $q(y) = q(z)$. However, this is a contradiction of P2. Hence, every monomial q in $p(x)$ is a conjunction of exactly N literals.

Combining P3 with P1, it follows immediately that $p(x)$ has exactly 2^{N-1} monomials, each of which contains N literals. Thus, $p(x)$ has a size of at least $N2^{N-1}$. A summary of this discussion follows.

Lemma 1: The minimum polynomial that computes the parity function over N variables has at least $N\,2^{N-1}$ literals.

Such a polynomial can be implemented as a two level circuit, with level 1 consisting of 2^{N-1} copies of *AND* gates each of fan-in N and one *OR* gate at level two of fan-in 2^{N-1}. In view of Lemma 1, this two level circuit is of *optimal size*[1] $1 + 2^{N-1}$, which is exponential in N.

C2. A Depth-Size Trade-off

An important question is: how much of reduction in size results from increasing the depth of the circuit? To get an idea of the depth-size trade-off for parity circuits, first consider the design of a depth-3 circuit. Let $N = n^2$.

Step 0   Divide the N input variables into n blocks each containing n variables.

Step 1   Compute the parity in each of the n blocks in parallel using the depth-two circuits based on the *OR* of *AND*s form.

Step 2   Compute the parity of the output of the n circuits in Step 1 using the depth-two circuits based on the *AND* of *OR*s form.

The resulting circuit is of depth 4. Refer to Figure 3(a) for an illustration. A number of observations are in order. While the output gates of the circuits in Step 1 and the input gates of the circuits in Step 2

---

[1] While it is customary to compute the size of unbounded fan-in circuits by the number of edges in the underlying directed graph, in tune with the literature on parity circuits, here we count the size by the number of gates as is usually done for the bounded fan-in case.

are all *OR* gates, since the input to Step 2 involves the complements of the output of Step 1, as is they *cannot* be combined. As a first step in reducing the depth from four to three, arrange to compute the complement of the output of each of the n parity circuits in Step 1 using the *OR* of *AND*s form depth-two circuits. Refer to Figure 3(b) for an illustration. Note that $\bar{y}_1$ and $\bar{y}_2$ are computed using the *OR* of *AND*s form quite like y_1 and y_2.

Now, the output *OR* gates of the circuits that compute the parity and their complements in Step 1 can be combined with the input *OR* gates of the Step 2 in a natural fashion to obtain the three-level circuit for computing the parity. Refer to Figure 3(c) for an illustration of the resulting three-level circuit.

Now, we compute the size of the resulting three-level circuit. The total size of the circuit for computing the parity and its complement in Step 1 is $2n(1 + 2^{n-1})$. The size of the circuit in Step 2 is $(1 + 2^{n-1})$. In combining the *OR* of *AND*s in Step 1 with the *AND* of *OR*s in Step 2, $2n$ copies of the *OR* gates in Step 1 are deleted. Thus, the total size is only $(2^n + 1)(1 + 2^{n-1}) - 2n = O(\sqrt{N} 2^{\sqrt{N}})$, as opposed to $(1 + 2^{N-1}) = O(2^N)$ size of the depth-two circuit. From this we readily obtain the following result.

Lemma 2: A depth-three circuit for computing parity is of size $O(\sqrt{N} 2^{\sqrt{N}})$.

In generalizing this to depth-d circuits, let $N = n^{d-1}$, for some integer n. In Step 0, divide the N inputs into n^{d-2} blocks each containing n variables. Step 1 computes the parity and its complement for each of the n^{d-2} blocks of n variables in parallel using the *OR* of *AND*s form. Step 2 computes the parity and its complement for n^{d-3} blocks each of n outputs of Step 1 using the *AND* of *OR*s form. Thus, starting with the *OR* of *AND*s form in Step 2, we alternate *OR* of *AND*s and *AND* of *OR*s through the entire design. After Step i, we have computed the parity of n^{d-1-i} blocks, each of n^i variables. Thus, after $d - 1$ steps, the parity of all the N variables is computed.

The resulting circuit is of depth $2(d - 1)$. But the output gates of the ith step and the input gates of the $(i + 1)^{th}$ step can be combined, for $1 \le i \le d - 2$. This reduces the depth by $d - 2$ leaving behind a depth-d circuit as required. This resulting circuit contains $\wedge$ gates fed by the inputs and has alternate layers of $\wedge$ and $\vee$ gates.

In computing the size, recall that Step i uses n^{d-i-1} subcircuits each computing a parity and another set of n^{d-i-1} subcircuits computing the

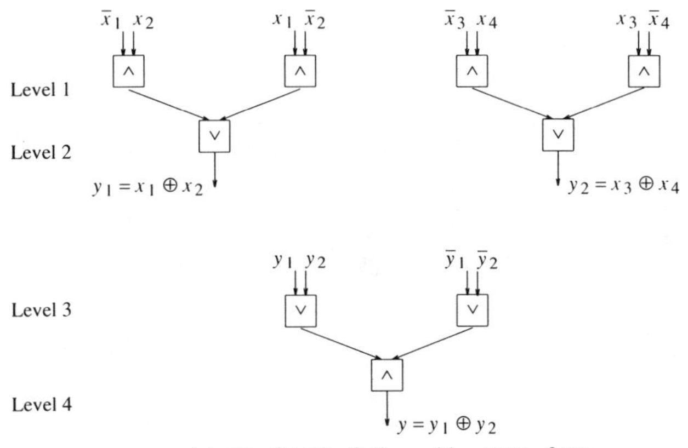

(a) *OR* of *AND*s followed by *AND* of *OR*s.

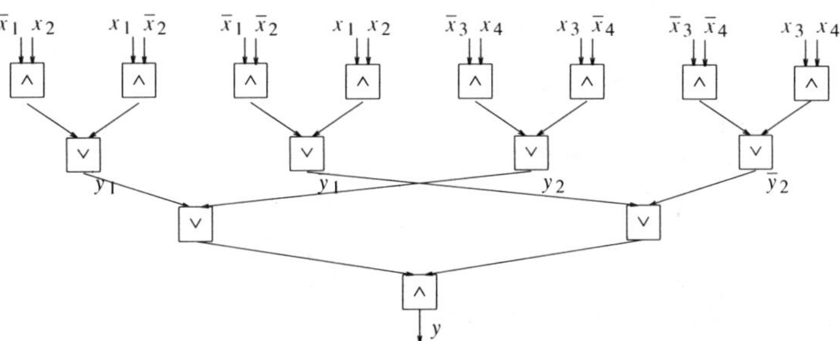

(b) $\bar{y}_1$ and $\bar{y}_2$ computed using extra copies of *OR* of *AND* circuits.

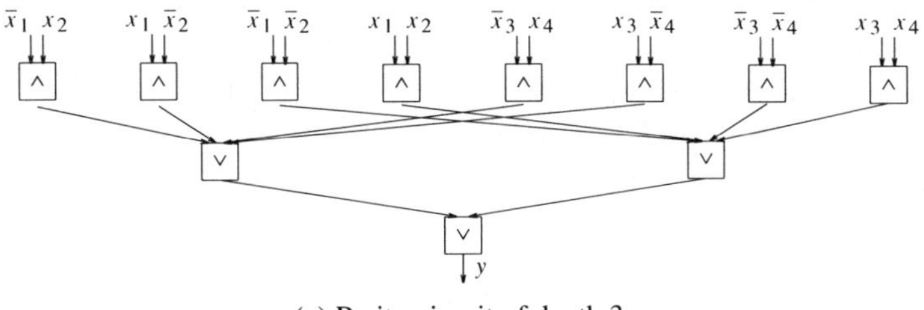

(c) Parity circuit of depth 3.

Figure 3. Development of a three-level parity circuit.

complement of the parity of n variables each. Thus, the total number of subcircuits used in the entire construction is given by

$$n^{d-2} + n^{d-3} + \cdots + n^2 + n + 1 = \frac{n^{d-1} - 1}{n - 1} \leq N.$$

Each subcircuit is of size $(1 + 2^{n-1})$. Thus, the total size of the $2(d-1)$ depth circuit is given by

$$\frac{n^{d-1} - 1}{n - 1} \times (1 + 2^{n-1}).$$

The total saving in the number of gates resulting from the combination of the output of Step i with the input of Step $i+1$, for $1 \leq i \leq d - 2$, is bounded by

$$2(n^{d-2} + n^{d-3} + \cdots + n^2 + n) = \frac{2(n^{d-1} - n)}{n - 1}.$$

Combining these, we obtain the net size of depth-d circuit as

$$\left[\frac{n^{d-1} - 1}{n - 1}\right](1 + 2^{n-1}) - \frac{2(n^{d-1} - n)}{n - 1} = \left[\frac{n^{d-1} - 1}{n - 1}\right]2^{n-1} - \frac{n^{d-1} - 2n + 1}{n - 1}$$

$$\leq \left[\frac{n^{d-1} - 1}{n - 1}\right]2^{n-1} = O(N^{\frac{d-2}{d-1}} 2^{N^{\frac{1}{d-1}}}).$$

In summary, we obtain the following.

Lemma 3: A depth-d circuit for computing parity is of size $O(N^{\frac{d-2}{d-1}} 2^{N^{\frac{1}{d-1}}})$.

In other words, for any d fixed, the size of the depth-d parity circuit is exponential. In search for a polynomial size circuits, we now extend the above design to circuits of depth-$d(N)$. In particular, consider [2]

$$d(N) = \frac{\log N}{\log\log N} + 1.$$

Then, clearly

$$N = n^{d(N)-1} \qquad \text{implies that} \quad n = 2^{\log\log N} = \log N.$$

As an example, if $N = 2^{16}$, then, $n = 16$ and $d(N) = 5$. By following the algorithm that leads to the depth-d circuits in $d - 1$ steps, we now develop the required $d(N)$-depth circuit in $d(N) - 1$ steps. The size of this circuit can readily be computed from the expression for the size in Lemma 3 by setting $d = d(N)$. First, observe

$$\frac{1}{d(N)-1} = \frac{\log\log N}{\log N}$$

$$N^{\frac{1}{d(N)-1}} = N^{\frac{\log\log N}{\log N}} = 2^{\log\log N} = \log N \qquad (\text{from } a^x = 2^{x\log a})$$

$$2^{N^{\frac{1}{d(N)-1}}} = 2^{\log N} = N \qquad \text{and} \qquad N^{\frac{d(N)-2}{d(N)-1}} = \frac{N}{N^{\frac{1}{d(N)-1}}} = \frac{N}{\log N}.$$

Combining these with Lemma 3, we obtain the following

Lemma 4: A depth-$d(N) = \dfrac{\log N}{\log\log N} + 1$ parity circuit is of size $O(\dfrac{N^2}{\log N})$.

While this circuit is of polynomial size, its depth is a slow varying function of N. Refer to Tables 1 and 2 for some typical values of N, depth and size.

Table 1. Depth of Exponential Size Circuits

N	Depth $= d$	Size $= N^{\frac{d-2}{d-1}} 2^{N^{\frac{1}{d-1}}}$
2^{16}	2	$2^{65,536} \approx 10^{19,727}$
2^{16}	3	2.97×10^{79}
2^{16}	4	2.24×10^{15}
2^{16}	5	2.68×10^{8}

Table 2. Depth of polynomial size circuits

N	Depth $(d(N) = \dfrac{\log N}{\log\log N} + 1)$	Size $(\dfrac{N^2}{\log N})$
2^4	3	2^6
2^{16}	5	2.68×10^8
2^{64}	12	5.32×10^{36}

C3. A Lower Bound on the Size

We conclude this Appendix by presenting a lower bound on the size of the constant depth circuits for computing parity. This result is from Hastad. For a proof of this result, refer to Hastad [1987] and Boppanna and Sipser [1990].

Theorem 5: For some constant N_0, and for $N \geq N_0^d$, depth-d unbounded fan-in Boolean circuits for computing parity must have a size at least $2^{c(d)N^{\frac{1}{d-1}}}$, where $c(d) = (\dfrac{1}{10})^{\frac{d}{d-1}} \approx 0.1$.

Consequently, constant depth circuits for parity must be of exponential size. Combining this lower bound result with Lemma 3, it follows that the algorithm for the design of constant depth parity circuits leading to Lemma 4 gives rise to constant depth near-optimal (size) circuits. Another interesting Corollary of Theorem 5 is the following result.

Lemma 6: A polynomial size parity circuit must have a depth of at least $\dfrac{\log N}{c + \log\log N}$ for some constant c.

Proof: If $s(N)$ is the size of the circuit of depth-d, then from Theorem 5, it follows that

$$s(N) \geq 2^{c(d)N^{\frac{1}{d-1}}}$$

where $c(d) \approx 0.1$. Taking logarithms twice and simplifying, we obtain

$$d - 1 \geq \frac{\log N}{c + \log\log s(N)}$$

where $c = -\log c(d) > 0$. The Lemma follows by requiring that $s(N)$ be a polynomial in N.

Again, combining this result with Lemma 4, it follows that the circuit described by Lemma 4 is optimal.

C4. Notes and References

The notion of the design of Boolean circuits of depth-two, based on DNF and CNF is now classic. The optimality of depth-two circuits for computing parity is from Lupanov [1961]. Analysis of complexity of unbounded fan-in, bounded depth Boolean circuits is virtually a post-1980 phenomenon. Refer to the monograph by Wegener [1987] and Dunne [1988] for an in depth coverage of the results in this area.

The first super-polynomial lower bound on the size of the unbounded fan-in depth-k circuits for computing parity is from Furst, Saxe and Sipser [1984]. They proved that the depth-d circuits must be of size, at least $N^{\log^{(f_d)} N}$, where $\log^{(k)} x$ denotes the logarithm iterated k times on x, and $f_d = 3(d - 2)$. Independently, Ajtai [1983] proved an improved lower bound, namely, $N^{c_d \log N}$ on depth-d circuits for some constant c_d. The first exponential lower bound on the size of the constant depth parity circuits is from Yao [1985] who showed that depth-d circuits require a minimum size of $2^{N^{\frac{1}{4d}}}$. Recently, Hastad [1987] derived near-optimal lower bound on the size of constant depth parity circuits. Refer to Theorem 5 for this bound. The proof of this Theorem is beyond our scope and we refer the interested reader to Hastad [1987] for details. For a succinct summary of the complexity of Boolean circuits, refer to Boppanna and Sipser [1990].

References

Abramson, N. [1963]. *Information Theory and Coding.* McGraw Hill, New York, NY.

Aho, A.V., J. E. Hopcroft, and J. D. Ullman [1974]. *The Design and Analysis of Computer Algorithms.* Addison-Wesley, Reading, MA.

Ajtai, M. [1983]. Σ_1^1 – Formulae on Finite Structures, *Annals of Pure and Applied Logic, Vol 24, pp 1-48.*

Akl, S. G. [1989]. *The Design and Analysis of Parallel Algorithms.* Prentice Hall, Englewood Cliffs, NJ.

Akers, S. and B. Krishnamurthy [1989]. A Group Theoretic Model for Symmetric Interconnection Networks, *IEEE Transactions on Computers,* Vol 38, pp 555-566.

Almasi, G. S. and A. Gottlieb [1989]. *Highly Parallel Computing.* The Benjamin/Cummings Publishing Company, New York, NY.

Amdahl, G. M. [1967]. Validity of the Single Processor Approach to Achieving Large Scale Computing Capabilities, *Proceedings of the AFIPS Spring Joint Computer Conference,* Vol 30, pp 40-54.

Anderson, D. A., J. C. Tannehill, and R. H. Pletcher [1984]. *Computational Fluid Mechanics and Heat Transfer.* Hemisphere Publishing Company, New York, NY.

Anderson, R. and G. Miller [1988]. Deterministic Parallel List Ranking, *Proceedings of the Third Aegean Workshop on Computing, AWOC 88, Corfu,* Greece. Springer-Verlag, New York, NY. pp 81-90.

Balcazar, J. L., J. Diaz, and J. Gabarro [1988]. *Structural Complexity, Vol 1.* Springer-Verlag, New York, NY.

Balcazar, J. L., J. Diaz, and J. Gabarro [1990]. *Structural Complexity, Vol 2.* Springer-Verlag, New York, NY.

Banerjee, U. [1988]. *Dependence Analysis for Supercomputing.* Kluwer Academic Publishers, Boston.

Bartels, R. H., J. C. Beatty, and B. A. Barsky [1987]. *An Introduction to Splines for use in Computer Graphics and Geometric Modeling.* Morgan Kaufmann Publishers, Inc., Los Altos, CA.

Blelloch, G. E. [1989]. Scans as Primitive Parallel Operations, *IEEE Transactions on Computers,* Vol 38, pp 1526-1538, 1989.

Bertsekas, D. P. and J. T. Tsitsiklis [1989]. *Parallel and Distributed Computation: Numerical Methods.* Prentice Hall, Englewood Cliffs, NJ.

Biggs, N. [1971]. *Finite Groups of Automorphisms.* Cambridge University Press, Cambridge, England.

Bilardi, G. and F. P. Preparata [1986]. Digital Filtering in VLSI, *Proceedings of Aegean Workshop on Computing, (Ed) F. Makedon,* Springer-Verlag, New York, NY, 1986, pp 1-11.

Bilardi, G. and F. P. Preparata [1987]. Size-Time Complexity of Boolean Networks For Prefix Computations, *Proceedings of the Symposium on the Theory of Computing,* pp 436-442.

Birkoff, G. and T. C. Bartee [1970]. *Modern Applied Algebra.* McGraw Hill, New York, NY.

Boppana, R. B. and M. Sipser [1990]. The Complexity of Finite Functions, in *Handbook of Theoretical Computer Science, Vol A,*

Algorithms and Complexity, (Ed) J. van Leeuwen, MIT Press, Cambridge, MA, pp 759-804.

Brauer, A. [1939]. On Addition Chains, *Bulletin of the American Mathematical Society,* Vol 45, pp 736-739.

Brent, R. P. [1970]. On the Addition of Binary Numbers, *IEEE Transactions on Computers,* Vol 19, pp 758-759.

Brent, R. P. [1974]. The Parallel Evaluation of General Arithmetic Expression, *Journal of ACM,* Vol 21, pp 201-206.

Brent, R. P. and H. T. Kung [1982]. A Regular Layout for Parallel Adders, *IEEE Transactions on Computers,* Vol 31, pp 260-264.

Chandra, A. S., L. J. Stockmeyer, and U. Vishkin [1984]. Constant Depth Reducibility, *SIAM Journal on Computing,* Vol 13, 423-439.

Chandra, A.,S. Fortune, and R. Lipton. [1985]. Unbounded Fan-In Circuits and Associative Functions, *Journal of Computers and Information Sciences,* Vol 30, pp 222-234.

Chen, C. Y. and S. Das [1990]. Breadth-First Traversal of Trees and Integer Sorting, *Technical Report CRPDC-90-4,* Department of Computer Science, University of North Texas, Denton, TX.

Chen, C. Y. and S. Das [1992]. Breadth-First Traversal of Trees and Integer Sorting, *Information Processing Letters,* Vol 41, No. 1, pp 39-49.

Cole, R. and U. Vishkin. [1986a]. Approximate and Exact Parallel Scheduling with Applications to List, Tree and Graph Problems, *Proceedings of the 27th Annual Symposium on Foundations of Computer Science,* pp 478-491.

Cole, R. and U. Vishkin [1986b]. Deterministic Coin Tossing with Applications to Optimal Parallel List Ranking, *Information and Computation,* Vol 90, pp 32-53.

Cole, R. and U. Vishkin [1988]. Approximate Parallel Scheduling. Part 1: The Basic Technique with Applications to Optimal Parallel List

Ranking in Logarithmic Time, *SIAM Journal on Computing,* Vol 17, pp 128-142.

Cole, R. and Vishkin, U. [1989]. Faster Optimal Parallel Prefix Sums and List Ranking, *Information and Control,* Vol 81, pp 334-352.

Cook, S. A. [1985]. A Taxonomy of Problems with Fast Parallel Algorithms, *Information and Control,* Vol 64, pp 2-22.

Cormen, T. H., C. E. Leiserson, and R. L. Rivest [1992]. *Introduction to Algorithms.* MIT Press, Cambridge, MA.

Dolev, D., C. Dwork, N. Pippenger, and A. Wigderson [1983]. Superconcentrators, Generalizers, and Generalized Concentrators with Limited Depth, *Proceedings of the 15th Annual Symposium on Theory of Computing,* pp 100-109.

Dweighter, H. [1975]. Elementary Problems (E 2569), *The American Mathematical Monthly,* Vol 82, p 1010.

Dunne, P. E. [1988]. *The Complexity of Boolean Networks.* Academic Press, New York, NY.

Eğecioğlu, Ö., E. Gallopoulos, and Ç. K. Koç [1989a]. Fast Computation of Divided Differences and Parallel Hermite Interpolation, *Journal of Complexity,* Vol 5, pp 417-437.

Eğecioğlu, Ö., E. Gallopoulos, and Ç. K. Koç [1989b]. Parallel Hermite Interpolation: An Algebraic Approach, *Computing, Vol 42, pp 291-307.*

Eğecioğlu, Ö., E. Gallopoulos, and Ç. K. Koç [1990]. A Parallel Method for Fast and Practical High-Order Newton Interpolation, *Bit,* Vol 29, pp 268-288.

Eğecioğlu, Ö., and A. Srinivasan [1992]. Optimal Parallel Prefix on Mesh Architectures, *Technical Report,* Department of Computer Science, University of California, Santa Barbara, CA.

Eğecioğlu, Ö., and Ç. K. Koç [1992]. Parallel Prefix Computation with Few Processors, *Computers in Mathematics with Applications,* Vol 24, pp 77-84.

Fich, F. E. [1983]. New Bounds for Parallel Prefix Circuits, *Proceedings of the ACM Symposium on Theory of Computing,* pp 100 - 109.

Flynn, M. J. [1972]. Some Computer Organizations and their Effectiveness, *IEEE Transactions on Computers,* Vol 21, pp 948-960.

Freund, R. F. and H. J. Siegel (Editors) [1993]. *Heterogeneous Computing - A Special Issue of IEEE Computer,* Vol 26.

Furst, M. J. Saxe, and M. Sipser [1981]. Parity, Circuits, and the Polynomial Time Hierarchy, *Proceedings of 22nd Annual IEEE Symposium on Foundations of Computer Science,* pp 260-270.

Garey, M. R., D. S. Johnson, and S. Lin [1977]. Solutions of Elementary Problems (E 2569), *The American Mathematical Monthly,* Vol 84, p 296.

Gazit, H., G. L. Miller and S. H. Teng [1987]. Optimal Tree contraction in EREW Model, *Proceedings of the Princeton Workshop on Algorithms, Architectures, and Technical Issues for Models of Concurrent Computation,* pp 139-156.

Gates, W. H. and C. H. Papadimitriou [1979]. Bounds for Sorting by Prefix Reversals, *Discrete Mathematics,* Vol 27, pp 47-57.

Golub, G. H. and C. F. Van Loan [1989]. *Matrix Computations.* Johns Hopkins University Press, Baltimore, MD.

Golumbic, M. C. [1976]. Combinatorial Merging, *IEEE Transactions on Computers,* Vol 11, pp 1164-1167.

Goldberg, A. V., S. A. Plotkin, and G. E. Shannon [1987]. Parallel Symmetry Breaking in Sparse Graphs, *Proceedings of the 19th Annual ACM Symposium on Theory of Computing,* pp 315-324.

Gustafson, J. L. [1988]. Reevaluating Amdahl's Law, *Communications of ACM,* Vol 31, pp 532-533.

Halverson, R., and Sajal K. Das [1993]. A Comprehensive Survey of Parallel Linked List Ranking Algorithms, *Technical Report CRPDC-93-12,* Department of Computer Science, University of North Texas, Denton, TX.

Han, Y. [1991]. An Optimal Linked List Prefix Algorithm on a Local Memory Computer, *IEEE Transactions on Computers,* Vol 40, pp 1149-1153.

Han, T., D. A. Carlson, and S. P. Levitan. [1987]. VLSI Design of High-Speed Low Area Addition Circuitry, *Technical Report,* Department of Electrical and Computer Engineering, University of Massachusetts, Amherst, MA.

Hastad, J. T. [1987]. *Computational Limitations for Small-Depth Circuits.* The MIT Press, Cambridge, MA.

Heller, D. [1978]. A Survey of Parallel Algorithms in Numerical Algebra, *SIAM Review,* Vol 20, pp 740-777.

Hellerman, H. and I. A. Smith. [1976]. *APL/360 Programming and Applications.* McGraw Hill, New York, NY.

Heydari, M. H. and I. H. Sudborough [1992]. On Sorting by Prefix Reversals and the Diameter of Pancake Networks, Preprint, Department of Computer Science, University of Texas at Dallas, Richardson, Texas.

Hicks, G. L. and A. J. Bernstein [1964]. On the Minimum Stage Realization of Switching Functions using Logical Gates with Limited Fan-in, *Proceedings of the Switching Circuit Theory and Logical Design,* Vol S-164, pp 149-155.

Hildebrand, F. B. [1974] *Introduction to Numerical Analysis, Second Edition.* McGraw Hill, New York, NY.

Hockney, R. W. and C. R. Jesshope [1981]. *Parallel Computers.* Adam and Hilger Ltd, Bristol, UK.

Hoover, H. J., M. M. Klawe, and N. J. Pippenger [1981]. Bounding Fan-out in Logical Networks, *IBM Research Report RJ 3184.*

Hoover, H. J., M. M. Klawe and N. J. Pippenger. [1984]. Bounding Fan-out in Logical Networks, *Journal of ACM,* Vol 31, pp 13-18.

Hopcroft, J. E. and J. D. Ullman [1979]. *Introduction to Automata Theory, Languages, and Computation.* Addison-Wesley, Reading, MA.

Huffman, D. A. [1952]. A Method for the Construction of Minimum Redundancy Codes, *Proceedings of the IRE,* Vol 40, pp 1098-1101.

Hwang, K. and F. A. Briggs. [1984]. *Computer Architecture and Parallel Processing.* McGraw Hill, New York, NY.

Hwang, K. and D. DeGroot [1989]. (Editors) *Parallel Processing for Super-Computers and Artificial Intelligence.* McGraw Hill, New York, NY.

Hyfil, L. and H. T. Kung. [1977]. The Complexity of Parallel Evaluation of Linear Recurrences, *Journal of ACM,* Vol 24, pp 513-521.

Iverson, K. [1962]. *A Programming Language.* John Wiley & Sons, New York, NY.

JáJá, Joseph. [1992]. *An Introduction to Parallel Algorithms.* Addison-Wesley, Reading, MA.

Jelinek, F. [1968]. *Probabilistic Information Theory.* McGraw Hill, New York, NY.

Karp, R. M. and M. O. Rabin [1987]. Efficient Randomized Pattern Matching Algorithms, *IBM Journal of Research and Development,* Vol 31, pp 249-260.

Karp, R. M. and V. Ramachandran [1990]. Parallel Algorithms for Shared- Memory Machines, in *Handbook of Theoretical Computer Science,* Edited by Jan Van Leeuwen, jointly published by Elsevier, Amsterdam, and The MIT Press, Cambridge, MA, Vol A, Chapter 17.

Knuth, D. E. [1969]. *The Art of Computer Programming,* Vol 2. Addison-Wesley, Reading, MA.

Krapchenko, V. M. [1970]. Asymptotic Estimation of Addition Time of a Parallel Adder, *Systems Theory Research,* Vol 19, pp 105-122.

Krishnamurthy, E. V. [1989]. *Parallel Processing: Principles and Practice.* Addison-Wesley, Reading, MA.

Kruskal, C. P., L. Rudolph, and M. Snir [1985]. The Power of Parallel Prefix, *IEEE Transactions on Computers,* Vol 34, pp 965-968.

Kruskal, C. P., T. Madej, and L. Rudolph [1986]. Parallel Prefix on Fully Connected Direct Connection Machines, *Proceedings of the International Conference on Parallel Processing,* pp 278-283.

Kuck, D. J. [1978]. *The Structure of Computers and Computations, Vol 1.* John Wiley & Sons, New York, NY.

Kung, H. T. [1980]. The Structure of Parallel Algorithms, in *Advances in Computers,* M. Yovits, (Ed), Academic Press, Vol 19, pp 65-112.

Leeuwen, J. van. (Ed). [1990]. *Handbook of Theoretical Computer Science, Vols A and B.* The MIT Press, Cambridge, MA.

Ladner, R. E., and M. J. Fischer [1980]. Parallel Prefix Computation, *Journal of ACM,* Vol 27, pp 831-838.

Lakshmivarahan, S., and S. K. Dhall [1985]. Parallel Algorithms for Solving Certain Classes of Linear Recurrences, in *Lecture Notes in Computer Science,* S. N. Maheshwari, (Ed), Vol 206, Springer-Verlag, New York, NY, pp 457-476.

Lakshmivarahan, S., and S. K. Dhall [1986]. A New Class of Parallel Algorithms For Solving Linear Tridiagonal Systems, *Proceedings of the Fall Joint Computer Conference,* pp 315-324.

Lakshmivarahan, S., Chi-Ming Yang, and S. K. Dhall [1987]. Optimal Parallel Prefix Circuits with $(size + depth) = 2n - 2$ and $\lceil logn \rceil \le depth \le \lceil 2logn \rceil - 3$, *Proceedings of the International Conference on Parallel Processing,* pp 58-65.

Lakshmivarahan, S. and S. K. Dhall [1990]. *Analysis and Design of Parallel Algorithms.* McGraw Hill, New York, NY.

Lakshmivarahan, S., Jung-Sing Jwo, and S. K. Dhall. [1993]. Symmetry in Interconnection Networks Based on Cayley Graphs of Permutation Group: A Survey, *Journal of Parallel Computing,* Vol 19, pp 361-407.

Liang, Y., S. K. Dhall and S. Lakshmivarahan [1991]. Finding Hamiltonian Circuits in Circular-Arc Graphs, *Proceedings of the 29th Allerton Conference on Control, Communication, and Computing,* pp 484-485.

Lubachevsky, B. D. and A. G. Greenberg [1987]. Simple, Efficient, Asynchronous Parallel Prefix Algorithms, *Proceedings of the International Conference on Parallel Processing,* pp 66-69.

Lupanov, O. [1961]. Implementing the Algebra of Logic Functions in Terms of Constant Depth Formulas in the Basis OR, AND and NOT, *Soviet Physics Doklady,* Vol 6, pp 107-108.

Maekawa, M., A. E. Oldehoeft, and R. R. Oldehoeft. *Operating Systems Advanced Concepts.* The Benjamin/Cummings Publishing Company, Inc., Menlo Park, CA, 1987.

Massey, W. [1993]. *Grand Challenges 1993: High Performance Computing and Communications,* A Report by the committee on Physical, Mathematical, and Engineering Sciences, National Science Foundation, Washington, DC.

McNaughton, R. and S. Papert. [1971]. *Counter-Free Automata.* The MIT Press, Cambridge, MA.

Mejier, H. and S. G. Akl [1987]. Optimal Computation of Prefix Sums on a Binary Tree of Processors, *International Journal of Parallel Programming,* Vol 16, pp 127-136.

Miller, G. L. and J. H. Reif. [1985]. Parallel Tree Contraction and its Application, *Proceedings of the 26th Annual IEEE Symposium on Foundations of Computing,* pp 478-489.

Miranker, W. [1971]. A Survey Parallelism in Numerical Analysis, *SIAM Review,* Vol 13, pp 524-547.

Modi, J. J. [1988]. *Parallel Algorithms and Matrix Computations.* Clarendon Press, Oxford, England.

Munro, I and M. Patterson [1973]. Optimal Algorithms for Parallel Polynomial Evaluation, *Journal of Computers and System Sciences,* Vol 7, pp 189-198.

Ofman, Yu. P. [1963]. On the Algorithmic Complexity of Discrete Functions, Soviet Physics Doklady, Vol 7, pp 589-591

Ortega, J. M. [1988]. *Introduction to Parallel and Vector Solution of Linear Systems.* Plenum Press, New York, NY.

Parberry, I. [1987]. *Parallel Complexity Theory.* Pitman Publishing, London, UK.

Pippenger, N. [1990]. Communication Networks in *Handbook of Theoretical Computer Science, Vol A, Algorithms and Complexity,* (Ed) J. van Leeuwen, The MIT Press, Cambridge, MA, pp 807-833.

Prasad, S., S.K. Das, and Calvin Chen. Efficient EREW PRAM Algorithms for Parentheses-Matching, *Technical Report CRPDC-92-14,* 1992 (Revised April 1993), Department of Computer Science, University of North Texas, Denton, TX.

Quinn, M. J. [1987]. *Designing Efficient Algorithms for Parallel Computers.* McGraw Hill, New York, NY.

Reif J. H. [1985]. An Optimal Parallel Algorithms for Integer Sorting, *Proceedings of the 26th Annual IEEE Symposium on Foundations of Computing,* pp 496-504.

Reif, J. [1986]. Logarithmic Depth Circuits for Algebraic Functions, *SIAM Journal on Computing,* Vol 15, pp 231 - 242.

Reingold, E. M. [1972]. Establishing Lower Bounds on Algorithms: a Survey, *AFIPS Spring Joint Computer Conference,* Vol 40, pp 471-481.

Rheinboldt, W. C. 1984]. Computational Modeling and Mathematics Applied to Physical Sciences, A Report of the committee on Applications of Mathematics, National Research Council, National Academy Press, Washington, DC.

Rye, K.W. and J. Ja Ja [1989]. List Ranking on Hypercube, *Proceedings of the International Conference on Parallel Processing,* pp 20-23.

Savage, J. E. [1976]. *The Complexity of Computing.* John Wiley & Sons, New York, NY.

Schonhage, A. [1975]. A Lower Bound for the Length of Addition Chains, *Theoretical Computer Science,* Vol 1, pp 1-12.

Schwartz, J. T. [1980]. Ultracomputers, *ACM Transactions on Programming Languages and Systems,* Vol 2, pp 484-521.

Siegel, H. J. [1985]. *Interconnection Network for Large Parallel Processing.* Lexington Books, D. C. Heath and Company, Lexington, MA.

Snir, M. [1986]. Depth-Size Tradeoffs for Parallel Prefix Computation, *Journal of Algorithms,* Vol 7, pp 185-201.

Stockmeyer, L. and U. Vishkin. [1984]. Simulation of Parallel Random Access Machines by Circuits, *SIAM Journal on Computing,* Vol 13, pp 409-422.

Stone, H. S. [1971]. Parallel Processing With Perfect Shuffle, *IEEE Transactions on Computers,* Vol 20, pp 153-161.

Stone, H. S. [1973]. An Efficient Parallel Algorithm for the Solution of Tridiagonal System of Equations, *Journal of ACM,* Vol 20, pp 27-38.

Stone, H. S. [1975]. Parallel Tridiagonal Equation Solvers, *ACM Transactions on Mathematical Software,* Vol 1, pp 289-307.

Strange, G. and G. J. Fix [1973]. *An Analysis of the Finite Element Method.* Prentice Hall, Englewood Cliffs, NJ.

Tarjan, R. and U. Vishkin [1985]. An Efficient Parallel Biconnectivity Algorithm, *SIAM Journal on Computing*, Vol 14, pp 862-874.

Vishkin, U. [1984]. Randomized Speed-ups in Parallel Computations, *Proceedings of the 16th Annual ACM Symposium on Theory of Computing*, pp 230-239.

Vishkin, U. [1985]. On Efficient Strong Orientation, *Information Processing Letters*, Vol 20, pp 319-333.

Volger, H. [1985]. Some Results on Addition/Subtraction Chains, *Information Processing Letters*, Vol 20, pp 155-160.

Wagner, W. and Y. Han [1986]. Parallel Algorithms for Bucket Sorting and Data Dependent Prefix Problem, *Proceedings of the International Conference on Parallel Processing*, pp 924-930.

Wegener, I. [1987]. *The Complexity of Boolean Functions.* Wiley-Teubner Series in Computer Science, John Wiley & Sons, New York, NY.

Wyllie, J. C. [1979]. *The Complexity of Parallel Computation*, Ph.D. Thesis, Cornell University, Ithaca, NY.

Yang, Chi-Ming [1987]. *Parallel Prefix Circuits*, M.S. Thesis, School of Electrical Engineering and Computer Science, University of Oklahoma, Norman, Oklahoma.

Yao, A. [1985]. Separating the Polynomial Time Hierarchy by Oracles, *Proceedings of the 26th Annual IEEE Symposium on Foundations of Computer Science*, pp 1-10.

Zima, H. and S. Chapman [1990]. *SuperCompilers for Parallel and Vector Computers.* Addison-Wesley, Reading, MA.

Index